AF477478

600 Moons

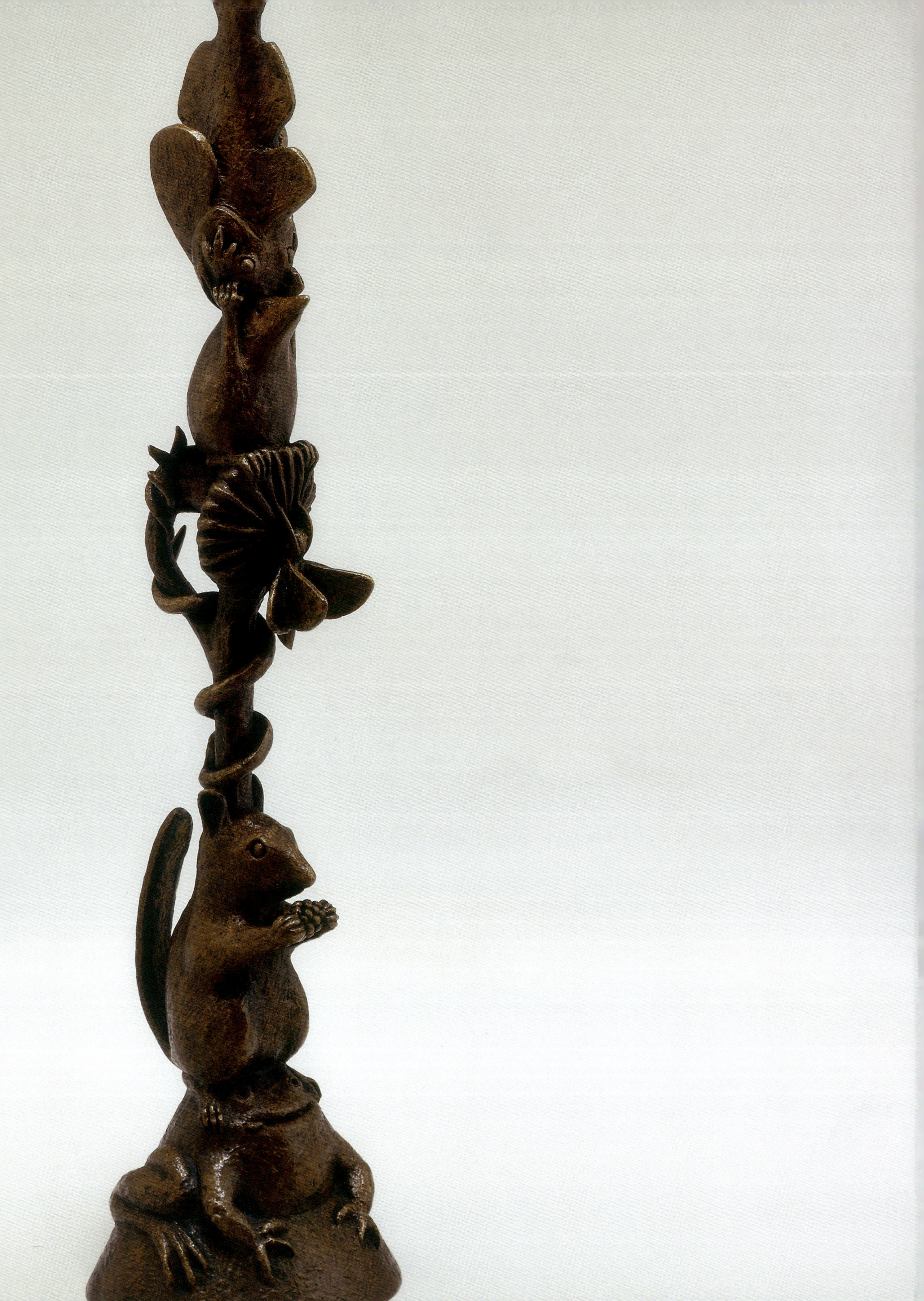

Deloris Tarzan Ament
with a foreword by Theodore F. Wolff

600 Moons

Fifty Years of Philip McCracken's Art

Museum *of* Northwest Art
La Conner, Washington

in association with
University of Washington Press
Seattle and London

600 Moons: Fifty Years of Philip McCracken's Art was organized by the Museum of Northwest Art.

Published in conjunction with an exhibition of the same title presented at the Museum of Northwest Art, July 17–October 17, 2004.

Museum of Northwest Art
121 South First Street
P.O. Box 969
La Conner, WA 98257
www.museumofnwart.org

In association with
University of Washington Press
P.O. Box 50096
Seattle, WA 98145-5096
www.washington.edu/uwpress

Library of Congress Control Number: 2003116239
ISBN: 0-295-98411-2

Jacket front: *Comet,* 1992, polychromed cedar, H. 31 in., collection of Mrs. William H. Bryant

Jacket back: *Beyond the Sun,* 1994, maple and epoxy, H. 19 in., collection of the artist

Front flap: Philip McCracken and owl, photograph by Anne McCracken

Back flap: *Night Bird* (detail), 1982, sandstone, H. 20 in., collection of Lance and J.P. Brigham, see page 117

Frontispiece: *Guemes Island Totem* (detail), 2001, bronze, H. 23¼ in., private collection, see page 148

Edited by Joseph N. Newland, Q.E.D.
Proofread by Sharon Rose Vonasch
Index by Olga K. Owens
Design, composition, and print production by Marquand Books, Inc., Seattle
Designer: John Hubbard; Compositor: Jennifer Sugden
Separations by iocolor, Seattle
Printed and bound by CS Graphics Pte., Ltd., Singapore

Contents

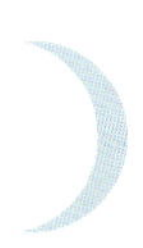

Director's Foreword

It is a pleasure for the Museum of Northwest Art to be associated with this fine book about Philip McCracken by Deloris Tarzan Ament.

McCracken's position as a major American artist is beyond question, and his roots strike deep in the Pacific Northwest. He grew up roaming its damp woods and beaches with fishing rod and hunting rifle, and rowing among the San Juan Islands. Although his artistic sense of place—so clearly evident in his work—sprang from the flora and fauna of the Northwest, he was deeply influenced by distinct personal experiences in England, New York, and the American Southwest. By choosing the Northwest as his home, he brought that knowledge and awareness back to us, and we are the better for it.

This book and the museum's related retrospective exhibition of McCracken's work were made possible by the contributions of many individuals and institutions, particularly the M*o*NA trustees, whose commitment to publishing the art history of the Northwest will benefit readers, students, and teachers for generations to come. We are grateful to the broad vision of collectors such as Marshall Hatch, whose erudite devotion to Northwest art inspired us to tackle this important project. We thank The Allen Foundation for the Arts, the Washington State Arts Commission, the Morris Graves Foundation, the Kreielsheimer Foundation, and the *Skagit Valley Herald.*

M*o*NA placed McCracken's story in the thoughtful hands of Deloris Tarzan Ament, who has become a friend and mentor to this museum. The warm foreword by Theodore F. Wolff brought historical perspective to her work, and we appreciate it. Dick Garvey's insight into McCracken's work is clearly evident in his photography, and the photographs by Mary Randlett are treasures, as is Mary herself. Working with editor Joseph N. Newland constantly buoyed our confidence and renewed our commitment to excellence. Our publishing partners, University of Washington Press and Marquand Books, have shown remarkable dedication to publishing the art history of the Northwest with us and this book simply would not have been possible without them, nor would it have been so beautiful without the work of designer John Hubbard. We add grateful thanks to chief curator Susan Parke, assisted by Lisa Young, for astute leadership of the exhibition, and to the many staff and museum members who invested so much heart in this important project.

My personal thanks go to Tim Bruce, M*o*NA supporter and knowledgeable enthusiast of McCracken's work. It was Tim who first envisioned this book and the related exhibition and led the initiative to accomplish it. We deeply appreciate it.

The late Frank and Alice Hull, longtime museum members, made thoughtful provision for M*o*NA through their estate and that gift helped make this book possible—a fitting tribute to two individuals so convinced of the power of the written word.

Although this book and the exhibition were made possible by a team of caring individuals, the beacons who guided our way were Phil and Anne McCracken. Their loving encouragement to this museum made even the most mundane element of the project seem like a treasured opportunity to serve.

Philip McCracken's work and his commitment to the Northwest exemplify the heritage on which the Museum of Northwest Art is based. His artistic integrity, and his lifelong spirit of adventure, serve to inspire our future.

Kris Molesworth
Executive Director

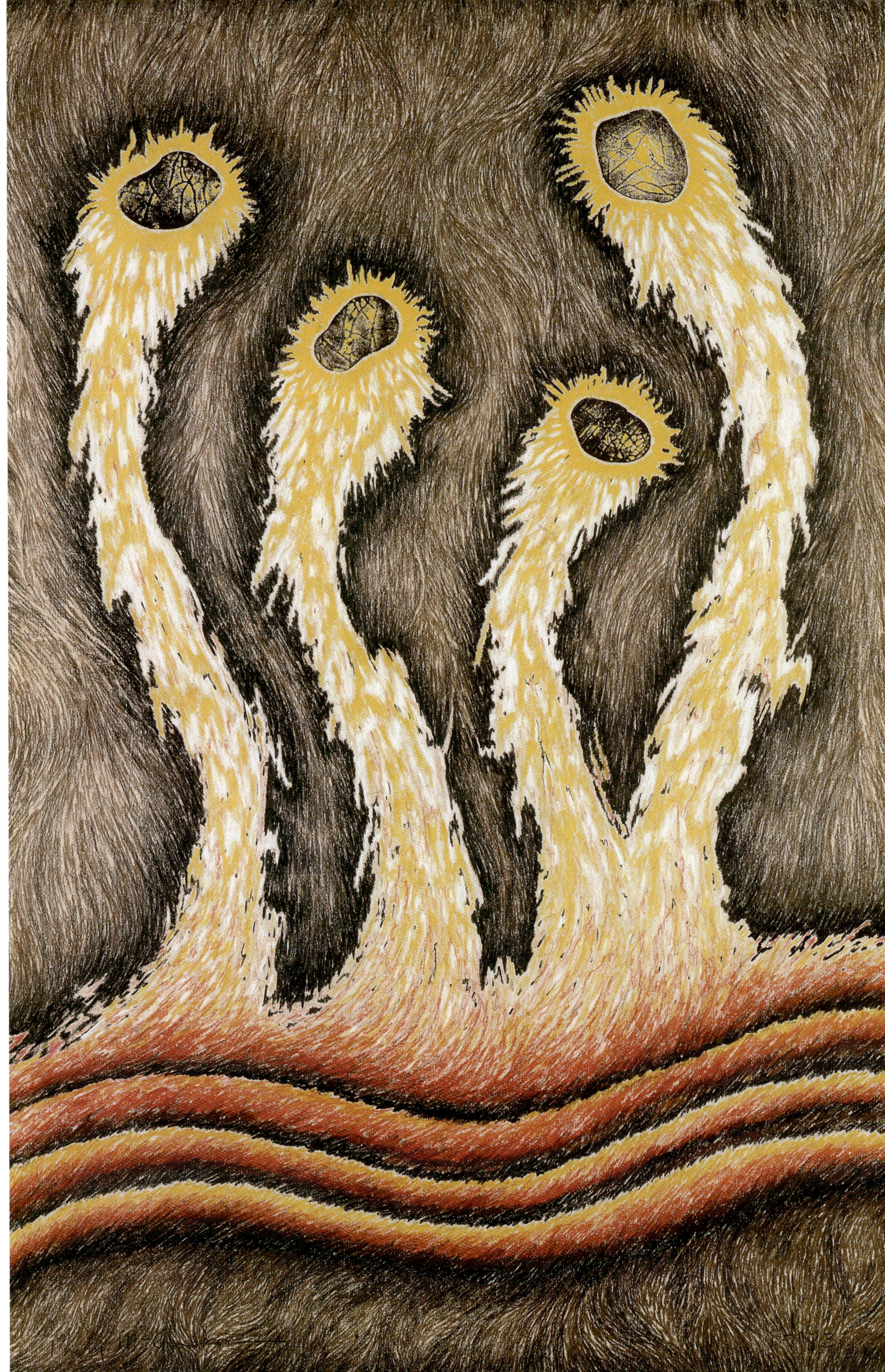

Theodore F. Wolff

Foreword: Philip McCracken

It's always a pleasure to write about Philip McCracken, not only because of the quality of his work, but also because of the delightful times I've had with the McCracken family and their wonderful assortment of furred and feathered friends. Some of these had been rescued from the woods, others would return to their native Guemes Island habitat once they had healed, and the rest consisted of a mixed bag of friendly cats and dogs. Among the last named was a lovable but unbelievably fat little dog named Meatloaf who could only waddle but who insisted on accompanying Philip and me on our evening walks. He could not keep up, but he was so serious and determined that I fell in love with him and promised myself that I would write about him one day—a promise I fully intend to keep before long.

Discussing an animal at the beginning of an introductory essay on an artist might seem like an odd thing to do. And with most artists it would be. In the case of Philip McCracken, however, it is altogether appropriate. How many of today's serious artists, after all, have devoted as much time and effort to depicting creatures of the wild as he? And how many have managed to fuse commitment to art's highest ideals with respectful attention to the nature and physical characteristics of animals and birds?

McCracken is that rarest of creative individuals, a formal purist with both heart and a rich and penetrating imagination. Henry David Thoreau, Constantin Brancusi, and Albert Einstein would have appreciated his work. The first for its delight in and faithfulness to nature. The second for the extraordinary clarity and integrity of its design. And the third for its attempts to give symbolic form to some of the most fascinating mysteries of our universe. More specifically, his work reveals a very personal concern for the birds, animals, and fish of his home state of Washington; an acute awareness of modernist formal and conceptual ideas; and a serious interest in how physics and mathematics can help clue us in to the secrets of time and space.

All these qualities combine in McCracken's art to produce work that defies categorization. He empathizes completely with nature's creatures and depicts them lovingly,

Earth Rhythms (detail)
1983 (see p. 67)

but he cannot legitimately be described as a wildlife artist. He reduces complex forms, feelings, and ideas to their essentials and then translates what results into something very close to pure form, but he is not a formalist. And finally, he has produced imaginative work of extraordinary conceptual ingenuity, but he cannot by any stretch of the imagination be classified as a conceptualist or indeed, as any other kind of orthodox modernist or post-modernist.

Who, then, is Philip McCracken the artist?

Perhaps the best clue is something he said during one of our evening walks with Meatloaf several years ago. "I want everything, both in my life and in my art, to be organic, to grow from the center out, to come together to form a perfectly integrated whole."

McCracken, in other words, is an artist who must be taken in his entirety, as someone totally committed to following his intuitions no matter where they might lead, be it toward the fashioning of a tiny, perfectly simple carved owl; the creation of dramatic monumental sculpture designed to fit into architectural settings; the production of mixed-media pieces intended to "explore time in terms of the speed of light"; or the execution of a delightful series of works devoted to the trials and tribulations of the lowly potato.

McCracken is not, in short, to be squeezed into one or another artistic category. He belongs in almost all—and in none—of them. And that includes the regionalist category that defines him as primarily, if not exclusively, an artist of the Pacific Northwest.

True, he is a member of the distinguished Pacific Northwest school, and is probably best known for his three-dimensional depictions of that region's flora and fauna. In actuality, however, he is no more a regionalist than was Mark Tobey or Morris Graves. Like theirs, his vision and accomplishments have always extended far beyond the borders of his home state. And like theirs, his work reflects ideas and formal approaches more national and international in scope than would be the case with someone more exclusively committed to the celebration of local places and events.

After all, it's very unlikely that a young, recent graduate of the University of Washington art department with a strictly regional view of art would have gone off to England in 1953 to work with Henry Moore, at that time one of the world's most innovative sculptors. And just as unlikely that he would, at that time and place, and later while living near New York City, have thoroughly familiarized himself with international modernism's most advanced notions of what was and was not relevant to twentieth-century art.

But that is exactly what McCracken did. True, he then returned to his home state, but he did so not in order to isolate himself from the pressures and demands of the art world, but in order to apply what he had learned abroad and in New York to the subjects and themes that were the most familiar to him and closest to his heart.

That he succeeded as an artist is a matter of record, as is the fact that the major impetus to his growing reputation occurred in New York as a result of a series of well-received one-person shows at one of Manhattan's leading galleries. These events and his inclusion in several important museum exhibitions throughout the country established, once and for all, that McCracken's significance as an artist extended far beyond the boundaries of the Pacific Northwest.

Having said all that I must go back to my earlier statement that McCracken is a formal purist with heart. For all his wide-ranging interests and talents and the remarkable things he has created because of them, I suspect that he ultimately will be best remembered for his numerous sculptures of birds, animals, and seafaring creatures. And with good reason, for what he creates in this area is both irreducibly simple in form and warmly appealing in content. He has the remarkable ability to translate such things as the "bearness" of a bear and the "owlness" of an owl into starkly elemental forms that yet somehow manage to embody and convey McCracken's affection and respect for the creatures depicted. Most impressive of all is the fact that he accomplishes this without undue stylization or sentimentality.

McCracken's creative integrity, artistic sensibility, and respectful regard for all creatures large and small set him apart from the vast majority of his contemporaries. As an artist he is both a modernist and a traditionalist. Most of all, however, he is a delightful and caring human being. The home he and his wife Anne have created on Guemes Island testifies to this. Everyone and everything—including some of nature's wildest creatures—quickly adjust to the sense of harmony that reigns there. Even "natural" enemies accept one another with equanimity. One of my most treasured mementos of my visits to their home is a photograph that shows McCracken seated on a chair with one of the family cats curled up on his lap. Standing on Philip's knee only a few inches away, and looking at him with total unconcern, is a young, very perky robin.

With any other artist, that would be an extraordinary event. In the McCracken household, however, it is only a mildly unusual occurrence.

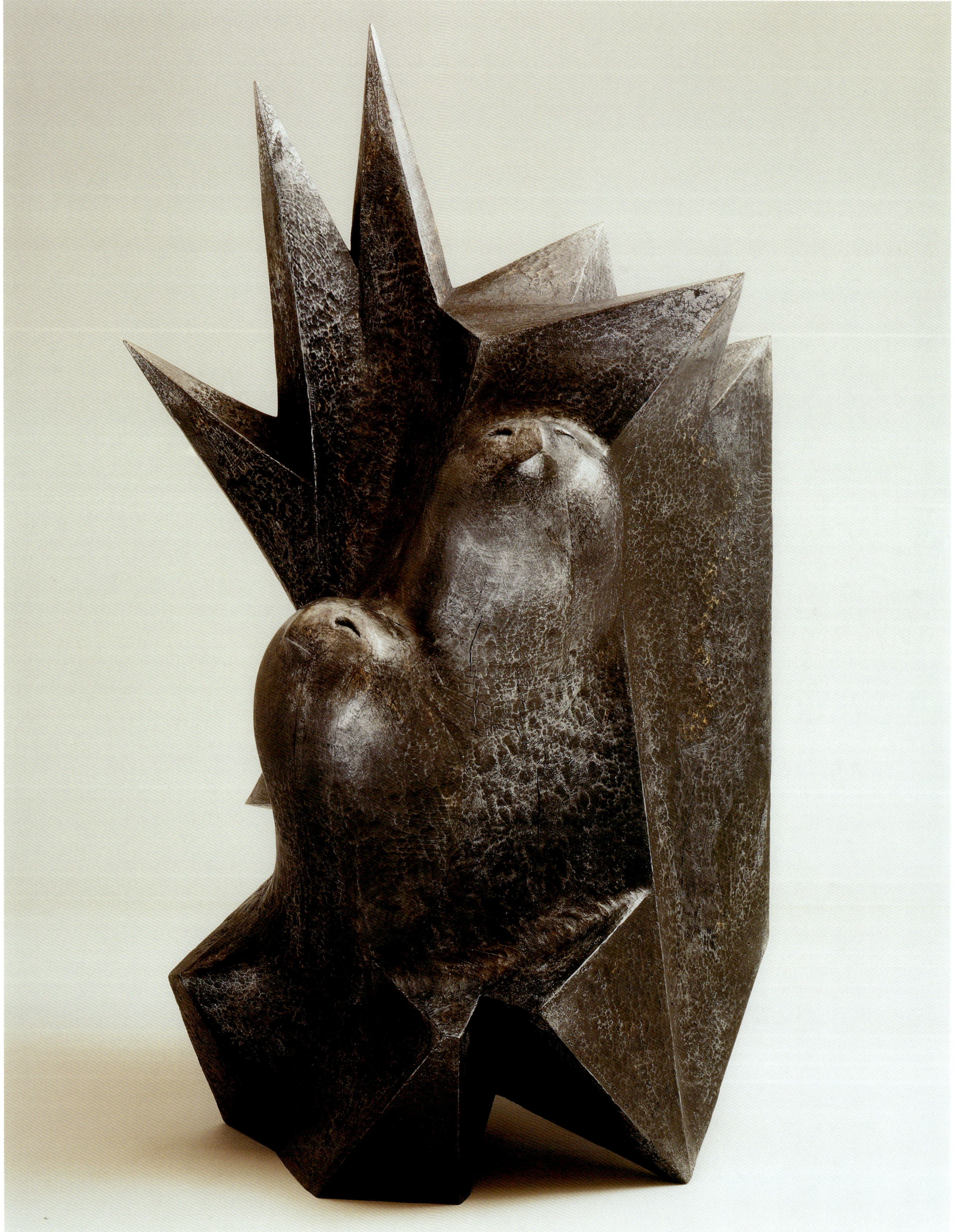

Introduction

"I remember a birthday party when I was a youngster. We played a game that involved carrying a peanut on a knife over a long distance and back to a goal line. We all lined up, balancing our peanuts, and waiting for the go signal.

"Now there was a prize that meant much to me: a little wind-up Indian on a tricycle. We all stood poised, sizing one another up, trying out different means of keeping the peanut on the knife. I noted with dismay that mine was strangely active. It had a savage determination to roll off one side or the other, and if not that, it was disposed to careen up and down the length of the blade.

"When the signal came, several racers immediately sprinted ahead thinking to cover the ground and back before gravity came to its senses. Thus the line was thinned. Of those remaining, I was last. All I saw was the peanut, but I knew space was opening around me as I went. As I neared the turning point, everyone else passed me, coming back. One boy was the essence of grace and assurance, and it made my heart sick to know I was his antithesis. His peanut sat majestically anchored to the bowels of the earth, and oriented to the stars. All I could do was barely keep mine under control.

"By the time I got to the turning point, all thoughts of winning had left me, and been replaced with a burning desire to simply get back at any cost with the peanut still on the knife. However, my joy knew no bounds when I turned to find a marvelous scene of carnage near the finish line. Everyone left was desperately pushing on, and with each falling peanut the race hastened. Every peanut fell but mine, my errant, beloved peanut, and I knew I had won, still out there alone, with all the distance back yet to go. I felt, for the first time, that peculiar and indefinable ecstasy when one discovers that one's own way was, in the end, the best. To feel the air charged with the agony of despair and envy of those who had lost did nothing to dispel my joy."[1]

Philip McCracken's childhood experience doubtless bolstered his determination to trust his instincts and follow his own path—an independence that has marked his life both personally and professionally.

Comet Birds
1996
Cedar
H. 30 in.
Collection of Ron and Mila Hart

His inner compass has as its lodestone a select group of writers, composers, artists, and philosophers he thinks of as his board of directors; it includes Henry David Thoreau, on how to conduct himself; and Sufi poet Jalal al-Din Rumi, whose ecstatic, nature-based mysticism includes such lines as "I am wind, you are fire," and "Oh if a tree could move and wander with foot and wings . . . ," and (significantly) "Let the beauty we love be what we do. / There are hundreds of ways to kneel and kiss the ground." Also on this internal board of directors are composers Claude Debussy and Gustav Mahler; Chinese poet Han Shan, who wrote "My heart is like the autumn moon"; and Romanian sculptor Constantin Brancusi, for the purity of his forms. The board is chaired by the ancient Chinese philosopher Lao-Tzu, who wrote the *Tao Te Ching* (The Way and Its Power). Honorary members include sculptor Henry Moore, potter Paul Bonifas, artist Morris Graves, and Pulitzer Prize–winning poet Lisel Mueller.

If any ideas could be said to characterize each and all of them, they would be an orientation to nature, a propensity for reflection, and a predisposition to look beyond the surface of things to sense their eternal nature. These standards, coupled with a patient perfectionism in the matter of craft, have led McCracken to create a body of work remarkable for its range of materials and its embrace of subjects formerly thought to be outside the bounds of possibility for sculpture.

To pigeonhole him as a bird artist, as a shortsighted critic once did, is to vastly underestimate the breadth of his reach and the heights of his creative imagination. His wide-ranging interests have given him an uncommonly broad scope. His work has ranged from realism to conceptualism, and from subatomic particles through geology, zoology, astronomy, physics, and themes from nature, to abstruse philosophical concepts. He is quite possibly the only sculptor in history to give form to written poetry, and to bird song.

His core message honors the profound mysteriousness of nature, and the oneness of all things, expressed in ways such as the patterns of spiral galaxies reiterated in the growth checks of the wood of an apple tree. He has taken as a subject a single cell (*Genesis*), and delved further into a cell's infinitesimal components (*Birth of a Charmed Quark*). He has worked with wood, with metal, with stone, with bone, with owl down, and with plaster. He has even created his own material, making artificial amber (*Dot.com*). "Each new medium reveals new ways of saying things," he said. Theodore F. Wolff, as art critic for the *Christian Science Monitor,* found McCracken's work "a perfect fusion of form and content."

As a form-giver, McCracken has rendered nature permeable, in the most exact way, to the language of style. This is the result of not only close but ecstatic observation of the natural world. His assumptions are unabashedly transcendentalist; that has been visible in his work for the past five decades.

A fifty-year retrospective exhibition is a major landmark for any artist. Few artists have the sustained output to make such an event possible, much less meaningful. To see the long arc of McCracken's work brings into focus the common ground of the pieces he has brought forth.

Only in retrospect can one perceive the tracks of his fascination with the interface between nature and technology, perhaps best exemplified in *Hornet's Nest.* And only in the last decade has it become possible to gauge the full range of his gifts, and his talent, quite possibly unique, for exploring in equivalent sculptural terms the explosive energies of outer space, the world of living creatures, and the microscopic world, all wrapped in the mysteries of time. It is difficult to think of another contemporary artist who has tackled themes so ambitious.

McCracken's art is that of a man enchanted by the universe, fully cognizant of its dark side. Sculptures such as *War Bird, Lights Out,* and *Cain's Hammer—Kosovo* evidence his recognition of violence. His work crests with emotion. One cannot look at his birds behind bars (*Caged Bird*) without feeling the surge of wanting to break free, or at *Bird Family* without basking momentarily in the downy warmth in which the adults enfold the chicks. Even destruction, which he has evoked with gun barrels and bullet holes, is presented in emotional terms.

While calculation and deliberation go into the planning and execution of each piece, fundamentally his ideas spring from deep wells in the subconscious mind. His exceptionally sure and direct access to these wells doubtless accounts for the authentic power of his images. Those wellsprings have never failed him. In half a century of making images, he has never had one of those dry periods that stall the progress of many—perhaps most—artists.

In 1964, when an annual Washington State Governor's Award was created to honor an outstanding Washington State artist, the first one went to McCracken. In 1994, he received a second honor from the State, the Governor's Arts Award. In 1999, Cornish College of the Arts presented him with a Lifetime Achievement Award. An earlier book on Philip McCracken by Colin Graham, published in 1980,[2] treated McCracken's career up to that point. This book reprises his early works in brief and emphasizes McCracken's later career, from 1980 to 2003.

More than once he has claimed that he doesn't understand the full meaning of his creations, saying candidly, "If I knew what they meant I might never do them." He was working on the Fragments of Night Sky series in the early 1990s when he said, "In a recent conversation with friends, the question arose as to whether I knew what I was doing, and I found myself saying no, I didn't. I realized that I not only didn't know what I was doing, but that I didn't want to know. I wanted to explore this new world without bringing past knowledge and perceptions to it."

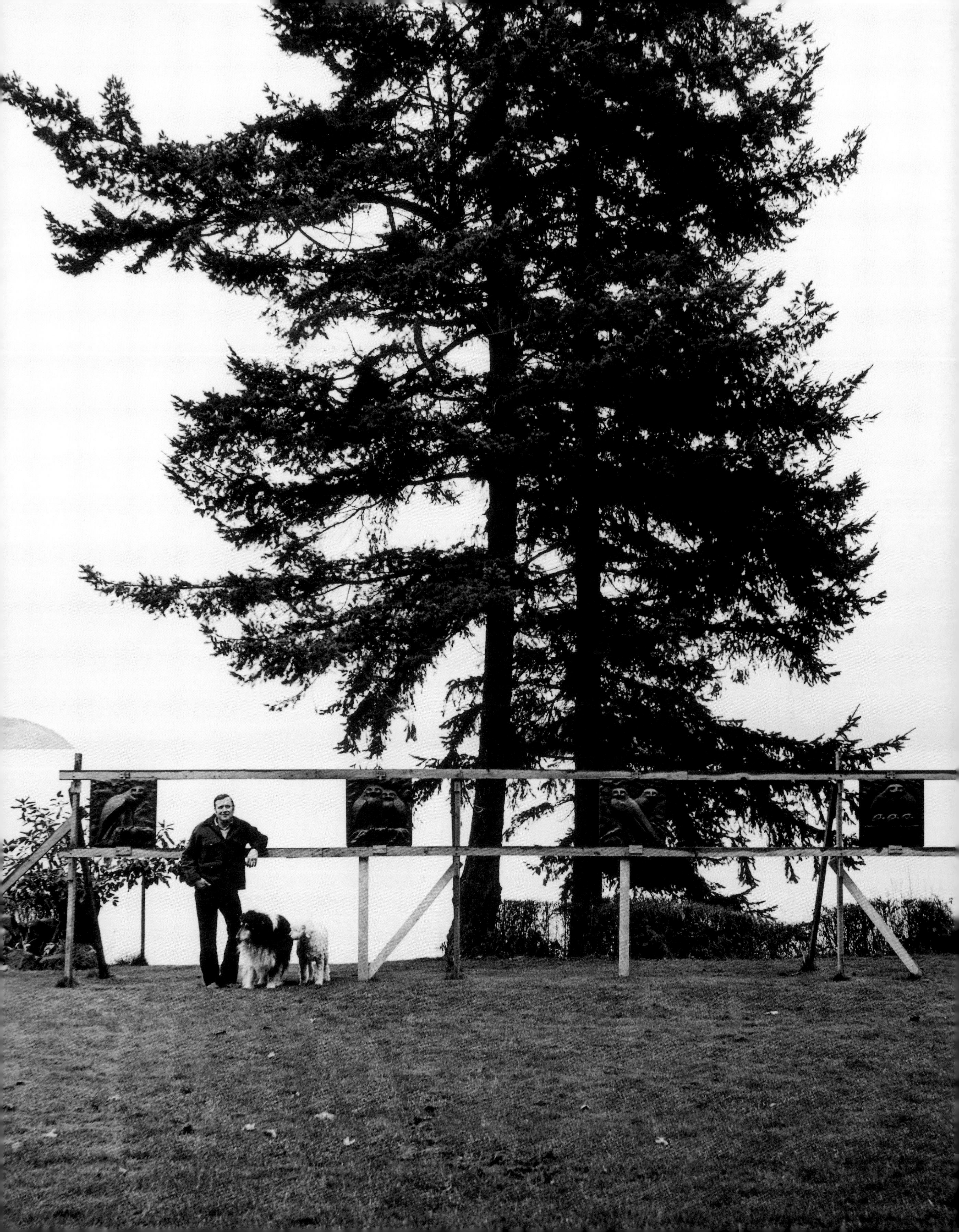

The Artist's Life

)

If Thoreau had been an artist, his work would likely have looked much like that of Philip McCracken. It celebrates the natural world—animal, vegetable, mineral, and the stuff of stars. He has put into sculpture bird song, poetry, and the motion of gasses. No theme is too daunting.

McCracken fears no challenge except, perhaps (like Keats[1]), dying before he can put form to the swarm of ideas that crowd his mind. He is a man of rare abilities, proficient at nearly anything mechanical or structural that comes to hand. He has worked as a commercial fisherman, been a weapons mechanic, and filled the family larder as a hunter. He has done building and landscaping. He is a well-read philosopher, whose musings range from archeology and astronomy to nuclear physics.[2]

His greatest eloquence is with form, into which he pours wide-ranging thoughts. His sculpture testifies to his admiration of animals great and small, especially birds, and their kinship to humans—a relationship he has had ample opportunity to experience.

If ever the lion lies down with the lamb, the McCracken household would be its likely setting. It has been home over the years to a diverse, ever-changing menagerie, from young goats to monkeys and a wide array of birds. As this is written, a great blue heron has taken up residence in the McCrackens' beachfront yard, pacing outside the windows, picking its way across the lawn with that considered statesman's gait peculiar to creatures with front-hinged knees. The heron looks forward to a daily ration of salmon strips that McCracken buys in frozen quantities.

Months ago it was an undernourished young bird with an uncertain future. Then it became the latest in a long line of wild creatures to enjoy the nurturing attention of the McCracken household. When Philip and Anne's three sons were growing up, they had such commonplace pets as hamsters and rabbits. But then came the bad-tempered possum, a delicate fawn, a great horned owl, a mischievous crow, a demanding skunk, and a couple of monkeys bent on wreaking havoc. There was a period when a cat, a dog, and a skunk regularly lined up at the table to beg during family meals, and

Kingdome bas-reliefs in the studio yard, October 1977
(detail of photograph by Mary Randlett)

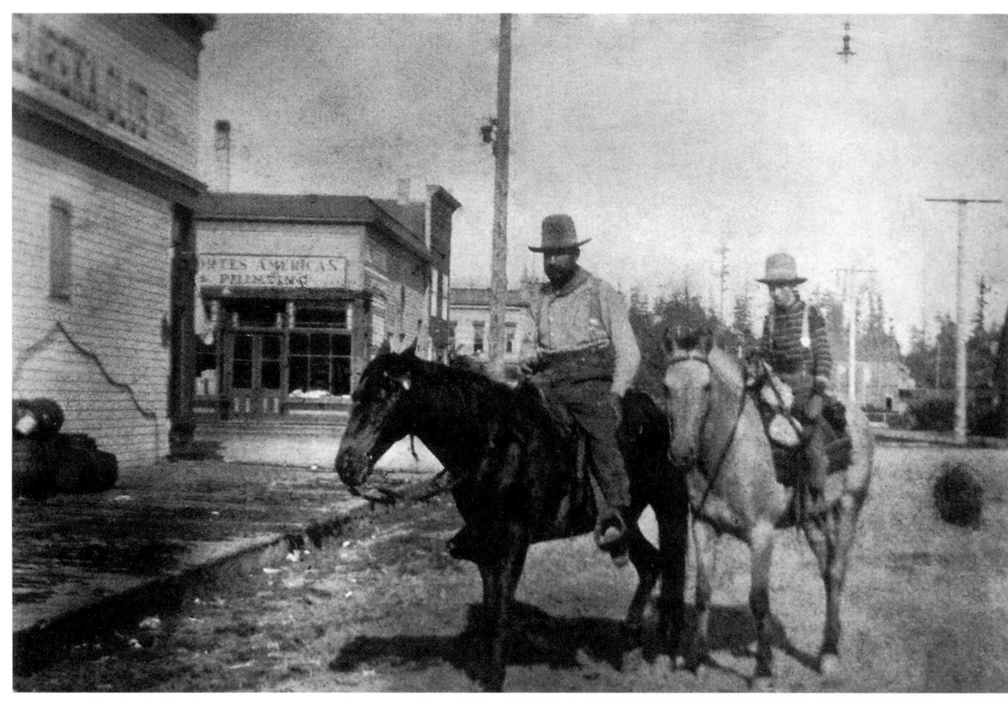

Philip McCracken's father and grandfather outside the Eureka Club Saloon, Anacortes, c. 1906 (McCracken family)

at times, baby goats whom they bottle-fed gamboled through the house, springing from bed to bed.

Although that scenario suggests otherwise, McCracken is not a sentimentalist. He knows life in the wild as a matter of predator and prey. He hunts to keep venison in the freezer. As he once explained to a guest at their table, "If you eat meat, you either kill it yourself, or go to a butcher counter and pay a hired assassin."

Hunting does not preclude his affectionate delight in birds and animals, and their often antic behavior. His absorption in the wildlife of the Pacific Northwest coast is a birthright. His family, now in its fifth generation in Washington State, set down roots when his grandfather traveled west from Colorado as a mining prospector. Although he and his son worked claims in the Marblemount area for many years, he struck gold only when he opened the Eureka Club Saloon in Anacortes, a town on the coast of Puget Sound some eighty miles north of Seattle.

McCracken's father, William, used to bed down on the saloon's pool table when he was small. Later, he was sent off to military school. He had a brief career as a boxer. Family lore has it that he once appeared on the same ticket as John L. Sullivan, before he returned to Anacortes to marry. He opened a store selling feed, grain, and ice. He prospered, and eventually served in the Washington State legislature. Philip, the family's third and youngest child, was born November 14, 1928. His sister, Patricia, was already thirteen; his brother, William, eleven. His father steered the family through the Great Depression of the 1930s without privation. Their vacations were spent at a summer cottage on Guemes Island, a short ferry ride from Anacortes.

Artists' creative passions are often believed to originate in childhood experiences. McCracken's seminal experiences included beach life on Guemes Island during the summer, where he was accustomed to row a skiff down the shore of the island to a dairy farm, and wait at the kitchen table while the milk was pasteurized on the farmer's stove. He fished off the wharves of Anacortes, and joined his brother on duck hunting trips on the Skagit flats. Both his parents liked to fish, and many of his happiest teenage times were spent fishing on the Upper Skagit River. The family home was two blocks from the mile-wide Guemes Channel that

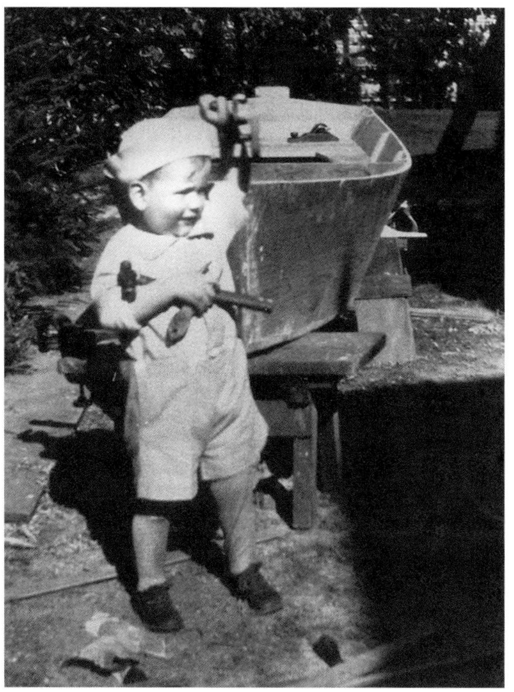

Philip as a child, with tools, 1932 (McCracken family)

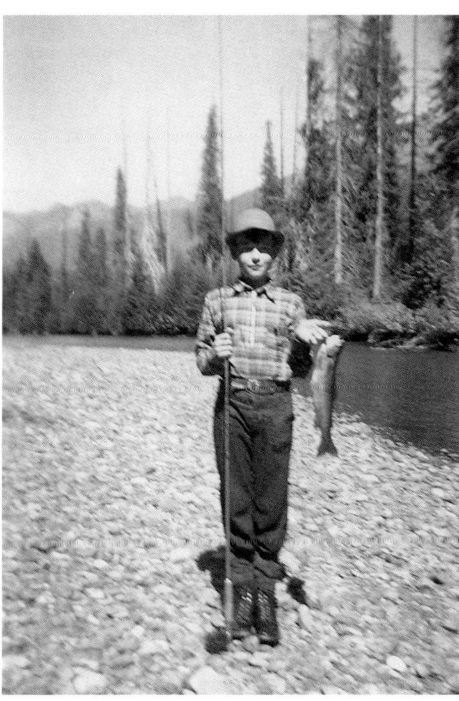

Philip with fishing pole beside the Upper Skagit River, c. 1942 (McCracken family)

separates Guemes Island from Anacortes. One of his favorite high school–age activities on Guemes was to shove off in the family skiff, and row from island to island with his dog.

His family had implicit trust in his ability to take care of himself. He recalls an occasion when he had built a raft and was paddling it fifty yards off the beach. In full view of his parents on the shore, he lost his balance and fell into the water, wearing a heavy Cowichan sweater. The glacier-fed waters of Puget Sound are notoriously cold. They can paralyze even a strong swimmer, much less one weighed down by thick, wet wool. He recalls that his parents didn't show the least concern. They watched calmly while their son rescued himself and got back on the raft.

That sense of confidence in his abilities to solve whatever problem emerges has remained with him all his life, as has a robust physical constitution—an asset nearly a necessity in a sculptor. He played tackle on his high school football team, but he often came home from scrimmages to paint. He had already discovered that drawing and painting were as engrossing as sports. In the small-town climate of Anacortes, however, art seemed a wholly impractical choice as a career. In the autumn of 1947, he enrolled in the prelaw curriculum at the University of Washington in Seattle. It was a course of study his parents recommended, in light of his argumentative nature.

When the Korean War broke out in 1950, McCracken joined the Army Reserves, hoping that would enable him to stay out of the war and remain in school. The plan backfired. The reserves were called up, and after basic training at Fort Ord, McCracken was assigned to El Paso, Texas, as a weapons mechanic. He became a specialist in working on the firing mechanisms of .50-caliber machine guns mounted on the turrets of half-tracks. He had always been interested in firearms, having grown up to think of them as tools to get food. Now he was dismayed to find the Army teaching him refined techniques for killing people with that tool.

The country around El Paso was his first experience of southwestern desert. Coming from the perpetually moist and verdant Northwest, McCracken was initially repelled by the desert. Then he began to be aware of the animal life that came out after sunset. Geckos and small creatures that live in the cracks of masonry walls were far more fascinating to him than gun mechanisms. Much to the bewilderment of his friends, he volunteered for watering detail after his usual workday. He discovered that directing a spray of water behind the stone retaining walls sent a variety of bugs scurrying out into view. The species were different from any he was familiar with. He began to drop some of the more interesting insects into jars stashed in the pockets of his fatigue pants. Once he went off duty, he dipped the insects in successive coats of varnish to preserve them as specimens.[3]

He spent much of his Army time trying to decide what he really wanted to do with his life. Creating art in his high school years had touched an inner need and revealed unsuspected talent. When he was discharged, he returned to Seattle with the backing of the G.I. Bill. He reenrolled at

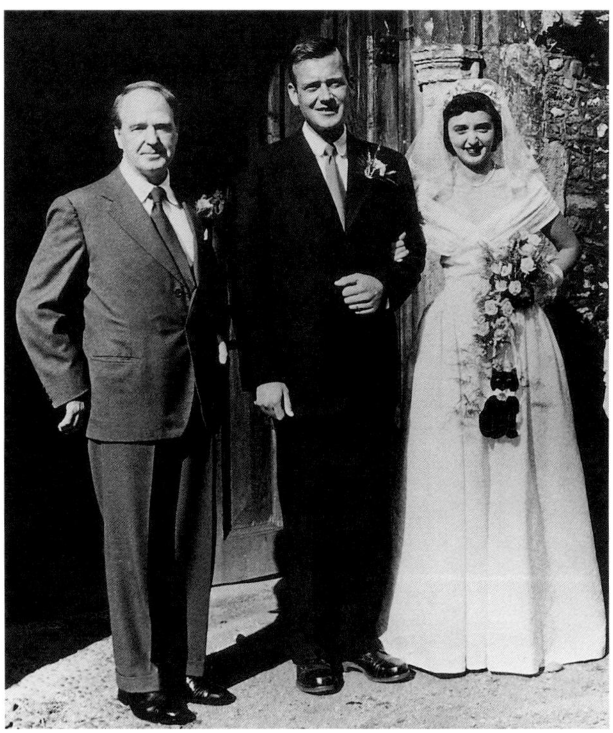
Philip and Anne's wedding, with Henry Moore, 1954 (McCracken family)

the University of Washington, this time in the art department. The art faculty was headed by Everett DuPen, who was supportive of experimentation, as was the French potter Paul Bonifas, who headed the ceramics division. With his exacting standards and his warm humanity, Bonifas came to serve as a role model for McCracken. He met Mark Tobey and Morris Graves, Northwest artists who were exhibiting in New York, and the painter Guy Anderson, whose background had much in common with his own. Their examples made a career in art seem feasible.

McCracken was the only member of his family to graduate from college, much less to consider a career as anomalous as art. His brother and sister had gone to work in their father's business. McCracken's path was clearer to his family when he supplemented the G.I. Bill with money he earned from commercial fishing each summer.

McCracken was awarded the School of Art Prize when he graduated in 1954. Two sculptures he created in art school were prophetic. Although a mobile he fashioned in the style of Alexander Calder was little more than a pastiche, its title, *Rain Forest Forms,* forecast the direction his art was to take. Even more predictive was *Heron,* a wood carving that entered the collection of Morris Graves (p. 110).

In his senior year of art school, McCracken wrote to the noted English sculptor Henry Moore, asking to be taken on as a studio assistant, to learn the practicalities of studio management. "Art schools teach you how to teach, but not how to make a career out of being an artist," McCracken said. "I needed to know things like how to pipe a fountain, and how to write a contract." After Moore examined photographs of McCracken's work, he invited him to England. McCracken lived initially in a pub a short distance from the studio, then took a room in a house across the road from Moore.

From his acquaintance with Graves and Tobey, McCracken had conceived that being an artist meant living as a romantic loner. Like most creative people, McCracken valued a measure of privacy, and time for introspection. Yet he is also sociable, and family oriented. He was delighted to find in Moore a happily devoted family man who, despite living in the country, enjoyed an active social life.

Moore and McCracken enjoyed watching wrestling on TV—a predilection that McCracken explains as having to do with the shapes and volumes of the massive forms. When visiting artists and critics came to tea, McCracken was often thoughtfully invited to join them. He learned a good deal from the artists' conversations about galleries, exhibitions, and patrons. He also learned some vital skills such as stone carving, and how to scale up a three-dimensional maquette into a larger size—an ability essential to public commissions.

Moore joined Bonifas, Graves, and the natural world as influences on McCracken's work. "I embrace influences," he said. "I find a part of me all over the place. That's what makes an artist: putting things together in a new way. Moore said the main ingredient for a sculptor is just to endure. He had been gassed in World War I, and he was happy to be alive. He would come into the studio whistling. Morris Graves said that art comes before life. But Moore said life comes before art. For me, the answer is balance."

Moore's devotion to his family came as a timely revelation to McCracken who, on the ship to Britain, had met and fallen in love with Anne McFetridge, a graduate of Mount Holyoke and Cornell who was headed to London to study the arts of the eighteenth century. On August 14, 1954, Philip and Anne were wed in the Norman church at Much Haddam, near Moore's studio. Moore graciously acted as best man.

That autumn found them living in Mahopac, in Putnam County, New York. McCracken found studio space in a building that was the cookhouse for a summer stock theater. By happy coincidence, sculptor Dudley Pratt, a former U.W. art professor, lived in nearby Croton Falls. When he was studying at the university, McCracken had lived for a while in Pratt's former studio, in Seattle's Madison Park district. McCracken delighted in Pratt's Croton Falls studio, which was laid out in a way that influenced how he organized his own studios in subsequent years. In addition to his tools and sculptures in progress, Pratt's studio held two whimsical features: a candy machine that rewarded children who moved the right levers with a spray of candies, and a sink with three taps labeled hot, cold, and whiskey. Pratt discontinued the latter practice when neighborhood kids persisted in washing their hands in whiskey. During McCracken's time in Mahopac, Pratt taught him how to cast in metal.

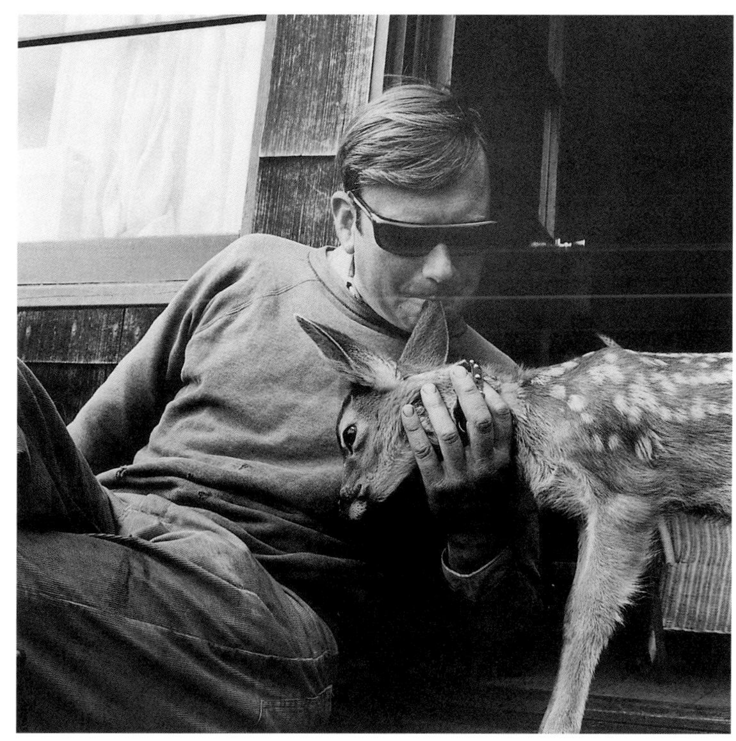

Philip with fawn, June 1968
(photograph by Mary Randlett)

McCracken made the most of every chance to go into the city to visit museums and art galleries. He took his portfolio around, looking for a venue to exhibit his work. The reception was discouraging. At the Kraushaar Gallery he was told, "Young man, you are the twenty-fifth artist this morning who has come in looking for a gallery." One of the most discriminating possibilities was Marian Willard's eponymous Willard Gallery, which began representing the work of Morris Graves and Mark Tobey in New York in the early forties. Graves drew Willard's attention to McCracken, and it was an

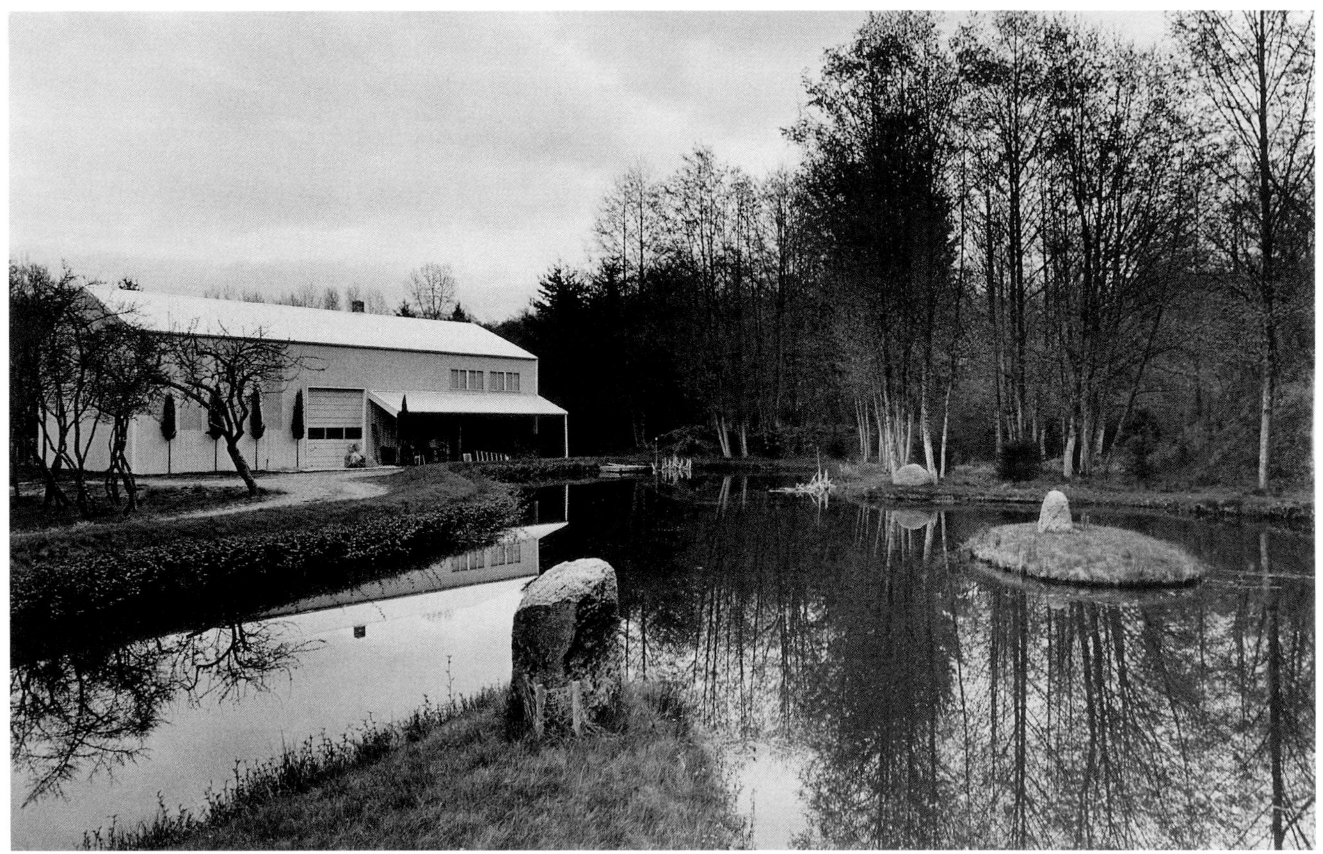

Looking across the pond at McCracken's new studio, April 1990
(photograph by Mary Randlett)

instant fit. Willard held the first solo exhibition of his work in 1960. Five years later, the *New York Times* hailed his sculpture as "Brancusi variations on a Thoreau theme."[4] The *Long Island Press* proclaimed, "McCracken handles wood like a wizard," calling his exhibition "a must";[5] and *Vogue* magazine included his show among the things "People Are Talking About."[6]

Satisfying though it was to participate in the vibrant arts scene in New York, McCracken realized that he was homesick for the water, the woods, and the animals of the Pacific Northwest. Marian Willard had given him one strong piece of advice: don't move to New York City. She recognized the special connection of his work to the natural world, and predicted that if he moved to an urban environment, that connection would be lost.

By the spring of 1955, Philip and Anne had moved to the McCracken family's Guemes Island cottage, a one-room cabin with a two-part sleeping loft. There they reared their sons, Tim, Bob, and Dan. They raised vegetables and kept a few goats. Once the boys were school age, Anne took the eight-minute ferry ride to Anacortes to teach high school English.

McCracken fished and hunted to stock the larder. One afternoon when he was foraging for berries on the interior of the island, he came across a deserted barn and some surrounding acreage. He liked the feel of the place. He made inquiry, and discovered that it was for sale.

He bought the 15-acre farm, using some of the land for livestock, and the barn for his studio. It was set in a clearing surrounded by a phalanx of cedar, hemlock, and fir trees that harbored owls, hawks, eagles, voles, and squirrels. The snapping of a twig often announced the unseen presence of a browsing deer. It is small wonder that such creatures formed the central inspiration for his work.

The studio barn was amply spacious, but it had one serious impediment: it was so drafty as to be virtually unheatable. In the winter his casting water froze, and snow filtered in to cover his tools. He soon moved his work to a small beachfront house that he converted into a serviceable studio.

Anne recalls finding him outside his studio one day putting watercolor in the mud puddles so the mud daubers could build a colorful home. On another occasion, she found him stroking the back of a bumblebee that was wriggling in ecstasy. Those same qualities of imagination and empathy went into his art. Northwest collectors were quick to realize that a sculptor of unusual quality had appeared in their midst. Together with a perceptive following in New York, they saw to it that his nature-based works went quickly into their collections.

By the late 1970s, when he was working on a series of bronze bas-reliefs commissioned for the new Kingdome stadium in Seattle, he had outgrown his studio. He constructed a framework that stretched across the yard to lay out the installation. It was clear that he needed a larger studio.

This time he enjoyed the luxury of designing one to suit his needs. He created a studio building more than seventy feet long and two stories high, set in a clearing in the woods. He made two large ponds for the animals with whom he shared the woods. One, just outside his studio door, curls away into the woods, with an island hummock of grass to welcome water birds. A second, smaller pond is hidden in the trees some distance away. When he set free a tangle of seedling plum trees, the place became complete. The plum branches are thickly covered with lichen and moss, rendering the trees as beautiful in winter as they are in spring blossom and summer leaf. From the bare wood of his studio building to the surrounding evergreens that filter light onto the pond, and the gnarled plum trees with lichen flecked branches, the site is a pitch-perfect reflection of Northwest aesthetics. It is simple, functional, and utterly in harmony with nature.

In his plans for the place, McCracken had drawn the pond with three large rocks punctuating it like a Japanese garden. When the pond was dug, three such rocks—and only three—were found in the excavation, and brought up to be placed in the landscape. It was but the latest of many synchronicities that have enriched his life.

Looking back over their young lives and the many animals with whom they shared their home, Anne shakes her head. "We didn't know any better," she says. Philip replies with a fond smile, "I don't think there is any better."

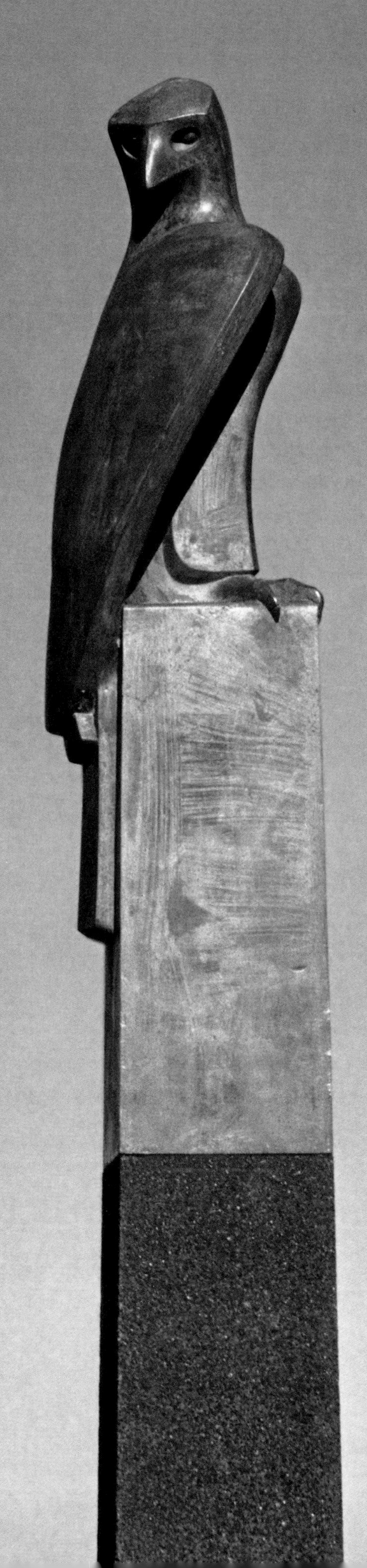

Early Sculpture

Animal imagery that speaks to aspects of the human spirit predominated in McCracken's work in the late 1950s and early 1960s. In the damp dark of Northwest forests, and the mists that hang in towering cedar trees, Northwest Coast Native Americans found reason for belief in animal powers. They understood that any animal might be a shape shifter, a changeling with the power to alter lives. It is always well, then, to treat animals with courtesy, and when they appear at the doorstep, to regard them as honored guests. The same spirit of place and sense of animal strengths communicated with McCracken.

In centuries past, his sculptures *Black Mask* and *Piping Rabbit* might well have added to the repertoire of stories of Northwest changelings. *Black Mask,* produced late in 1953, was McCracken's first breakthrough into a piece that communicated a potent presence. The simple burnt cedar shape is redolent of dark spirits and impenetrable forest depths. The mask form lends it the disturbing quality that something watches through its eyes.

Visored Warrior (1956) was the first in a long line of McCracken's sculptures to be composed of several different, sometimes surprising, materials. A marriage of cedar, pewter, and jasper, *Visored Warrior* is an oddly off-balance creature fifteen inches high, neither human nor animal but suggestive of both. The undulant body, of carved and polished cedar, suggests a toga draped from a shoulder. Inspiration for the helmeted head and the shield inlaid with jasper came from McCracken's trips to armor galleries in the British Museum and in New York's Metropolitan Museum of Art. It is notable that although the figure is helmeted, it is curiously unthreatening.

Soon after he returned to live in the Northwest, McCracken entered *Visored Warrior* and a watercolor from his student days into a juried exhibition in Bellingham. Jurors rejected *Visored Warrior,* but accepted the watercolor, awarding it first prize. The prize was a silver engraved crumb catcher, which McCracken tried in vain to trade for second prize—a ten-dollar cash award. Curators at the Whitney Museum of American Art in New York held *Visored Warrior* in considerably higher esteem. The piece was purchased for the Whitney's permanent collection.

Mountain Bird (detail)
1966 (see p. 33)

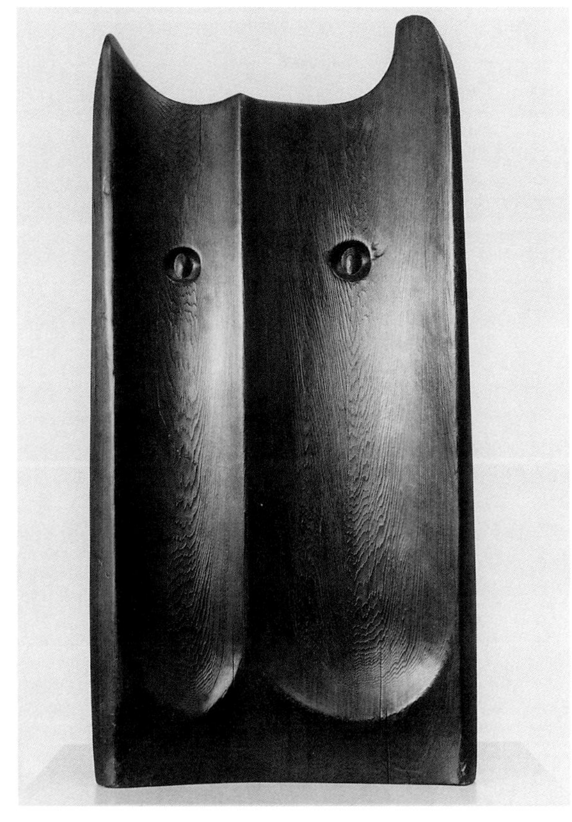

Black Mask
1953
Cedar
H. 28¼ in.
Collection of
Lang and Anne Simons

The charming *Piping Rabbit* (1957) is the antithesis of the darkness exuded by *Black Mask.* An insouciant rabbit (the only one McCracken has ever sculpted) who could have been lifted from a nursery rhyme sits jauntily playing a flute. The music could be for magic, for dancing, or for mischief. McCracken made a clay maquette for a pewter casting, and buried the mold in the ground, to be sure it would have good support when he poured the molten pewter into it. To his dismay, the mold broke apart, and molten metal puddled out into the ground. The piece was so strongly fixed in his mind that he went back into the studio immediately, and made it anew. A mold later taken from the pewter piece was used to make a bronze edition of five.

Caged Bird (1958) introduced a claustrophobic theme. The abstracted form of a life-size owl, carved in red cedar, sits staring out of a steel cage whose bars are almost widely spaced enough for the bird to slip through. The piece speaks to the human tendency to confine animals, but stands with equal eloquence as a symbol of humanity confined by a technological straightjacket beyond its comprehension. The central bar against which the bird pushes bulges noticeably, suggesting the confinement cannot last. The bird is almost greater than that which confines him.

The piece was first shown in New York, in a 1959 group exhibition at the Willard Gallery. It appeared in Paris in 1960 at the Claude Bernard Gallery, and was featured in

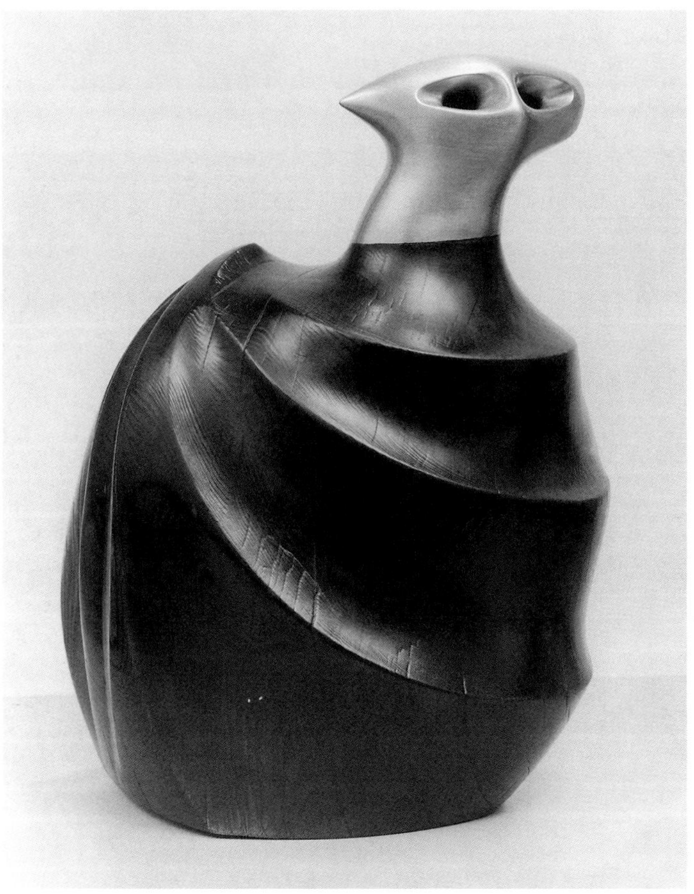

Visored Warrior
1956
Cedar, pewter, and jasper
H. 15 in.
Whitney Museum of American Art

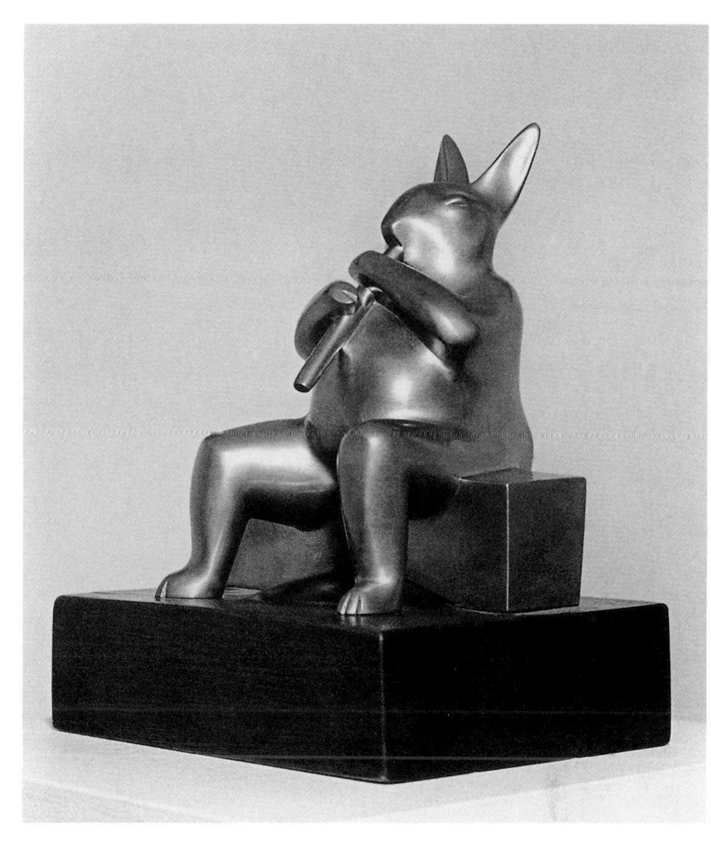

Piping Rabbit
1957
Pewter on wood base
H. 10½ in.
Private collection

McCracken's solo exhibition at the Seattle Art Museum in 1961. *Caged Bird* was purchased by the Frederick Davis family, who made a gift of it to the then-new Seattle Center Playhouse, where it was installed in the lobby in 1962. It is at present a part of the City of Seattle's Portable Works collection.

Birds of Passage (1958) was McCracken's first major sculpture commission, though his second commission for a public place. A year before, he had filled a three-hundred-fifty-dollar commission for a cast-stone and mosaic planter for Canlis Restaurant—not something he thought of as sculpture. *Birds of Passage* was created for the front of the First Federal Savings & Loan Bank in Mount Vernon, Washington. The piece consists of three cast-stone panels that anchor the bronze forms of a trio of birds, and their parallel swooping tracks. With outspread wings, they soar like swallows. But they may be something closer to phoenixes, considering the history of the sculpture.

Some years after its installation, the bank closed, and the sculpture was taken down. No one knows what might have become of it had not Art Hupy, a photographer who was responsible for the organization of the Valley Museum that later became the Museum of Northwest Art, rescued it. He took it to the Gaches Mansion in La Conner, where the museum's early exhibitions were held. For some years, it lay on the dirt floor of the building's basement. The sculpture was installed

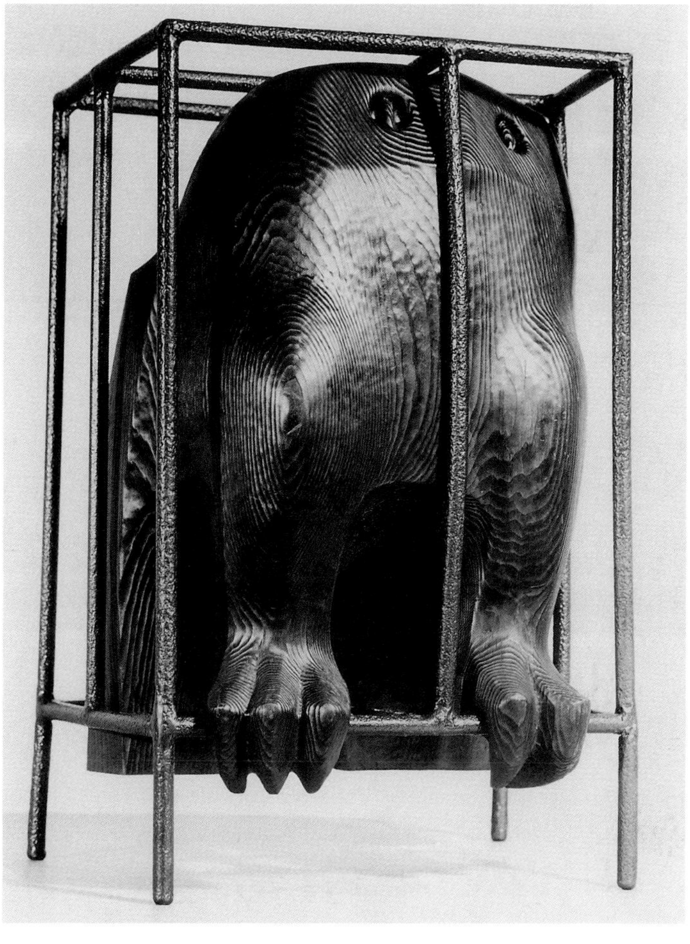

Caged Bird
1958
Cedar and steel
16¼ × 9½ × 8½ in.
Mayor's Office of Arts & Cultural Affairs,
City of Seattle 1% for Art Program

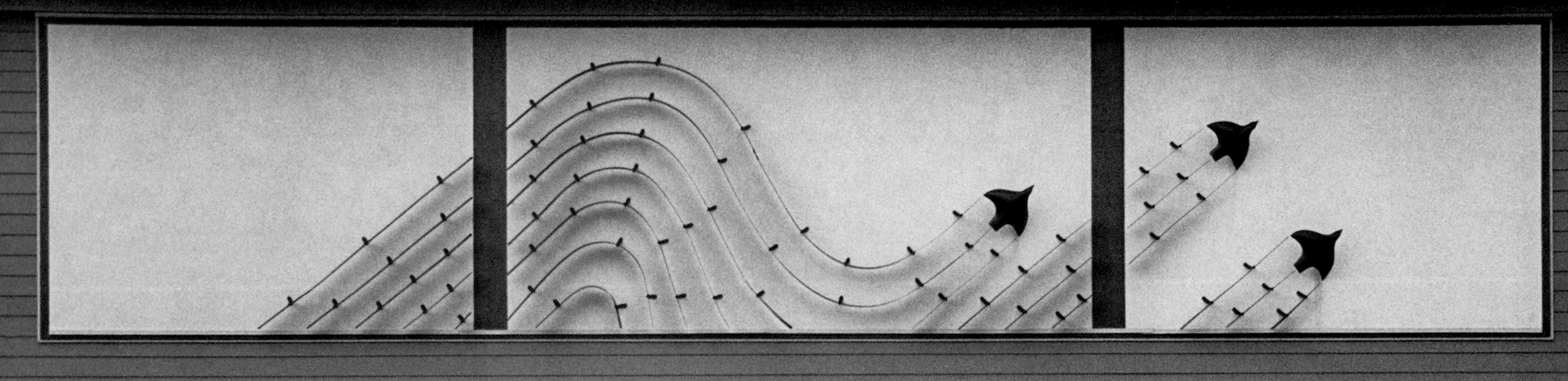

Birds of Passage
1958
Bronze
H. 84 in.
La Conner Middle School,
La Conner, Wash.

Out of Darkness
1959
Juniper
H. 10 in.
International Minerals and Chemical
Corporation, Skokie, Ill.

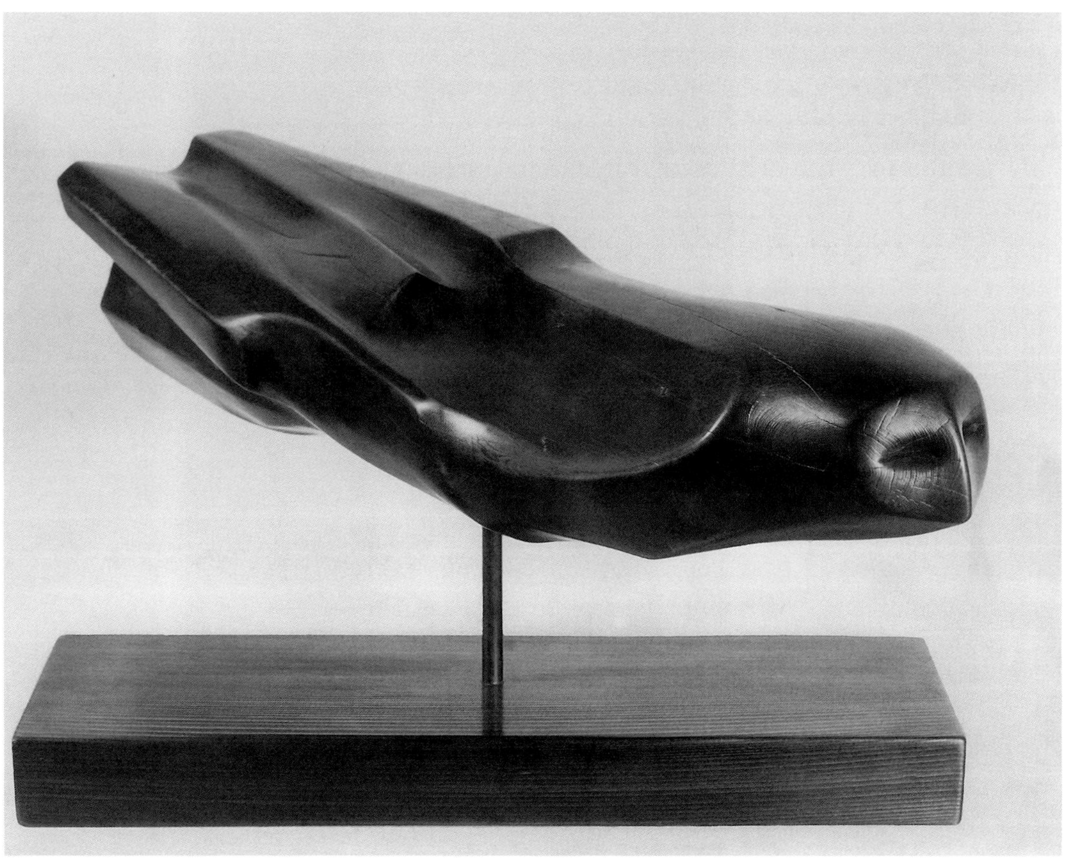

in 2000 at the La Conner Middle School, a placement that appears eminently appropriate for it.

Colin Graham noted that *Out of Darkness* (1959) evokes an old Anglo-Saxon parable likening human fate to that of a night-flying bird that plunges briefly into a lighted hall, only to pass swiftly into the oblivion of night.[1] Made of carved and polished juniper, the piece looks as aerodynamic as a delta-wing plane. The surface invites the hand's caress.

Restless Bird (1959) was made for the plaza in front of the Norton Building, at 801 Second Avenue, the first private office building in Seattle to commission art for a public area. To create the nine-foot piece, McCracken used the technique he learned from Henry Moore to scale up the size of a small maquette. *Restless Bird* is a raptor with its eye on prey, poised to move in a strike. The fabricated stone is made of granite chips, granite sand, and white cement. It weighs four tons. The piece was cast at Olympian Stone (now Precast, Inc.) in Redmond, in two sections joined by thick stainless steel rods through the legs.

Winter Bird (1961) carries the spare beauty of cold light and leafless trees. The abstracted shape of an emaciated, hungry bird is carved in juniper wood polished to a high sheen. Its most recognizable features are the eyes of its uplifted head, and the lengthened talons of its feet, which are curled around the irregular shape of a base whose curving top flows smoothly into crisp angles at its foot. This sculpture is nineteen inches high.

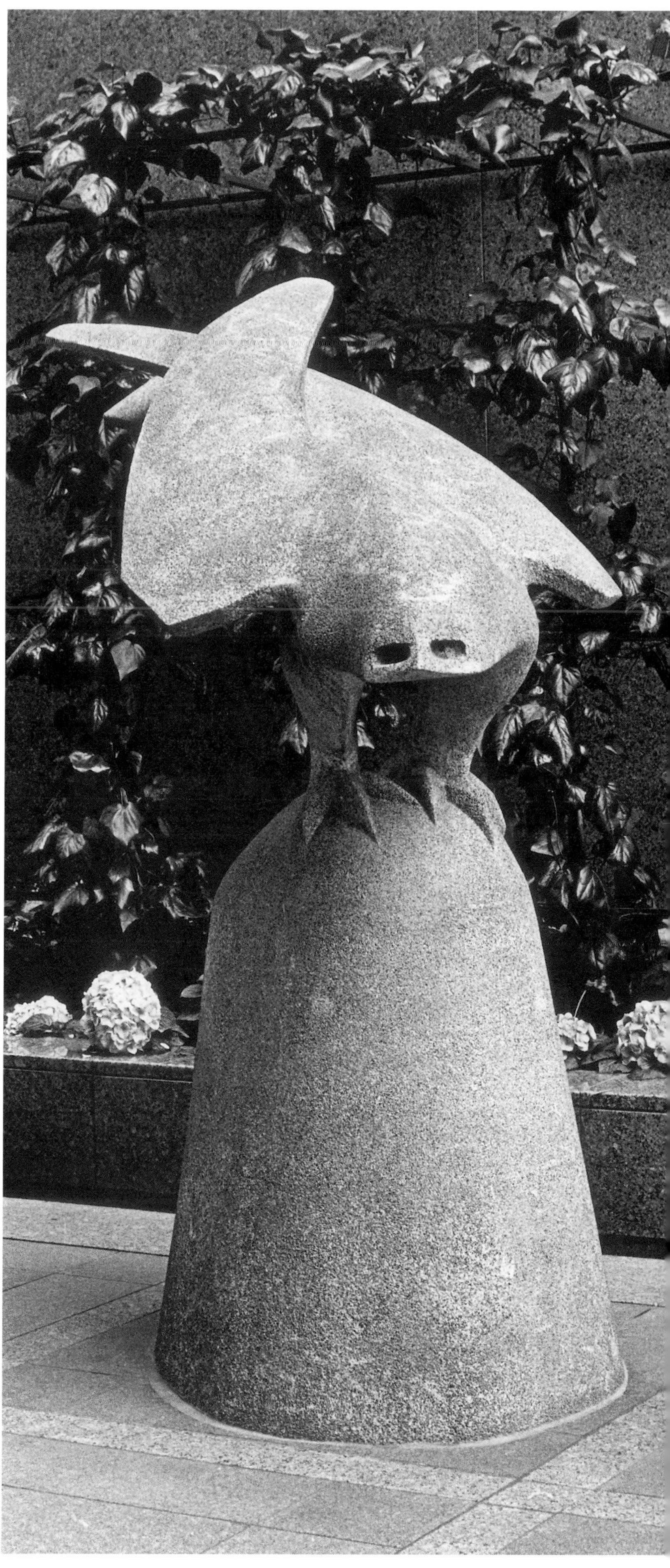

Restless Bird
1959
Cast stone
H. 108 in.
Norton Building, Seattle

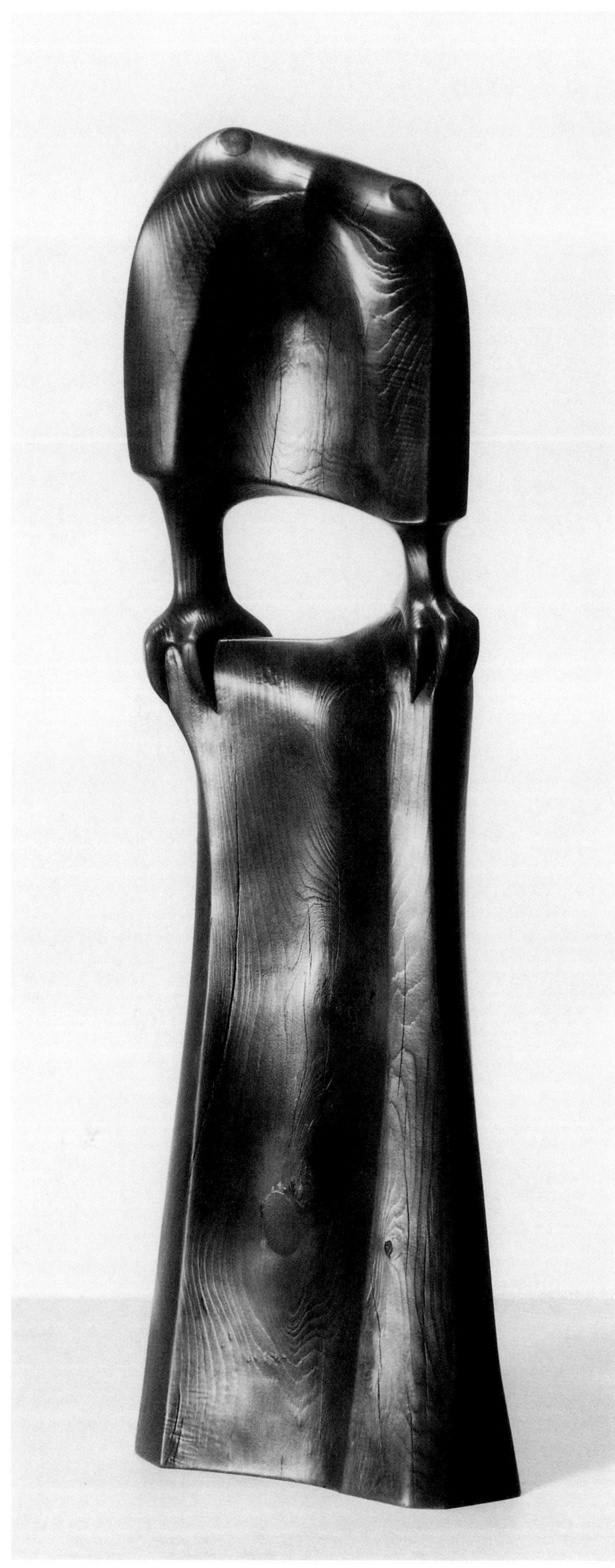

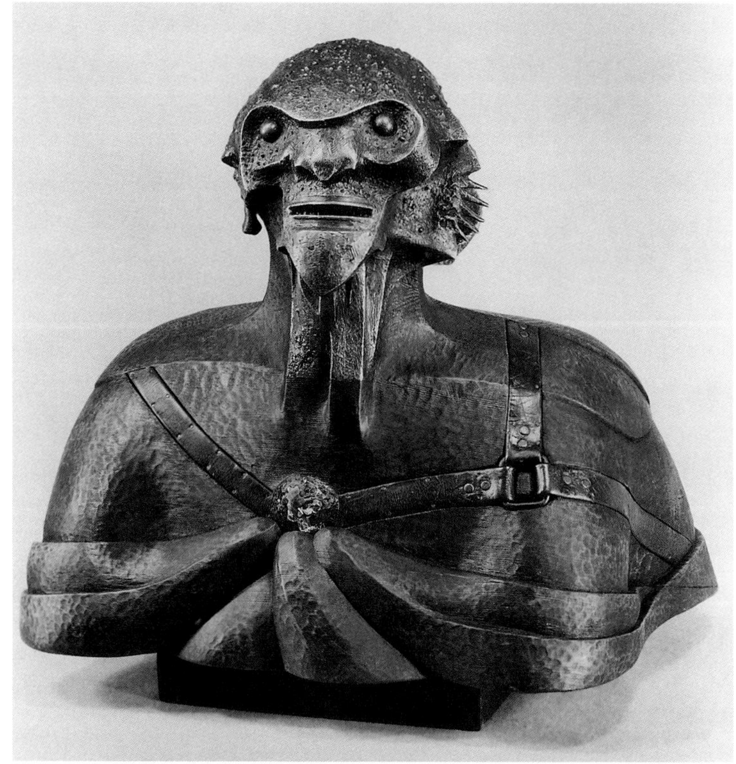

Winter Bird
1961
Juniper and petrified wood
H. 19 in.
St. Louis Art Museum,
Gift of Mr. and Mrs. Joseph Pulitzer, Jr.

Ocean Sorcerer
1961
Cedar, pewter, leather, and shell
H. 25 in.
Location unknown

Ocean Sorcerer (1961) is a remarkable image of a folk wizard from marine depths, a half-serious phantom bent on evoking a frisson of awe. The torso was carved of cedar. Leather shoulder straps that meet at the center of the breast are joined with a circular clasp of abalone shell. McCracken modeled the head of clay, inset with an extraordinary assemblage of materials that included ball bearings, salmon spine, part of an MJB coffee can, the carapace of a kelp crab, and sea urchin shells. All of those disparate elements lost their separate identities in the final pewter casting.[2]

Shortly after it was completed, *Ocean Sorcerer* was featured in an exhibition in Akron, Ohio. Short of a miracle, it will never again be exhibited. It was reported missing from the

Ivory Owl
1961
Fossil ivory and garnet
H. 9½ in.
Private collection

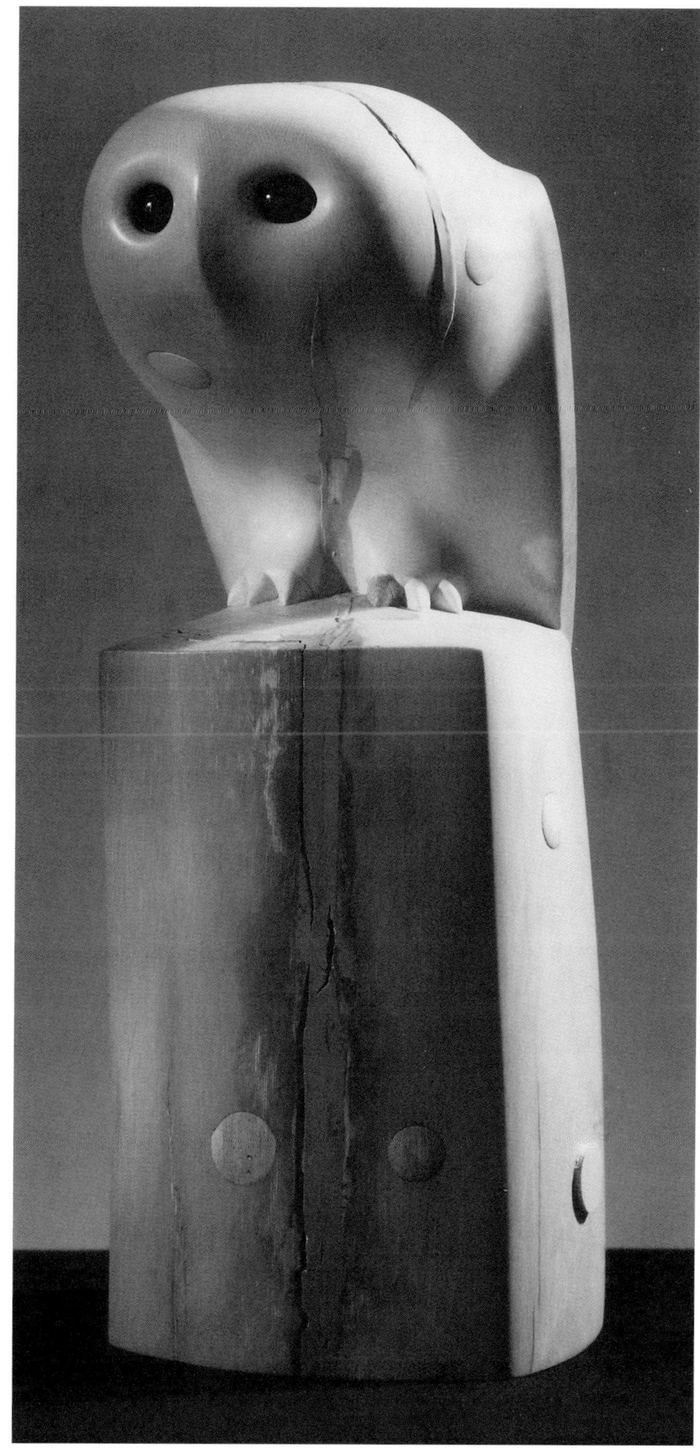

train on which it was being returned to Washington State. Inquiries revealed that the train had derailed somewhere along its route, and several boxcars had broken open. Most of the cargo consisted of paper, much of which had blown and scattered. To expedite cleanup, heavy equipment was moved in to push the ruined cargo into a ditch and bury it. *Ocean Sorcerer* is believed to be interred in a ditch somewhere along the rail line.

Ivory Owl (1961) bears testimony to McCracken's perennial willingness to experiment with new materials, and to the fact that no amount of skill can compensate for quirks in an unfamiliar medium. The piece was carved from the ivory of a mastodon tusk that McCracken received unexpectedly as a gift. He often chatted with the Guemes Island mailman. During one of their conversations, McCracken learned that the carrier had a brother in Alaska who was engaged in placer mining. Among other things, the brother had found a lode of fossil ivory. McCracken remarked that it was a material he'd like to work with some day. Shortly after, when he went out to collect the mail, he found a large section of mastodon tusk poking out of the box with a note saying, "Maybe you can make this live again."

He carved the smooth form of a white owl, with inset garnet eyes. Crouched on a plinth that is part of the same tusk, the whole stands just nine and a half inches high. The form is so direct and minimal that it could have come from an Ice Age shaman.

Fossilized ivory presents its own challenges, McCracken discovered, unlike those of any other material. He was accustomed to wood, which checks from the outside in as it dries. Mastodon ivory, by contrast, checks in layers around and around, as the tusk grows. He had sent the finished piece

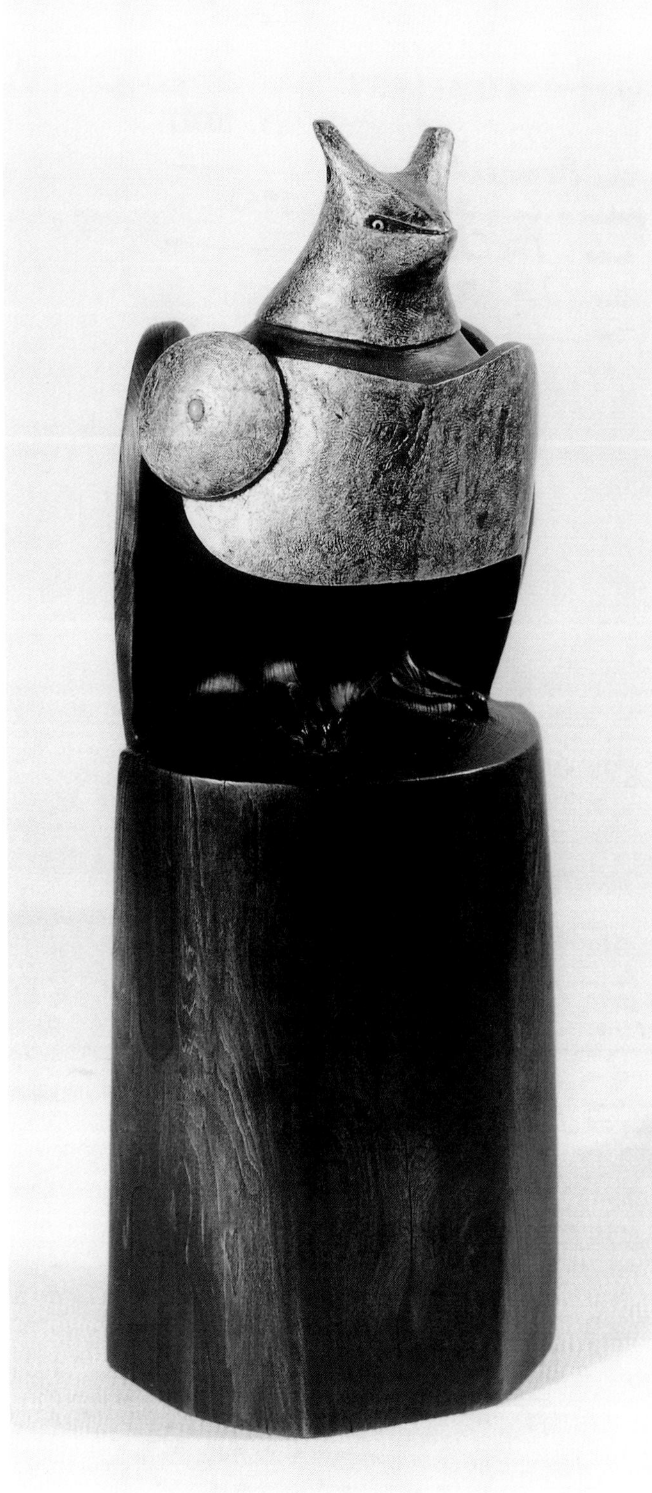

Armored Bird
1963
Juniper, gold leaf, gold chain, and opal
H. 10½ in.
Virginia Haseltine Collection of Pacific Northwest Art,
University of Oregon Museum of Art, 1975:3.21

to the Willard Gallery in New York, where winters are colder and dryer than those in the Pacific Northwest. In the dry, heated gallery air, *Ivory Owl* checked open, and was sent back to him for repair. He fixed it with filler and returned it to the gallery. Within a few months it came back to him a second time, after it shrank and checked again. This time McCracken bolted the form to hold it tight, and cut plugs out of fossil ivory, fashioning them into dowels to cover the bolts. Back in New York a third time, the dry air and the inner stresses of the ivory triumphed over the repair. It shrank and popped the dowels. By this time, Marian Willard's daughter Miani had taken a great fancy to the piece, and took it home with her. It is now in another private collection.

Armored Bird (1963) is another helmeted figure that, like *Visored Warrior,* bears no look of violence. But this bird's sharp eye (an opal) peering from the slot of the gold-leaf helmet, and the ears standing at sharp attention, as if listening for an imminent attack, give *Armored Bird* a more waspish aspect than the earlier *Visored Warrior.* Like *Ivory Owl,* the figure and its plinth are carved from one continuous piece. Gold leaf and juniper wood complement each other handsomely, and McCracken has made the most of it; the broad breastplate and the domed form of the round shield contrast with the broad wings. The gold breastplate casts the lower body in deep shadow, maximizing the differences of light and dark, and only the three-toed feet show on the pedestal.

Mountain Bird (1966), which depicts a predator, was commissioned with a bequest to the city of Anacortes from Gus Hensler, in gratitude for a lifetime of happiness there.

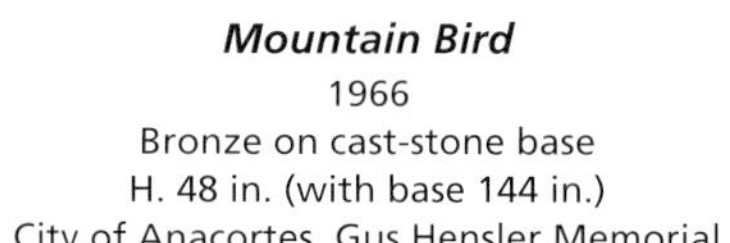

Mountain Bird
1966
Bronze on cast-stone base
H. 48 in. (with base 144 in.)
City of Anacortes, Gus Hensler Memorial

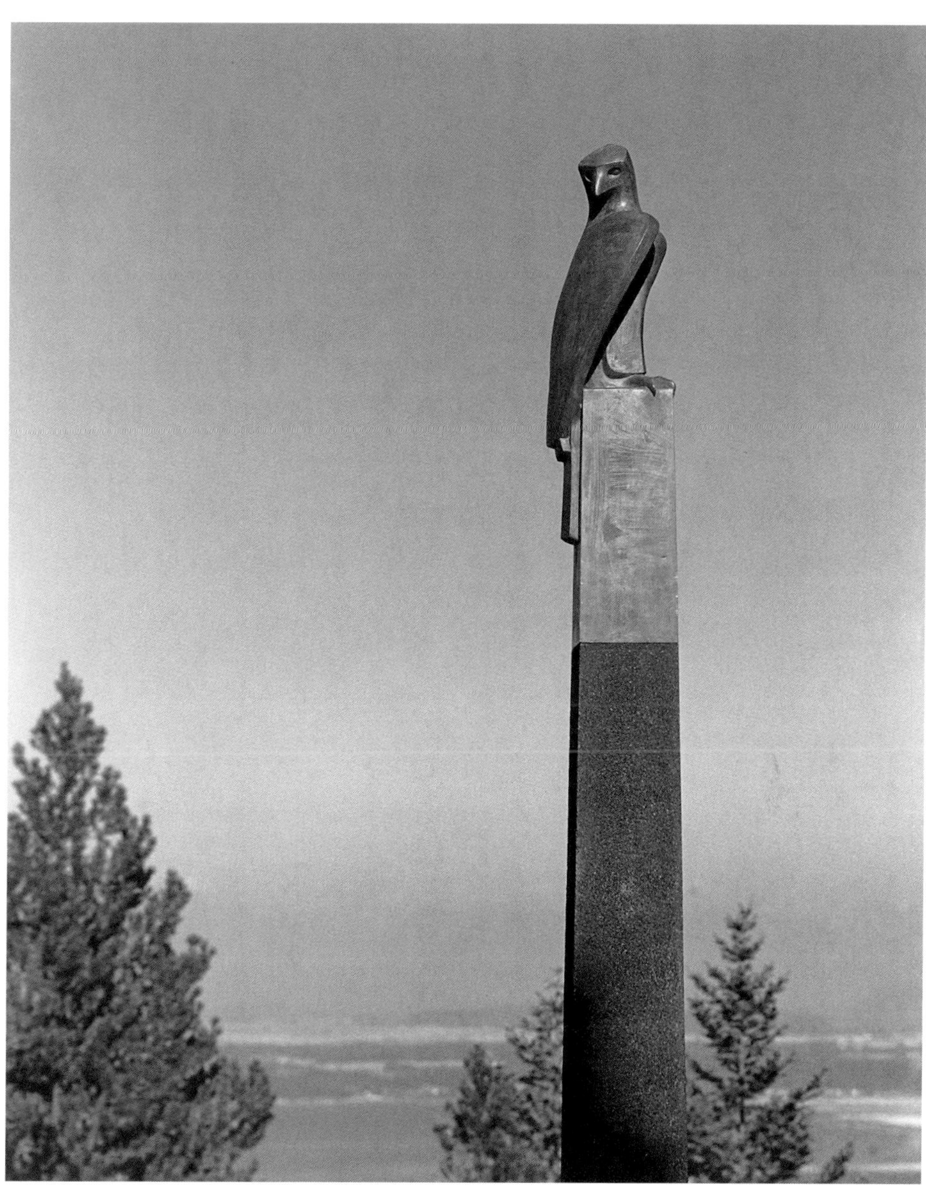

The piece stands as a sentinel on a twelve-foot column at the summit of nearby Mount Erie. The bird was cast in especially tough bronze to withstand possible damage from gunfire. McCracken knew that any object in a remote setting that can be used as a target is apt to be shot at. Within a week of *Mountain Bird*'s erection, shots had been fired at it, hitting the breast and the corner of one eye. McCracken found the evidence in the form of splattered lead. The bronze showed only the faintest traces of damage. Tiny chips had been blown off the corner of a wing and faceplate.

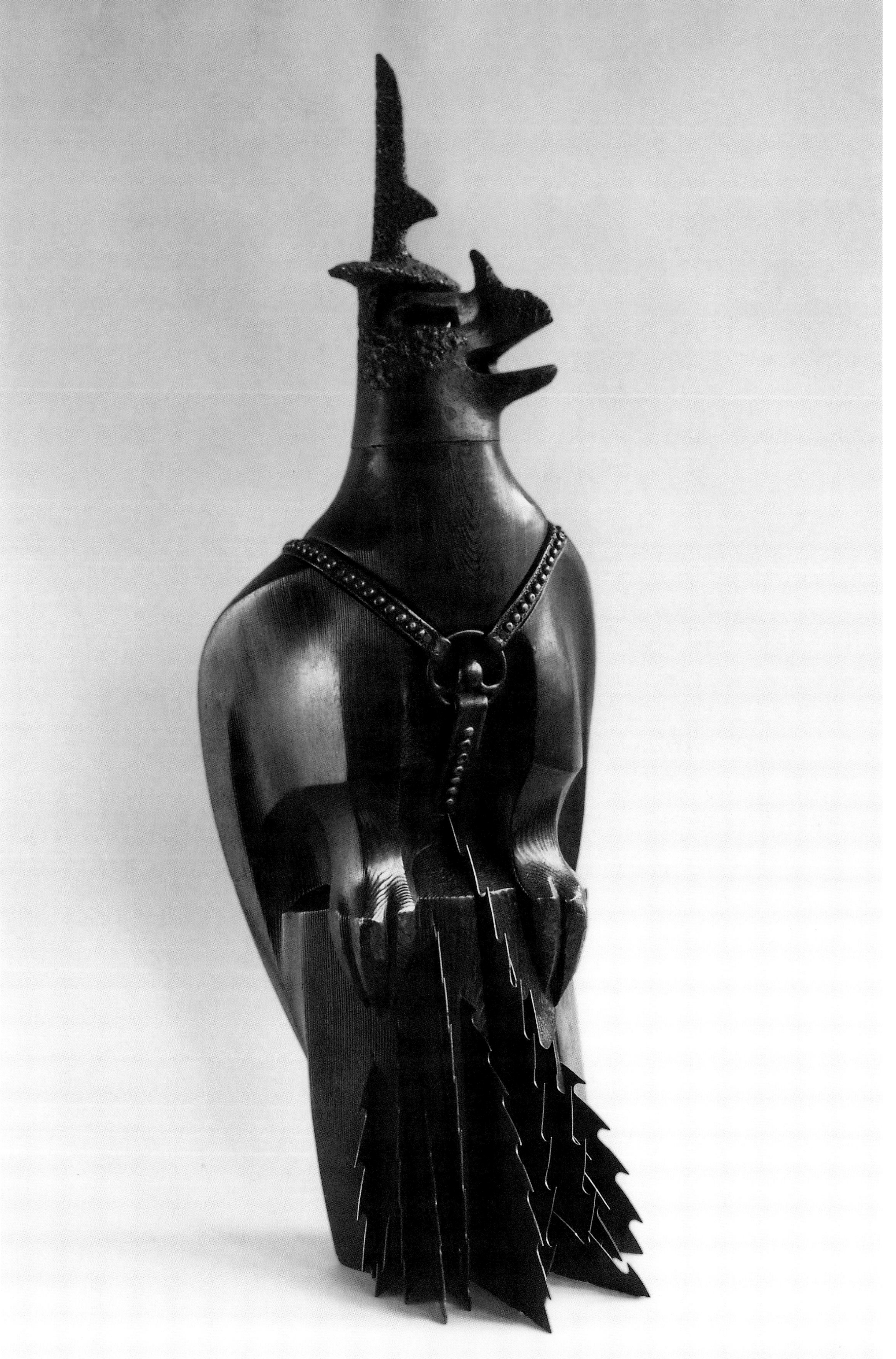

Violence

Violence is rarely a popular subject with art collectors, no matter how avid their appetite for it may be in films and television. Visual art is different. Unlike other media, in which issues are raised then resolved, a sculpture or a painting is in a frozen state; shapes and colors remain permanent once the artist is content with them. Black remains black. Bullet holes howl open-mouthed each time the eye passes over them.

A painting or sculpture on the theme of violence can feel like a never-ending scream. Yet nearly every artist at some time feels the need to express pain, or frustration at political events, in his or her most eloquent language: art. If the resulting artwork is painful to see, even ugly, that is part of the point for many artists. Not for McCracken. He could no more create deliberate visual dissonance than he could deliberately maim himself.

As a lifelong analyst of the natural world, McCracken knows intimately the extent to which violence is a part of nature. Yet the ubiquitous, gratuitous violence of the contemporary political world puzzles and appalls him. His fascination with that aspect of the world surfaces in many of his artworks. Such pieces emerged from his studio with particular force during the decade of the 1960s, when public protest was strong in the United States against the government's role in fighting an undeclared war in Vietnam. The intersection of beauty and violence is at the heart of many of these pieces.

War Bird (1960), the first of a series on the theme of violence, is an icon of aggression based on a hawk, a bird whose predatory prowess has made its name a byword for anyone avid for war. McCracken had been watching hawks strike at his chickens and admired their swift beauty. *War Bird* is carved of red cedar. Its helmeted iron head wears a wickedly down-turned beak with a spiked horn. The studded leather straps over the shoulders are the trappings of military might. For the first, but not the last time, McCracken used segments of a circular saw blade to invoke icy menace. Only intuition, not logical calculation, could produce such an organic fusion of materials so dissimilar.

War Bird summed up what McCracken later called "the elements of the human condition which I find most perplexing and arbitrary." His stated aim was "not to judge

War Bird
1960
Cedar, steel, leather, and copper
H. 40½ in.
Seattle Art Museum,
Gift of the Seattle Art Museum Guild

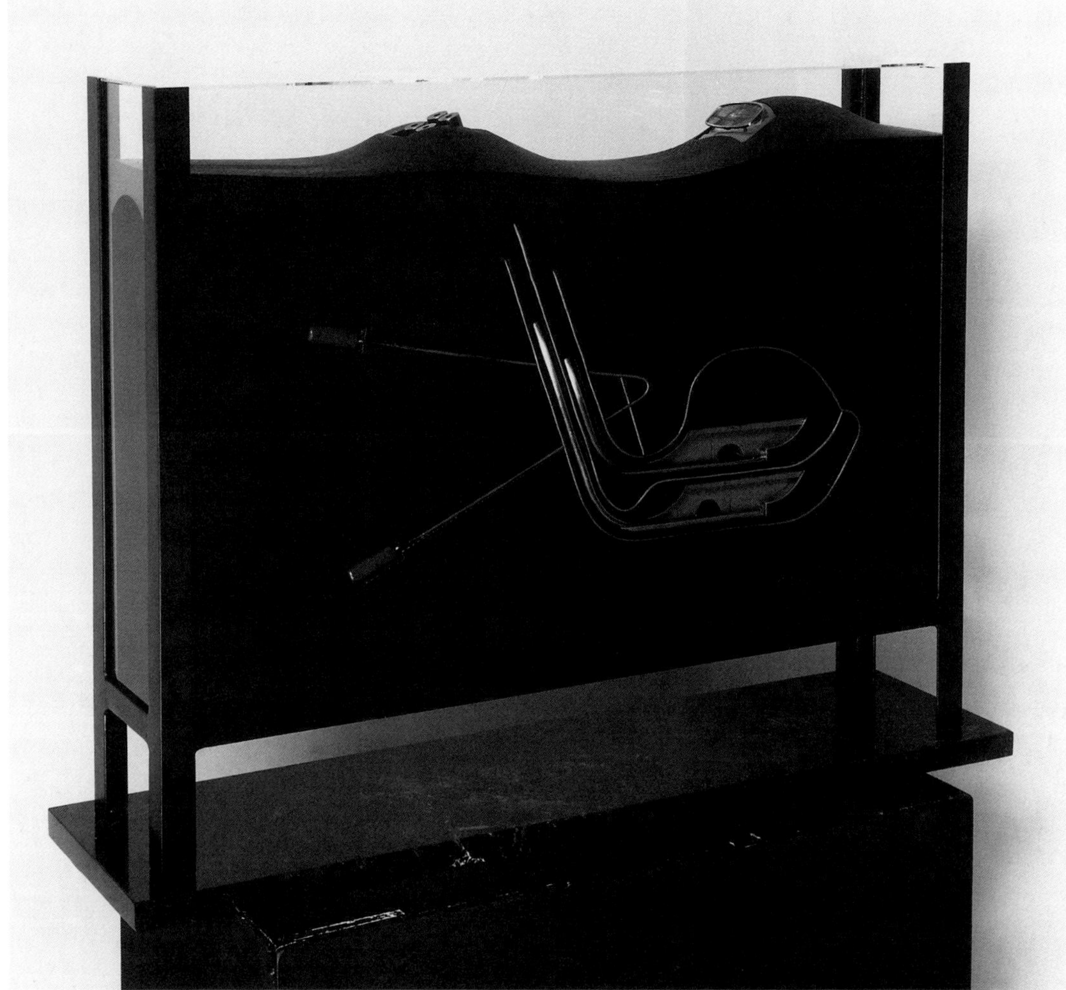

Insect Revolt
1966
Cedar, metal, and glass
22½ × 30¼ × 8 in.
United Nations Association,
New York

our condition, nor to condemn it, but to attempt to understand it." In that attempt, he emphasized, "Aesthetics always prevail over the temptation to become didactic. If I can't put a critical observation into an aesthetically adequate form, I don't make it."

He did not return to the theme of violence until 1966, when a stepping up of U.S. air strikes in Vietnam, and the reported suffering of U.S. combatants there, carried his focus into the arena of international crises. As vividly as any occupant of New York, London, or other major urban center, he was feeling the tensions of an increasingly savage world. He responded with bullets.

"Bullet holes in glass are expressive of violence, yet in themselves they are beautiful, like crystal stars, cold and timeless," McCracken said. He made use of their beauty in several pieces, each of which required that he first drop by neighboring homes to forewarn them they would hear gunshots from his studio later in the day, and should not be alarmed by them.

The first fully developed construction to utilize gunshots was *Insect Revolt* (1966). Based on an ant farm squeezed between two panes of glass so the ants' movements can be watched, McCracken's piece is an audacious assemblage of radio parts, gun barrels, and wires. The back pane of glass is shattered by bullet holes. The piece is a symbolic microcosm of human aggression, paranoia, and insane bellicosity. It speaks to the futility of self-destructive obsessions. Fittingly, the piece is in the collection of the United Nations Association in New York.

Bullet holes are also an integral part of *Healed Up Sky* (1967). A sheet of Plexiglas suspended over a painted cloud has been penetrated by four bullet holes that cast their shattered shadows against the white cloud and a gloriously blue sky. The bullets' points of entry are shown in the canvas as

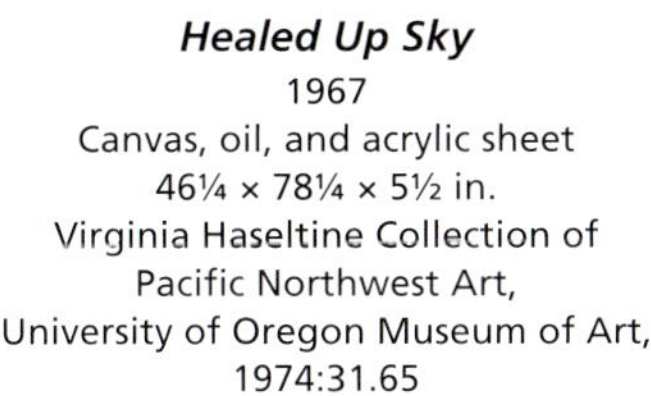

Healed Up Sky
1967
Canvas, oil, and acrylic sheet
46¼ × 78¼ × 5½ in.
Virginia Haseltine Collection of
Pacific Northwest Art,
University of Oregon Museum of Art,
1974:31.65

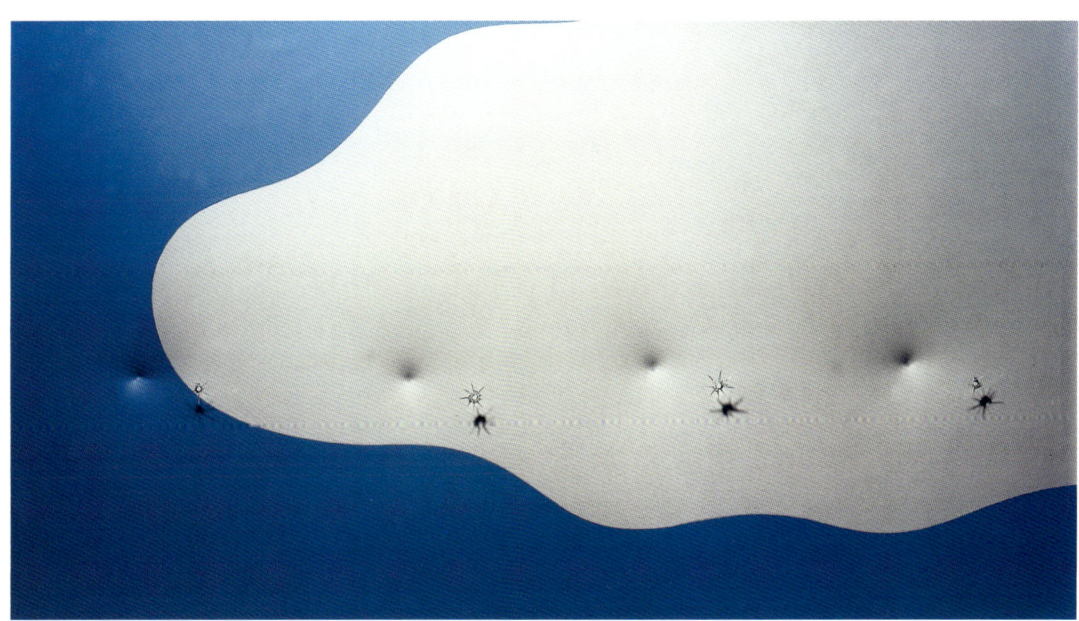

dimpled spots that appear to have healed up as the cloud moved, although the dark shadows persist. The painting has the hard edges and simplified contours artists loved in the mid-1960s. It is large enough—forty-six and a quarter inches high by eight feet wide—to pull the viewer in. Despite its stark beauty, the piece is ominous in no small part because the shape of the cloud can be read as the recumbent form of a white-swathed body.

In the mid-1960s great American cities were afire with riots, and the Vietnam War was approaching its climax. Undercurrents from those events are reflected in the ripping blade of *I Saw* (1967). The piece is a symbolic comment on the polite spin put by the media on deeds of annihilation. A sheet of transparent acrylic bears a cut that looks almost surgical in its neatness. Yet we can see all too clearly how, underneath, the circular saw blade has shredded the canvas through which it chews like a feeding shark. *I Saw* is as succinct a piece of antipropaganda propaganda as ever left an artist's studio.

The most chilling image came with *Lights Out* (1967), McCracken's final statement on gun-crazed folly. It is the coldest piece of McCracken's entire body of work; a response to political assassinations, including that of President John F.

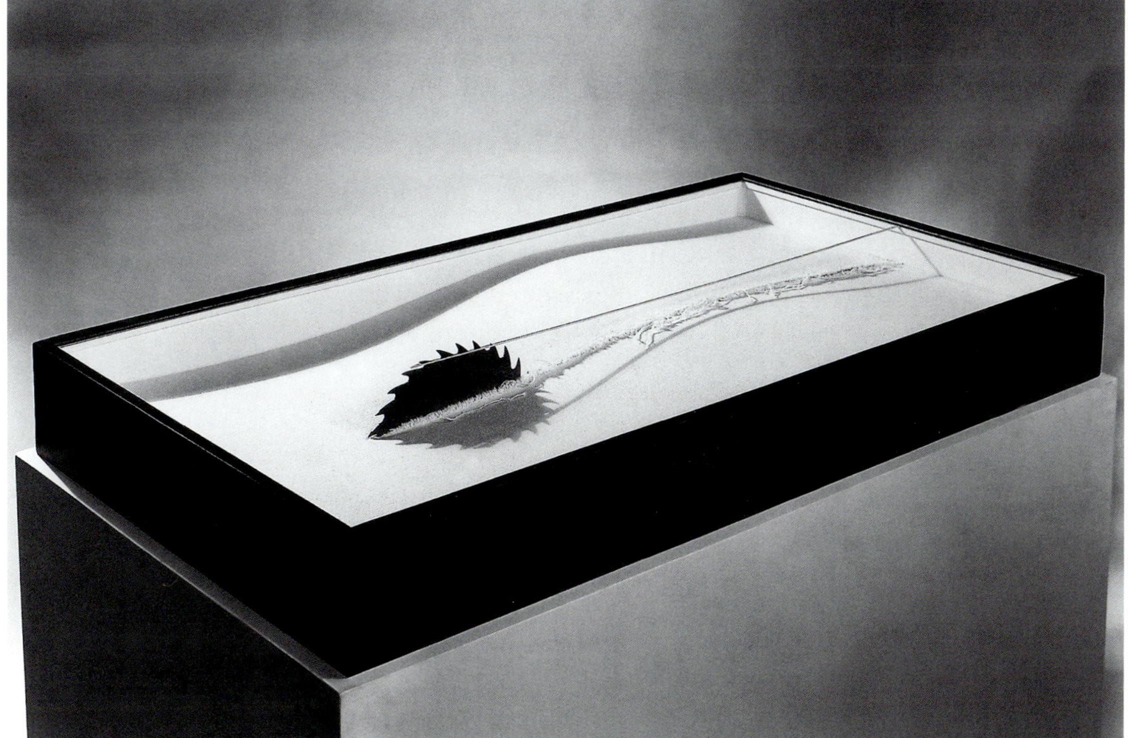

I Saw
1967
Acrylic sheet, canvas, wood,
and saw blade
5½ × 46½ × 25 in.
Museum of Contemporary Art
San Diego

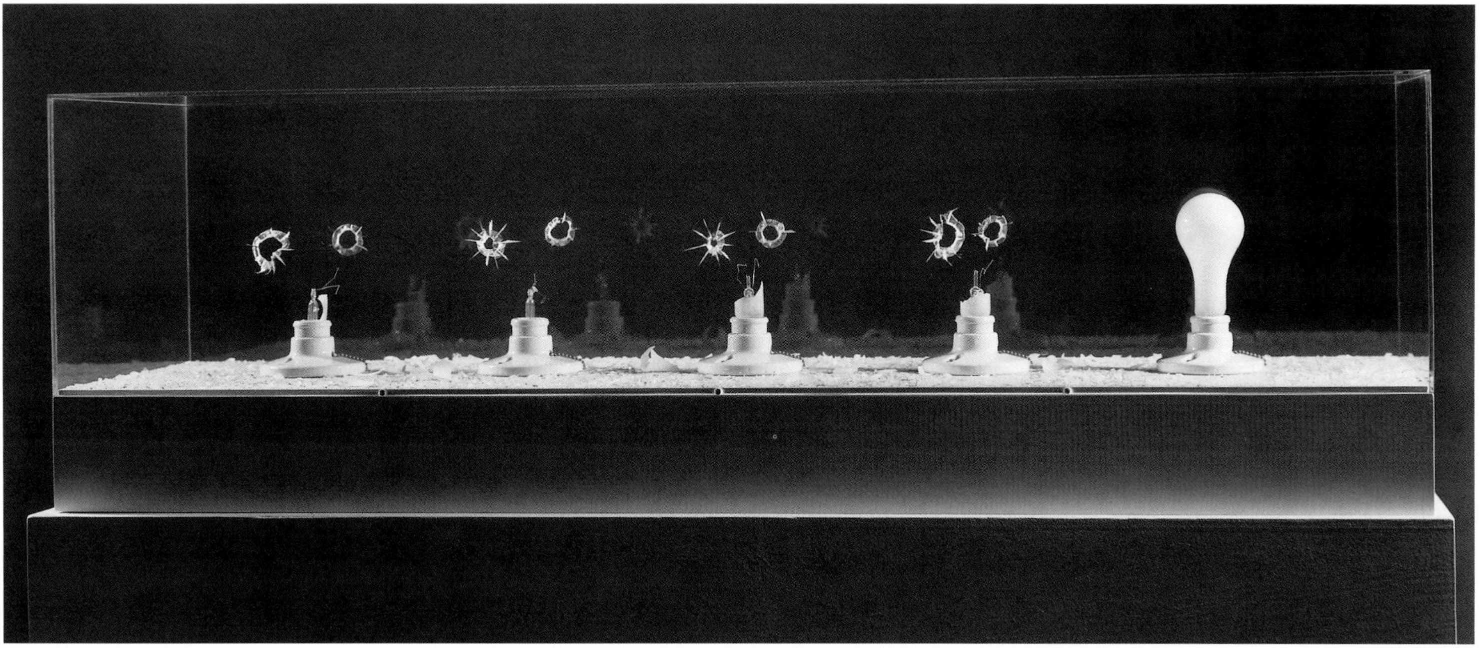

Lights Out
1967
Acrylic sheets, light fixtures, and wood
17¼ × 55¾ in.
Art Gallery of Greater Victoria

Kennedy. *Lights Out* evokes the cool, workmanlike sniper, whose invisible eyes are trained on the distance. Four gunshots have blown clean holes through both sides of a long Plexiglas case, which holds five evenly spaced electric light fixtures. The shots shattered four of the light bulbs. The fifth one, as yet untouched, carries the tension of waiting for another bullet. The terrible image has the seductive beauty of things lethal. Before he fired into the piece, McCracken coated the base surrounding the bulbs with glue, so the shards of broken glass would remain imprisoned where they fell, glittering and sharp-edged.

I Love You Tree (1967), produced the same year, is an image of utter simplicity. McCracken took down a handsaw hanging on his wall and cut through it the words "I Love You Tree." It was a nod to Marcel Duchamp's readymades—mass-produced items mounted and displayed as art. With the flourish of added words, McCracken brought the crosscut saw into the realm of Pop art with an ominous meaning: the paradox of loving that which you destroy.

Burning Through (1967) is one of McCracken's most potent pieces, lying somewhere in the territory between a painting and a wall sculpture. To create the image of a hot sphere burning through a still surface, a metaphor for violent entry into new territory, he first burned a hole through the stretched canvas, making sure to leave scorched edges. He then built up a domed form beneath, giving the leading edge

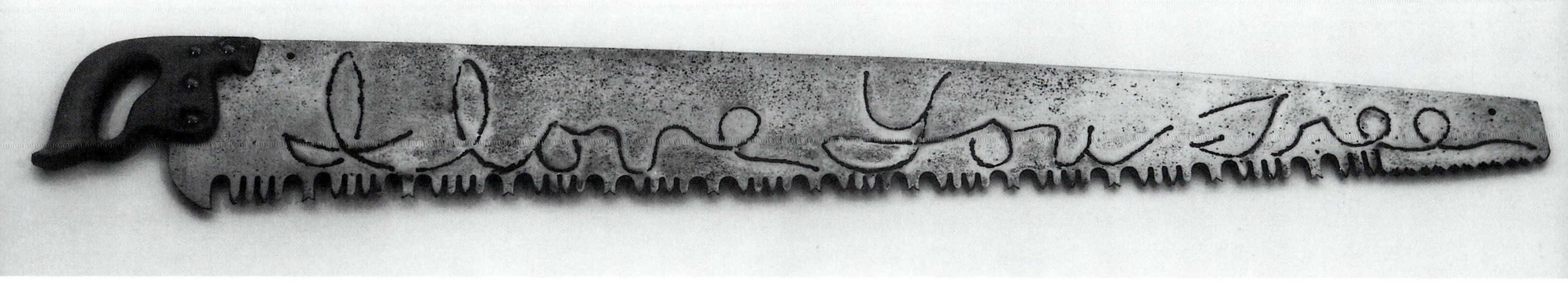

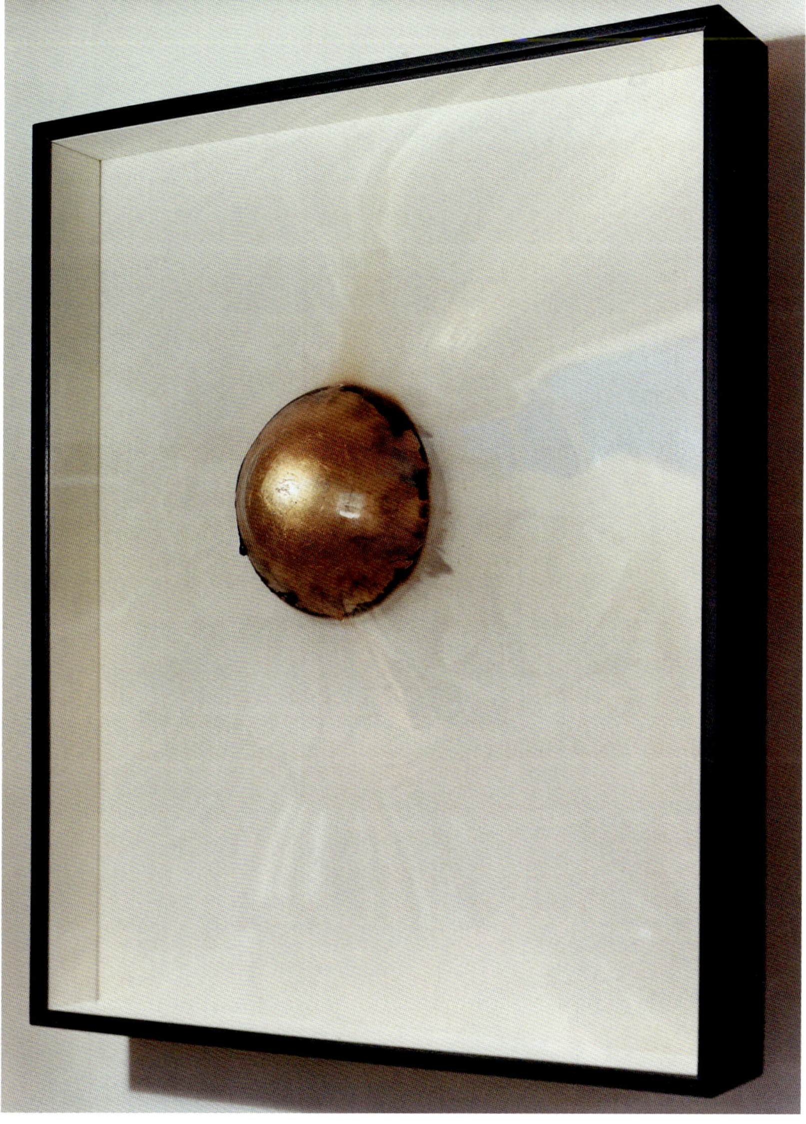

I Love You Tree
1967
Steel and wood
14 × 62 in.
Private collection

Burning Through
1967
Canvas, acrylic, and gold leaf
53½ × 43 × 9¾ in.
Collection of Anne Gould Hauberg

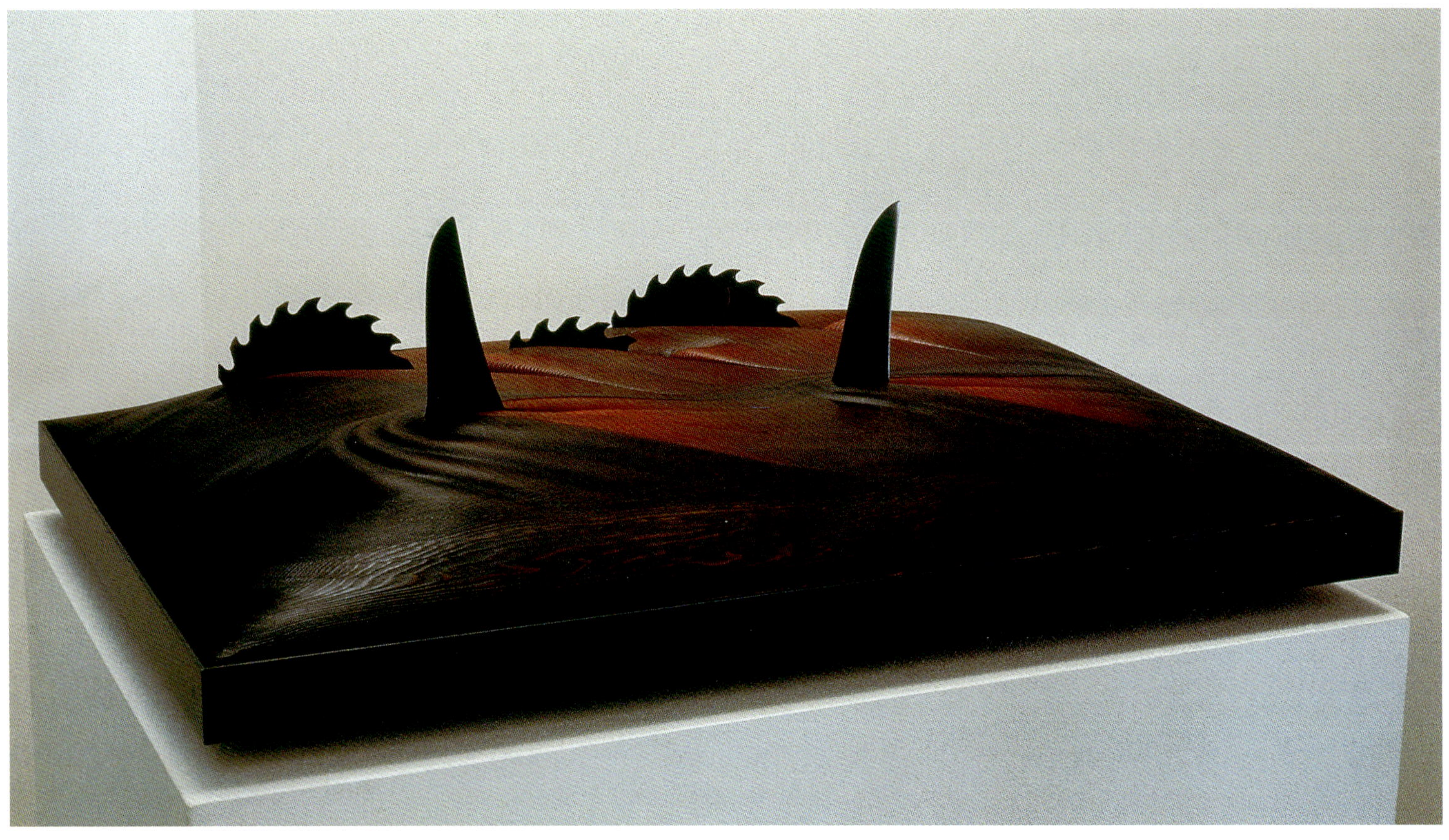

Red Inside
1981
Cedar and steel
H. 13 in.
Collection of
Marshall and Helen Hatch

a gold-leaf surface, which pushes through the canvas like a breakthrough into another dimension. To complete the effect, the acrylic faceplate that covers the piece was pushed out into a bulge that conforms to the yellow-hot nose that appears to be burning through the surface of the wall. It carries a visual clout that is almost visceral.

Red Inside (1981) is more overtly violent. Saw blades and steel dorsal fins shear through a substance suggestive of seawater—or of flesh—with an upwelling of red behind the fins. It is another of McCracken's explorations of forms, such as *I Saw,* which appear calm on the surface yet provide evidence of butchery taking place underneath. In equating the shark with a circular saw blade, the rending of flesh with the shearing of seawater, McCracken suggests an omnipresent threat. McCracken said he knew as he was making the piece that he was onto something because, "When I have that feeling that I just want one more day to get down this image that's coming out of the depths of my unconscious, I know I've got a good thing going."

Cain's Hammer—Kosovo, 1999
1999
Apple wood and mixed media
H. 14 in.
Collection of the artist

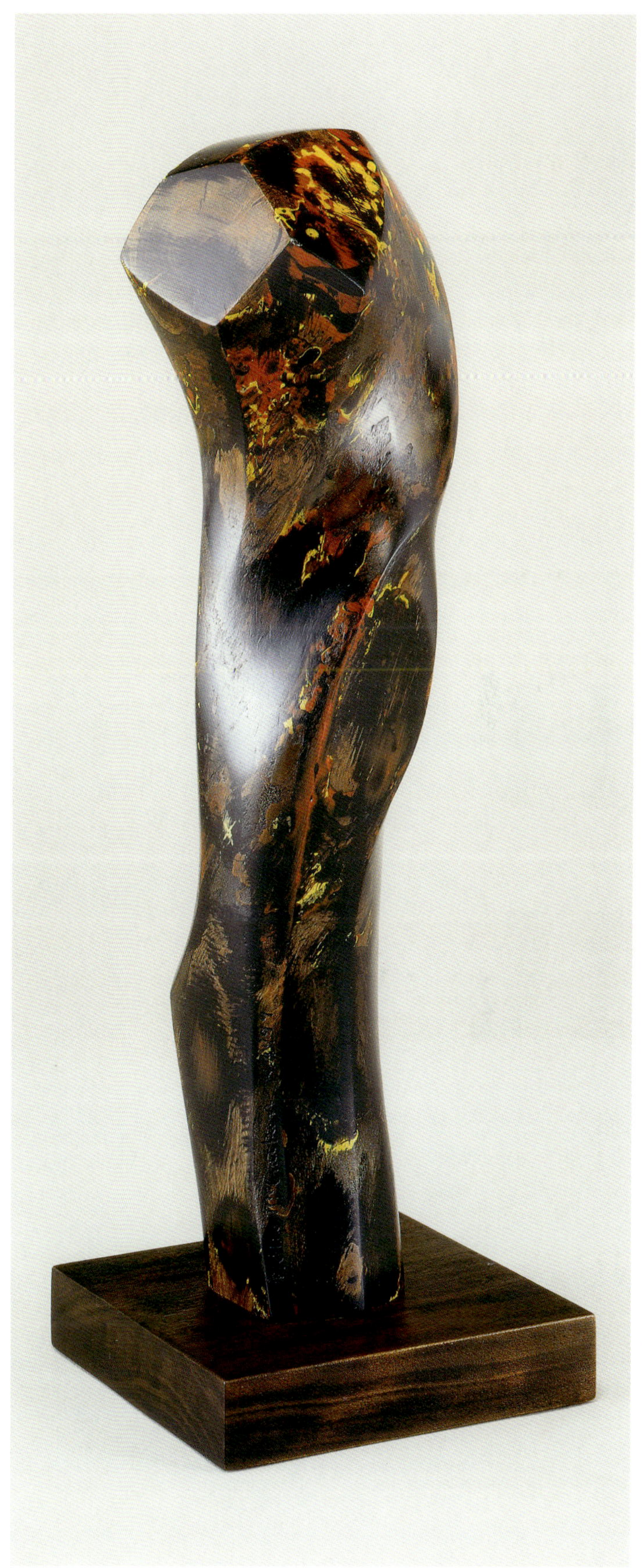

Throughout the pieces on violence, McCracken brought together natural media with forms and materials chosen for their abilities to express conflict and alienation, qualities of thorniness, or cutting, or piercing. But he had a deeper agenda: that of recognizing the underlying interdependence of seemingly disparate parts, and their ultimate compatibility when they are brought together in the context of a single form.

When the works that referenced violence were shown in New York, then later in Seattle in a dual show with Leo Kenney's paintings, critical acclaim and popular puzzlement went hand in hand. McCracken admitted at the time, "This is a dangerous group of works to show in terms of safe marketplace procedure. One is expected to carry on and extend what one does well, but the imagination is a siren—it draws one onward and one must hazard going on the rocks." Sales were meager, since few people were eager to have art emblematic of violence in their homes.

It was 1999 before he returned to the theme of violence, but when he did, it was with a work of resounding power. *Cain's Hammer—Kosovo* represents the prototype murder weapon. No indication is given in the book of Genesis about the weapon with which "Cain slew Abel," but it requires no stretch of imagination to think of it as having been done with a bludgeon, roughly shaped by nature, and adapted by primal man as a club. *Cain's Hammer—Kosovo,* with its resinous inclusions, takes on the look of an archeological find: the first murder weapon, miraculously preserved, and strangely beautiful.

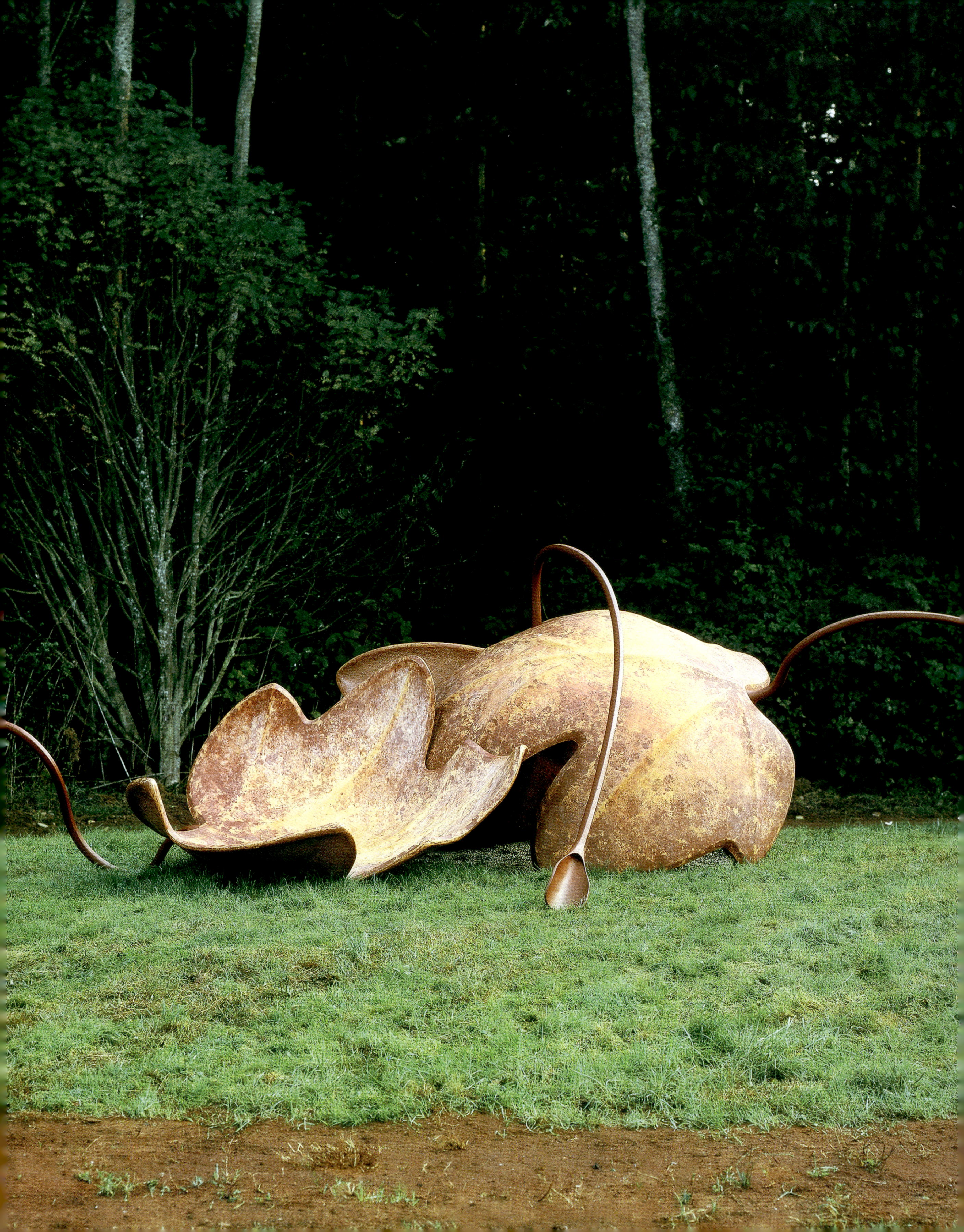

Early Lyricism

It is the mark of a great artist to express the inexpressible. To create poetry in form. Initially, lyricism described poetry sung to the accompaniment of a lyre. The term can describe a work that is emotional without being heavy, or, in the visual arts, an abstraction that uses color in a way seen as poetic.

McCracken's lyrical sculptures give visual motifs the "unfolding" quality of aural ones—a sense of rhythmic disclosure. They reveal a reality that underlies observable phenomena, thus expressing the belief that there are many other, latent realms beyond the visible world. His career has been a search for the visual metaphors that could make this belief manifest, and perhaps for that reason, the fanciful—sometimes extraordinary—subject matter has its feet in aboriginal art (*Dark Feathered River*), and in myth (*Pan*).

The originality of his conceptions is occasionally so radical as to be breathtaking. His subjects include clouds, and tension, and growing green force. And sometimes, song itself. McCracken may well be the only sculptor ever to attempt the subject of *Bird Song* (1964). The piece came about from a phenomenon other sculptors will appreciate. He was chopping wood one day when he looked down at a piece of alder and recognized an image in it: a bird with its head thrown back in song. He picked up the chunk of wood and took it into his studio. "Often, I arrive at an image by drawing something I'm planning to sculpt, or an image is revealed to me as I'm working on a piece. This was the first time I had the experience of seeing it in a flash, already in the material, waiting to be liberated."

The bird's "song" came to him with equal directness. "I was looking at an abalone shell, at the perforations around the deep part of the outer shell, and it occurred to me that their tapering shapes were like the intervals of a bird's song." He polished away the rough outer shell, leaving a strip of iridescent circles suggesting musical notes. Set so that the strip emerges from the bird's throat, it is transformed into a shining visual warble.

Poems (1966) tackles an equally unexpected subject: written poetry. The shape of an open book is carved in high relief against a stand. To give a visual equivalent to the

Autumn Leaves (detail)
1979 (see p. 53)

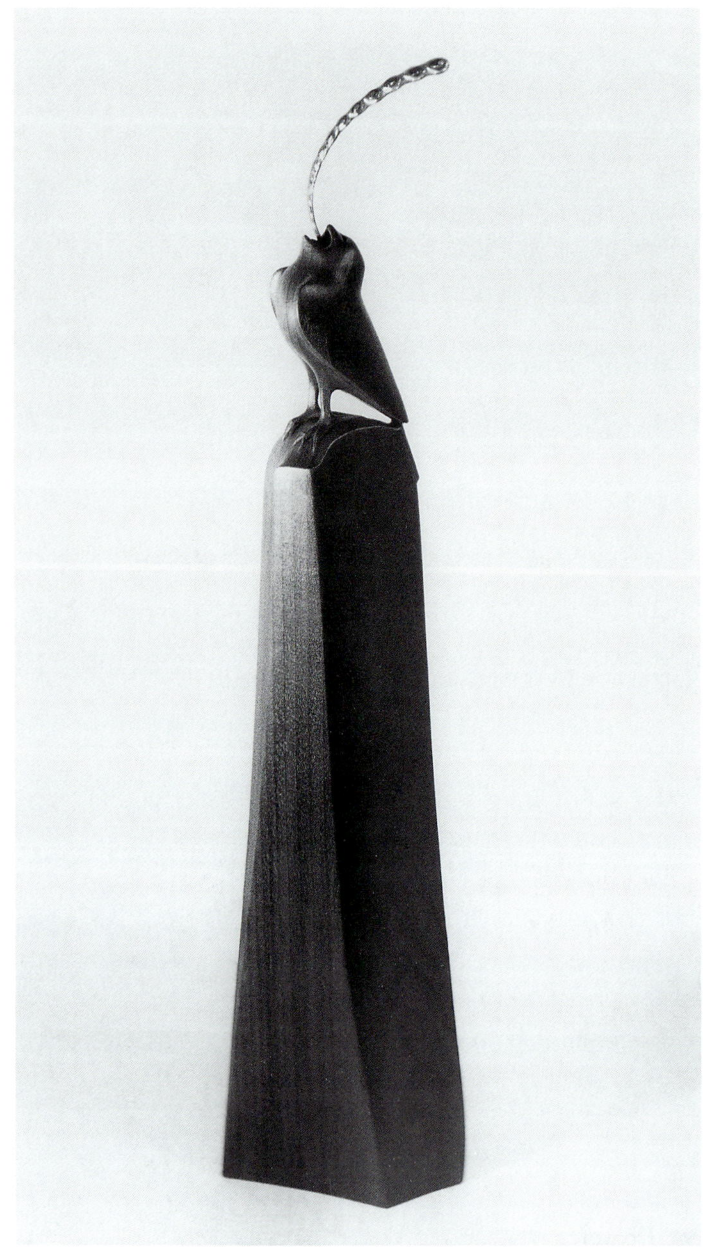

Bird Song
1964
Alder and shell
H. 25 in.
Private collection

sounds of poetry and the sensations a poem evokes, McCracken inset lines of small natural treasures: sea urchin spines, a bear claw, red leaves, a limpet shell, and other similar bits, like syllables in a haiku. Poetry occupies an important place in McCracken's life, especially since Anne is intensively immersed in the work of living poets. As one of the key organizers of the biennial Skagit River Poetry Festival in nearby La Conner, she adds another dimension to the household's artistic palette.

McCracken's body of work includes drawings that describe the movements of wind and water. In a 1966 mixed-media drawing titled *Errant Cloud,* he presents the whimsical idea that a small, solid-bodied cloud has broken off from a larger cluster formed of fractured volumes resembling stone, to sail away on its own through dark air, borne on currents visible only behind and below it.

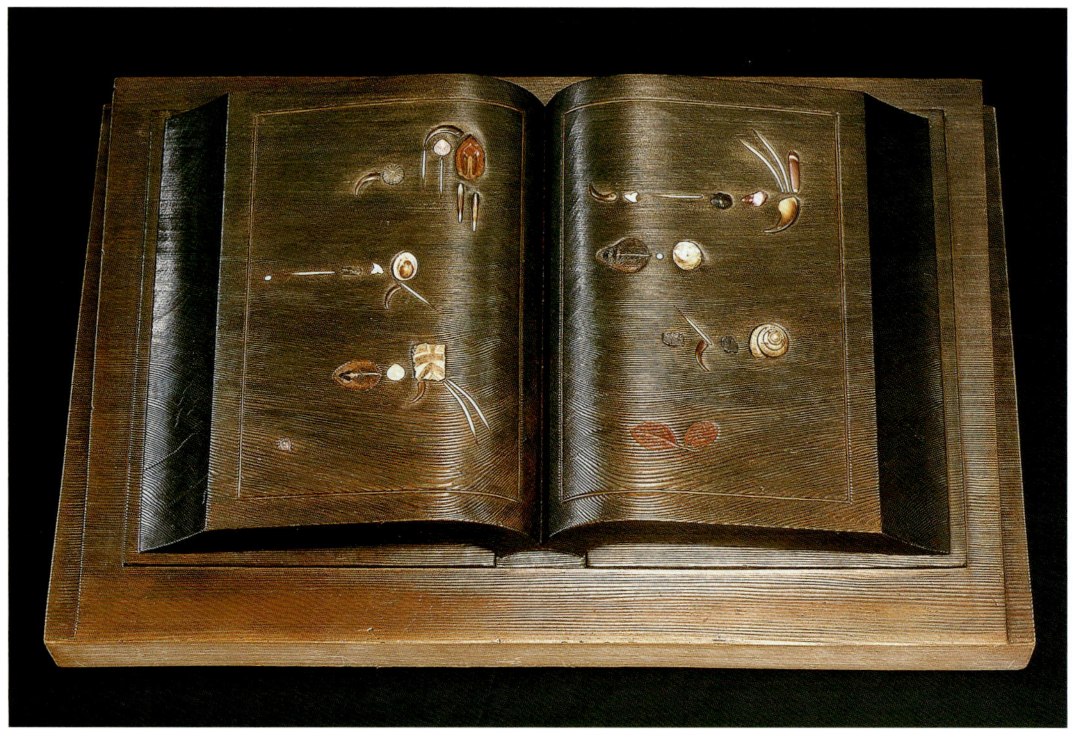

Poems
1966
Cedar and mixed media
5½ × 32 × 21¼ in.
Collection of Leeds and Wendy Gulick

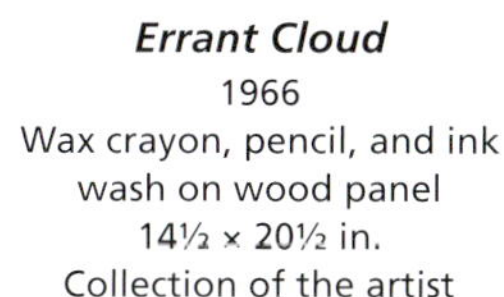

Errant Cloud
1966
Wax crayon, pencil, and ink wash on wood panel
14½ × 20½ in.
Collection of the artist

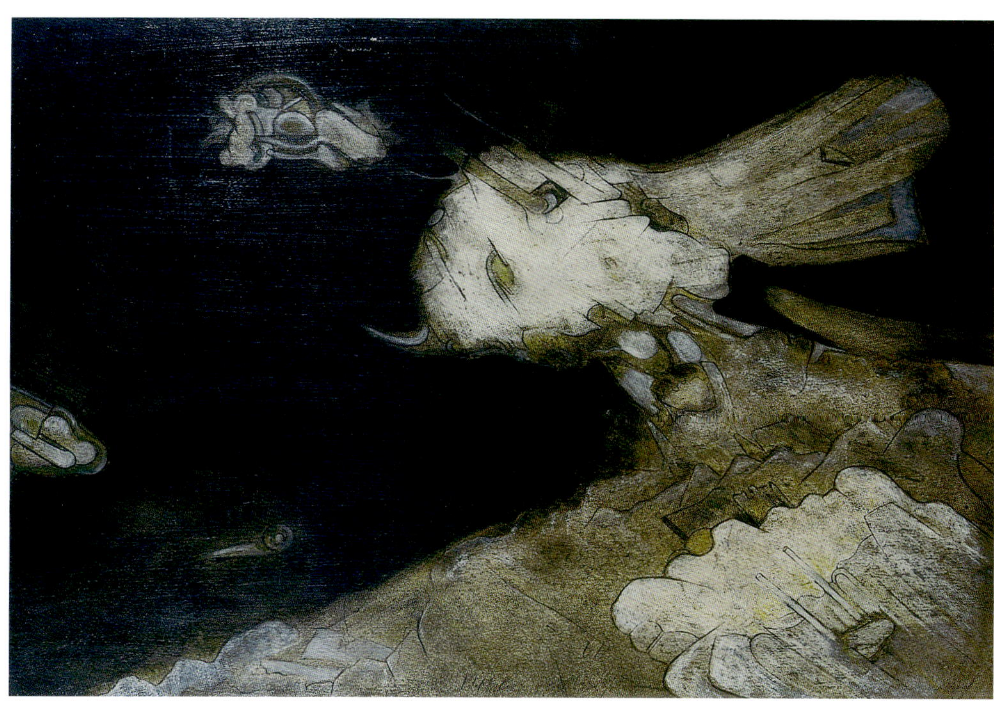

Tsunami, also completed in 1966, presents the power of a tidal wave as an onrush of overlapping arcs of breaking white water, each topping and overwhelming the one beneath it in a show of solid force.

"In *Hornet's Nest,* hornets are invested with the gift of imitating man," McCracken wrote. "It is a view of architectural inversion and insect plagiarism involving a viewpoint not of another human, but of another species of creature." He had watched yellow jackets fly through his studio, carrying flies whose legs and wings they had nipped off to carry their prisoners home. The parallels between hornets and men at war were unavoidable. But in this 1969 work, he cast the similarity in architectural terms, with a hornet's nest shaped like a brick. Hornets' nests are beautiful in themselves, with subtly striated layers. McCracken fabricated a nest in the squared-off form of a brick (a right-angled form peculiar to humans) by covering a wood form with hornet paper. He contrasted the hard geometric form (symbolic of a mind-set) with the free-form shapes of nature, by surrounding the nest with bare wild-rose branches to which a few dry rosehips still

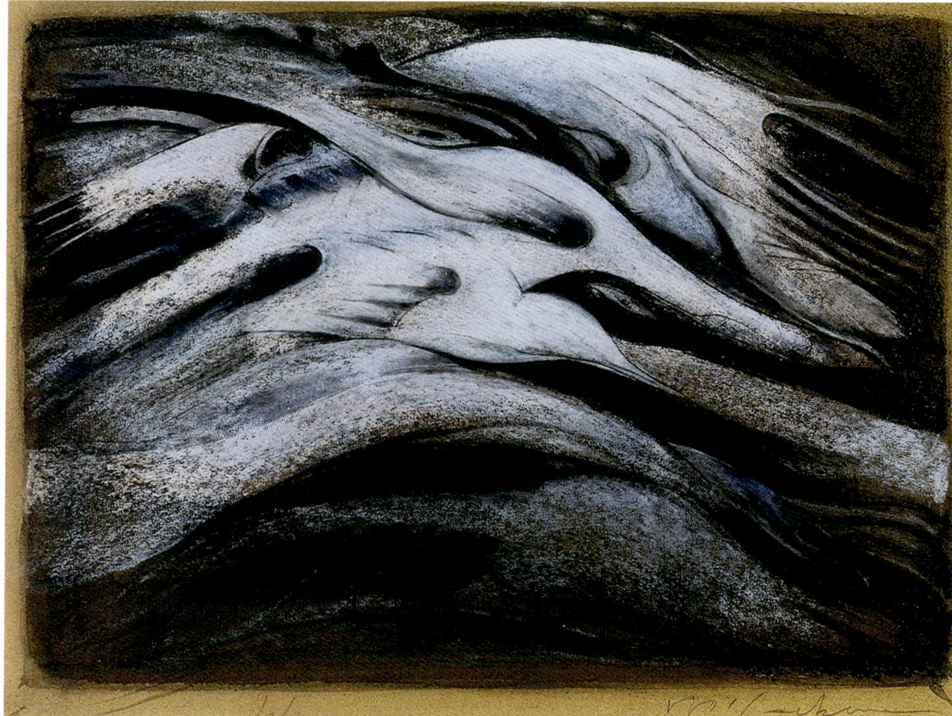

Tsunami
1966
Pencil and ink wash on paper
9 × 12 in.
Collection of the artist

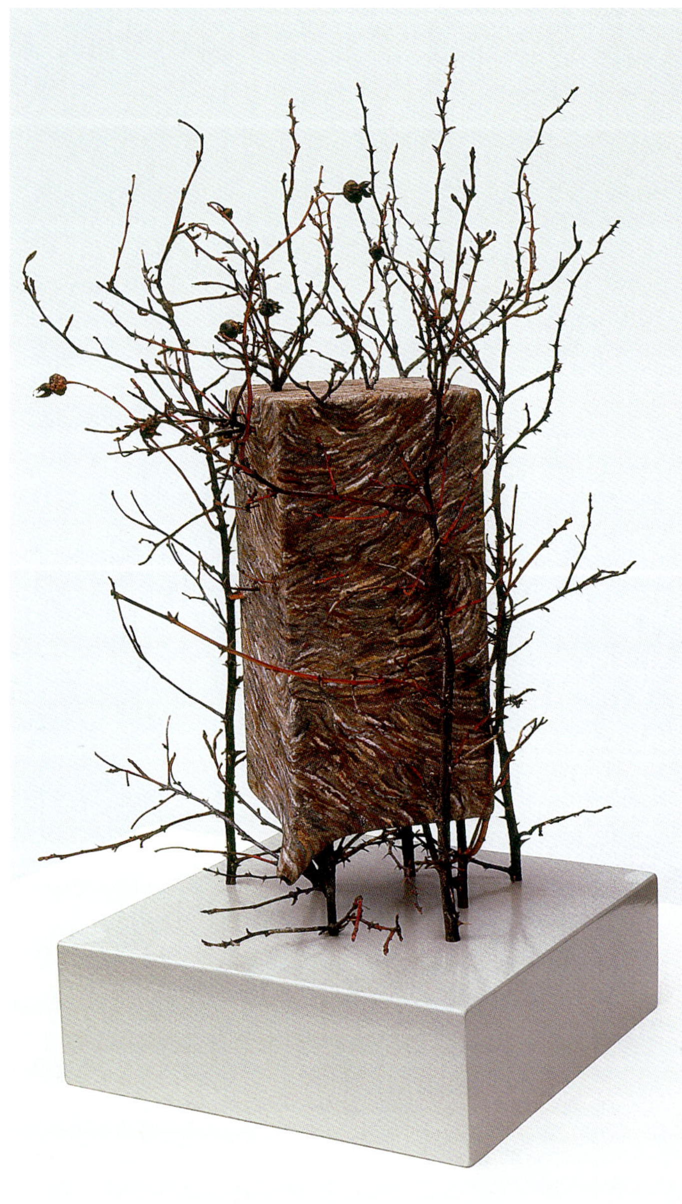

Hornet's Nest
1969
Wood, hornet paper, and wild rose bushes
H. 26 in.
Museum of Northwest Art, Gift of Anne Gould Hauberg

cling. There is some resonance between the rose thorns and the implied stingers of hornets. Yet the chief visual interplay is between the wild shapes of nature and the artificial symmetry of a manufactured object in the unexpected material produced only in the wild. Nature, it seems, abhors a right angle, whereas industrial man imposes it upon nearly everything he builds.

A display in the American Museum of Natural History in New York inspired *Aerial Nest* (1969), a crisply squared bird's nest holding a cache of cubic birds' eggs. The museum display was a pigeon's nest found somewhere in the Bowery. It had been built entirely of assorted metal debris, including rusty wire and paper clips. That unprecedented collision between nature and technology fascinated McCracken. He wrote, "Although I disavow the credit for doing it, or liability for causing it, I admit to its influence, and the debt I owe it for awakening the realization of the promise of new and sometimes frightening possibilities that exist in the forces at play between man and his environment." Or, he might have added (in view of the source of his awakening), "between bird and his environment."

The strange fusion of manufactured metal with instinctual nest building that he had seen in 1955 remained so luminous in his memory that more than a dozen years later, he was inspired to create the square *Aerial Nest,* with a support fabricated in the form of a television antenna. He used a real robin's nest (purloined after the birds deserted it), re-formed into a hollow cube, with speckled cubic "eggs" inside it, nestled in owl down—surely one of the more esoteric natural materials ever used in a sculpture.

After one recovers from the initial shock of the subject, the piece stands as a satisfying arrangement of shapes. The dark nest, elevated to stand at the center of the composition, visually anchors the extended rods that splay out like reaching birds' claws at one end, and stand in contrasting rigid verticality at the other. The triple arrow shapes on top lend the piece the feeling of soaring motion, suggesting the shape of the mechanical bird that might have laid such eggs, as well as directing vision off into some unseeable future.

The beauty of the arcing shape of a taut bow is the crux of *Silver Bow* (1969). Moving from wood and other natural materials to metal and fiberglass gave McCracken a fresh field for the exploration of form. Rather than exploring a man-and-nature interface, he looked at pure mechanical beauty. Yet the shapes created by the bow and its pulled string unmistakably evoke the outline of the outstretched wings of a soaring bird, with the arrow's protruding point as its head, and

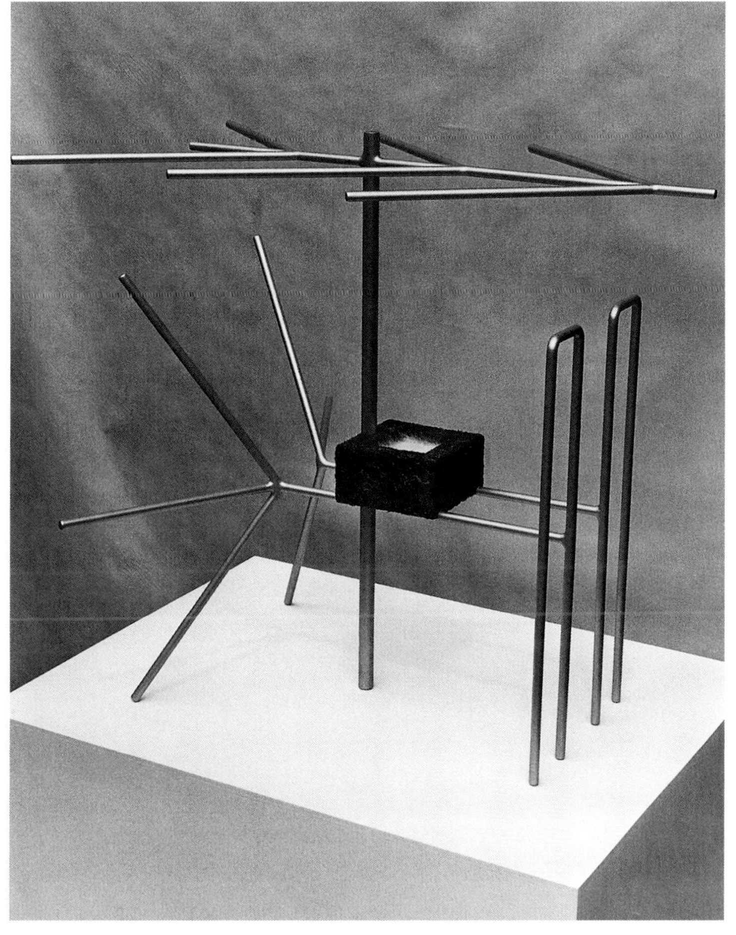

Aerial Nest
1969
Glass, wood, steel, and bird's down
H. 31 in.
Collection of the artist

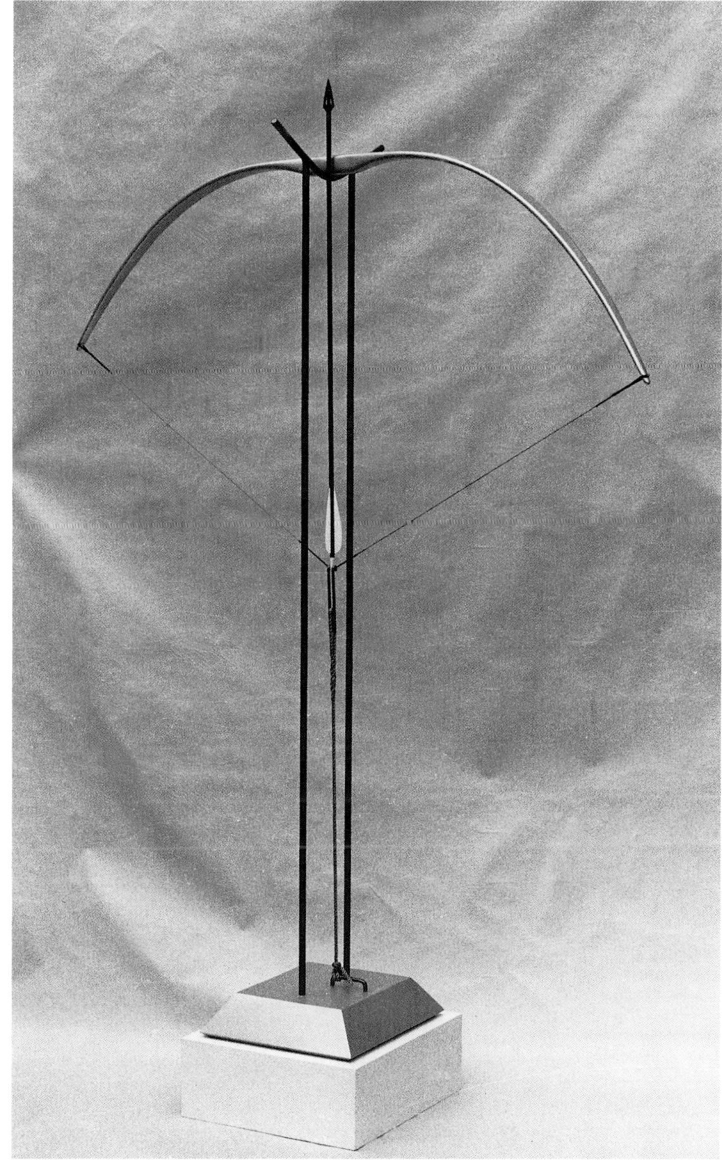

Silver Bow
1969
Steel, fiberglass, and wood
H. 77½ in.
Collection of Anne Gould Hauberg

the slender black rods of the stand as its extended legs and feet. The piece can be viewed as a cartoon image of a slender figure with stick legs and a pointed-arrow head spreading a transparent batwing cape. Moreover, seeing the spare lines of *Silver Bow* as a drawing is probably inevitable. Yet the forms created and these associations are more likely an accidental by-product of the piece rather than having been intended by the sculptor, whose stated purpose was to explore the idea of tension. The silver bow (actually steel) is drawn to full extension, nocked with an arrow, and suspended in that state. The concept is similar to that of his earlier piece *Lights Out,* except that the lethal weapon awaiting firing here is a bow rather than a gun.

McCracken realized the danger inherent in such a form when he had the finished piece in his library, and arrived home one day to discover that the arrow had released, and hung embedded in the ceiling.

McCracken returned to the use of cedar, the material which one New York critic said he handled "like a wizard," for an impression of one of the sweetest phenomena found in the woods, *Wild Honey* (1970). Like an X-ray view of a hive in a tree chosen by bees to be their home, McCracken re-created

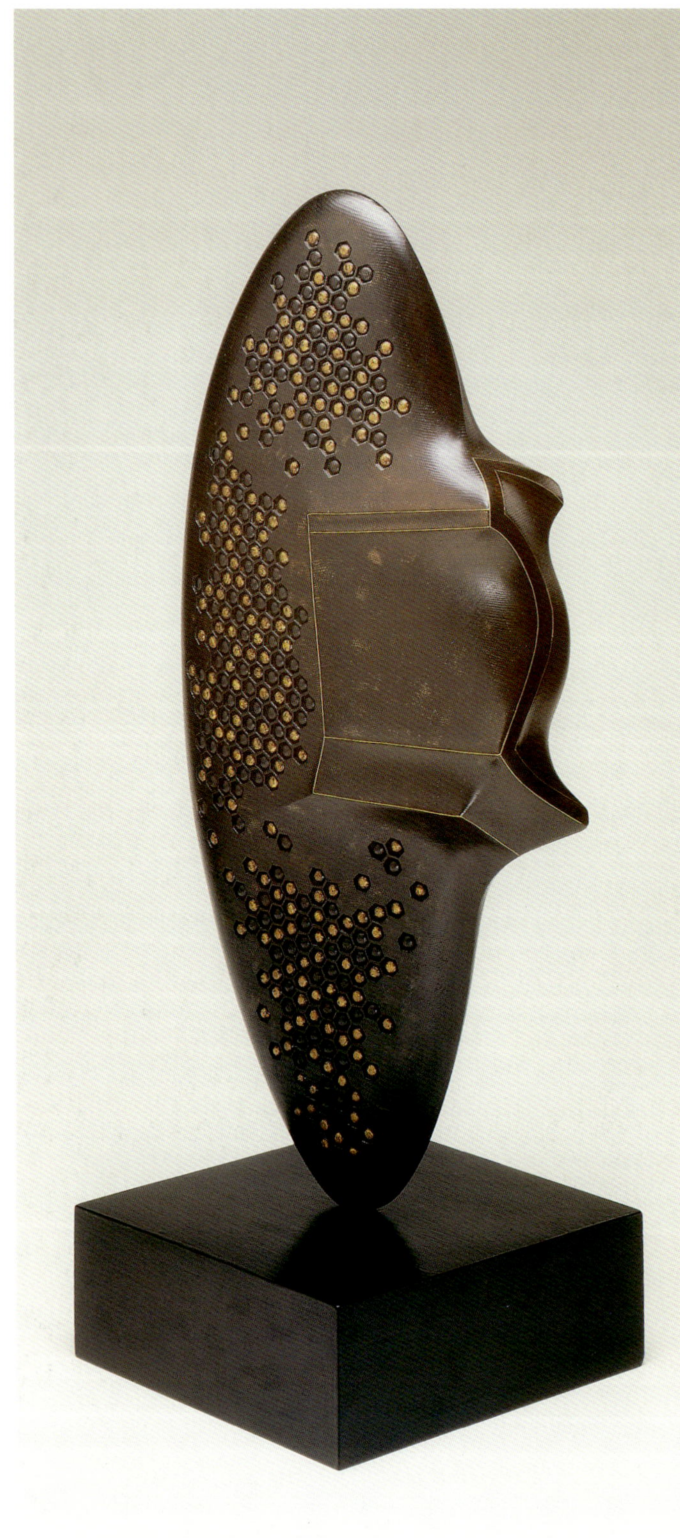

Wild Honey
1970
Cedar, gold wire, and gold leaf
H. 21¼ in.
Collection of Marshall and Helen Hatch

the tight hexagonal cells of honeycomb, and filled them with golden nuggets of "honey." Inlaid gold wire outlines the geometric shapes that create the mouth between the hive and the exterior of the tree.

In its geometries and its inlays, this piece prefigures McCracken's series Fragments of Night Sky, of twenty years later. In many ways, this piece is among the most satisfying of his entire *oeuvre.* Its shape is an inspired abstraction that nonetheless is as true to its subject as it is possible to be.

McCracken carved the quavering shape of a moon crossed by clouds to create a piece that stands unsurpassed as a pure expression of Pacific Northwest art: *Moon* (1971). Faint traces of white pigment define the orb and suggest its radiance. The soft shadows of clouds crossing the moon are created by carved indentations. Clouds are among a number of subjects previously thought to be outside the range of sculpture that McCracken has tackled. Creating their shapes by inference, by shadow rather than by substance, reflects the influence of Asian art in his work. The Seattle Art Museum was opened in 1933 with a fine collection of Asian art. Since it was the earliest museum collection to which McCracken had access, it made a deep impression on him.

McCracken had made an equally poetic form in 1972 when a Guemes Island resident gave him a commission for a major sculpture in wood. *Spring,* a towering cedar form sixteen feet tall, evokes Dylan Thomas's reference to "the force that through the green fuse drives the flower." In a rhythmic disclosure of growth, *Spring* rises from the earth in a series of softly unfolding layers to a top that appears about to burst open

Moon
1971
Cedar
H. 26¼ in.
Collection of Anne McCracken

in blossom. The base is set in a concrete sheath that allows the piece to be turned to present different faces to the light.

Its shape and cedar material link it to traditional Northwest Coast totem poles, which customarily are made from the same material, at a similar height. But here, rather than a series of totemic animals, McCracken has shaped the wood into a single thrusting form. He wrote a poem during the time he was carving it:

In the early morning light
Dried cedar blood
Sparkles
Under the flashing blade.

The term "medicine wheel" describes the Big Horn Medicine Wheel, situated on a high, bare shoulder of land at about 10,000 feet, above the tree line south of Sheridan, Wyoming. The site consists of a central cairn from which lines of stones radiate like the spokes of a wheel out to a surrounding stone circle. The lines are thought to have pointed to the rising of prominent stars on key dates, to function as a calendar presumed to have been used to time important rituals.[1]

McCracken's *Medicine Wheel* (1974) was conceived with more wide-ranging function. He began with drawings of instruments such as barometers and seismographs, which record phenomena beyond ordinary human perception. In

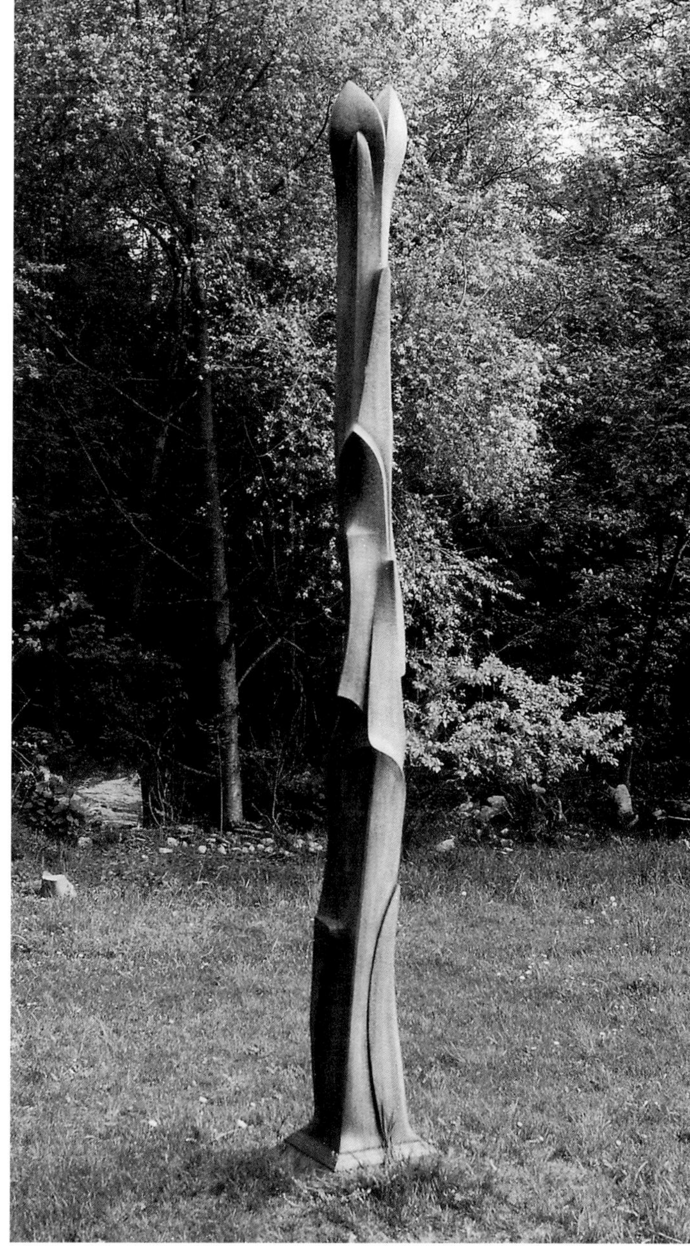

Spring
1972
Cedar
H. 192 in.
Private collection

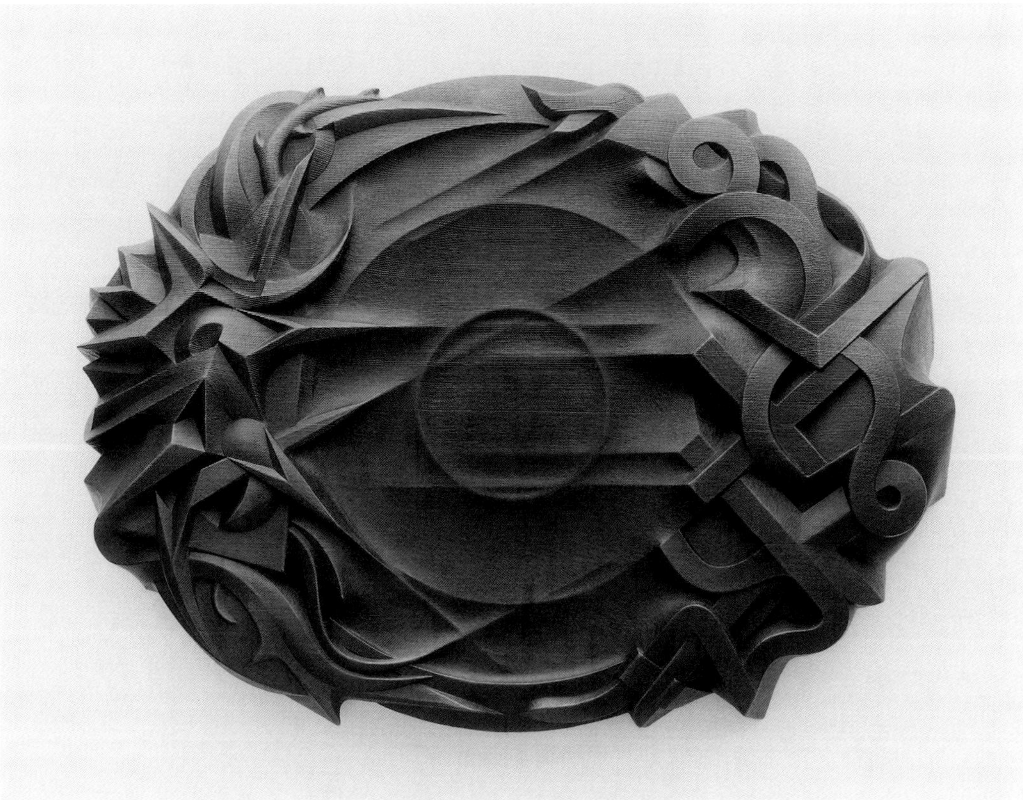

his drawings, readings such as high-low and fair-stormy took on additional dimension as continuums expressing good-evil, love-hate, and yin-yang. It was the subtle space between such extremes that was of greatest interest to him.

Translated into sculpture, the idea began with a central circle that denotes the great cosmic sea of Vedic lore, out of which everything was created. The partial rings of two additional, larger circles are visible beneath the overlying forms. On one side, the invented shapes suggest the entangled characters of an unknown language; on the other side, forms of no known earthly objects emerge into the third dimension as if they were coming into being, or perhaps subsiding back into the cosmic sea. Lines reach across the gulf of the central circle toward the sides, while a diagonal line thrusts up from below on a similar mission.

Medicine Wheel is all the more satisfying for being incomprehensible on any logical level. It must be understood on a preverbal level, appreciated for the shape and movement of its forms. The rhythmic concentric circles that underlie the piece are forerunners of a later series of Mandala sculptures (see p. 140).

"Every new medium is a new language capable of expression in a different and distinct way," McCracken has found. The fresh spectrum of artistic possibilities may be inherent in the way a medium carries color, or in the forms intrinsic to such things as its weight-bearing capability, its flexibility, its hardness, or its ability to flow and be molded. In 1974, McCracken turned for the first time to the use of colored plaster. He explained, "I was drawn to this medium in order to express a new awareness of light, a certain dim yet luminous quality which I had not found in any medium I had used up to this point. The resulting essay into fresco plaster relief sculpture includes, in addition to older ideas which were incompatible with the media I was using at the time, new ideas stimulated by the exploration of fresco."

His first major piece in fresco was *Pyramids and Seascape* (1974), a semi-abstract exploration of shape and surface. Rhythmic repetitions of jutting triangles that read as pyramids

Medicine Wheel
1974
Cedar
26½ × 35 in.
Private collection

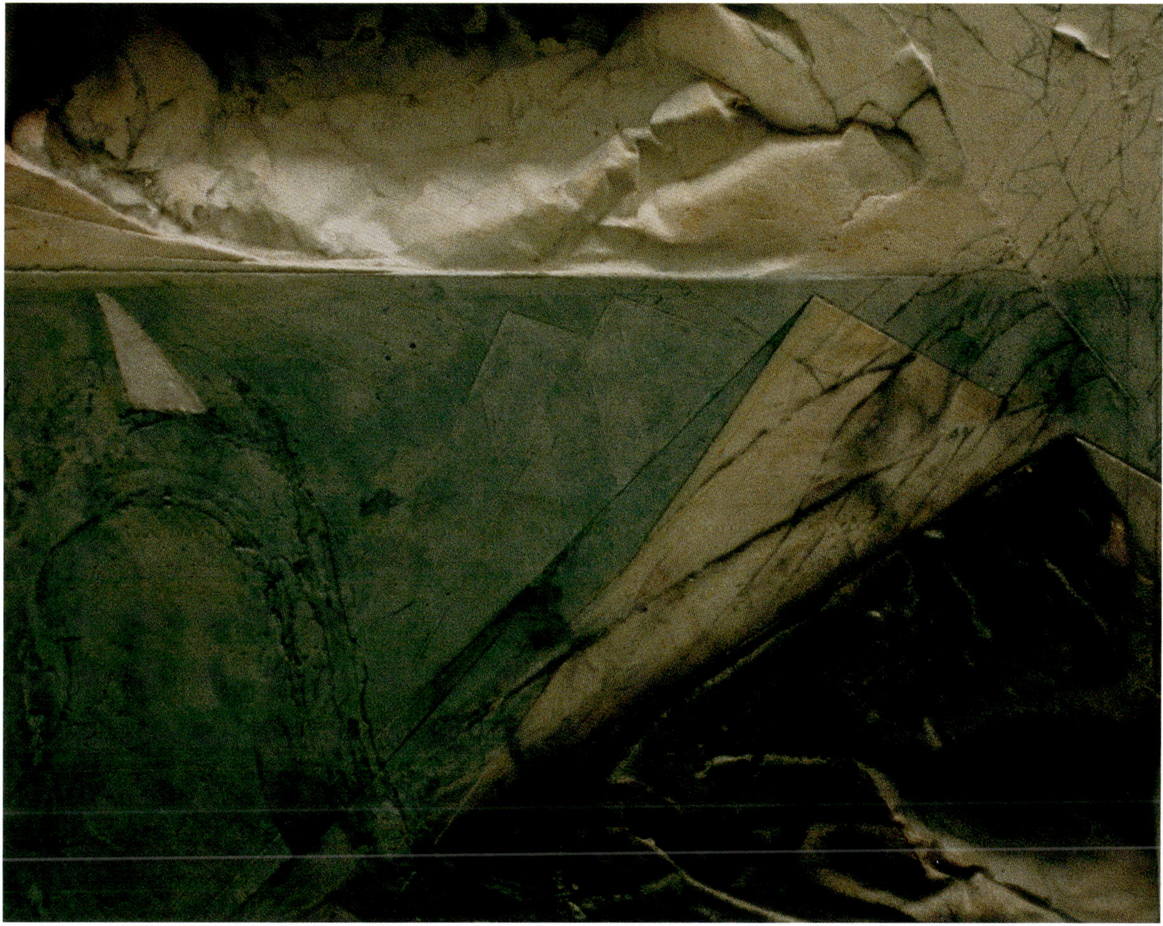

appear to recede into the distance. One of the assets of fresco is that it ages nobly. McCracken has evoked that quality with a distressed surface, which in addition to suggesting great age, carries the tangible richness of impasto painting. The drawn outline of a tree rises up the right side. A thickened surface current that makes a sharp rise and descent creates a cataclysmic landscape of torrential water flowing to the base of pyramids under heavy skies.

McCracken wrote, "In these plaster relief sculptures the dominant color medium is fresco in the broad sense of the word, meaning water-based color on plaster. *Fresco buone,* paint on wet plaster, and *fresco secco,* painting on dry plaster, have both been employed, as well as integral color—i.e., color mixed directly into the plaster.

"The text of the work is based in a deep regard for nature. The richly diverse experimentation found in nature inspires me, as do new combinations of ideas and means in my approach to sculpture. They make possible a refocusing of vision on old familiar objects, illuminating them in new and often (to me) surprising ways, and encourage 'what-if-ness' in the configurations of imagination. There is great freedom in knowing there are no laws one must follow *a priori* to making a piece of sculpture. Anything is possible, and the governing laws that apply to the developments are those that evolve during the course of creation."

Surface texture cast from wrinkled paper, pulled and crimped to conform to a rectangle with an inset circle, forms the background of *Green Wing Shield* (1975). The shield's emblem is a domed circle with a marbled veining of blue-green color through its top half, overlaid with a copper color in the bottom half. The shapes of bird wings, cast from actual wings, stand out in bas-relief from the lower section of the dome.

Seven years after McCracken completed *Spring,* the patron who had commissioned that work lost a young son in an automobile accident. McCracken was asked to create a sculpture in his memory. The theme of fallen leaves seemed an appropriate choice. Because the sculpture was to be in a public place, it was essential to fashion it of materials

Pyramids and Seascape
1974
Fresco and mixed media
H. 11½ in.
Collection of Troy Tabor-Bourret

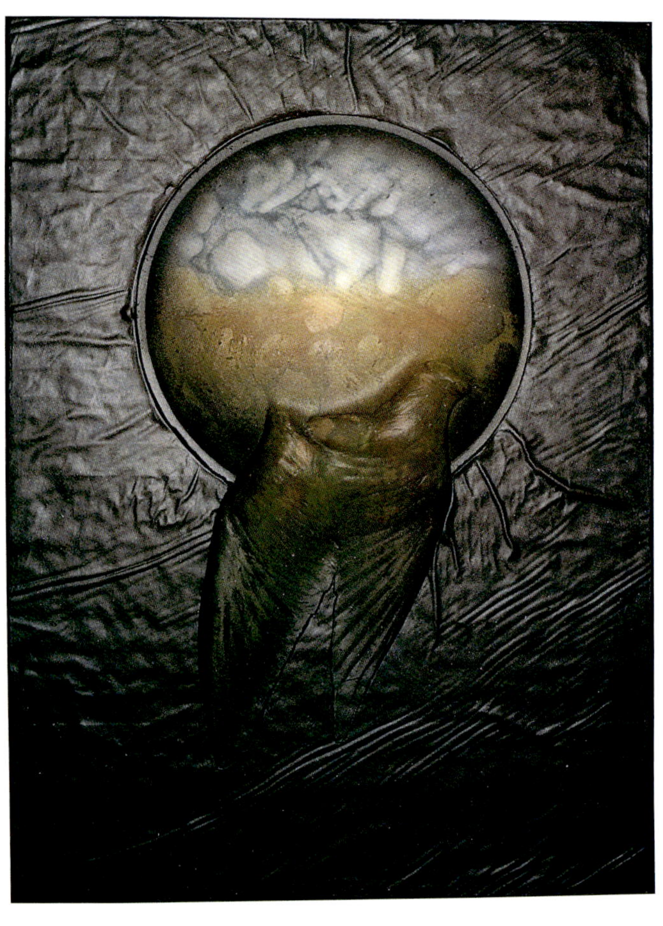

Green Wing Shield
1975
Fresco
H. 39¼ in.
Collection of Marshall and Helen Hatch

Red Dwarf
1975
Fresco
33½ × 30½ in.
Skagit Valley College,
Gift of Dr. and Mrs. Jack Reid

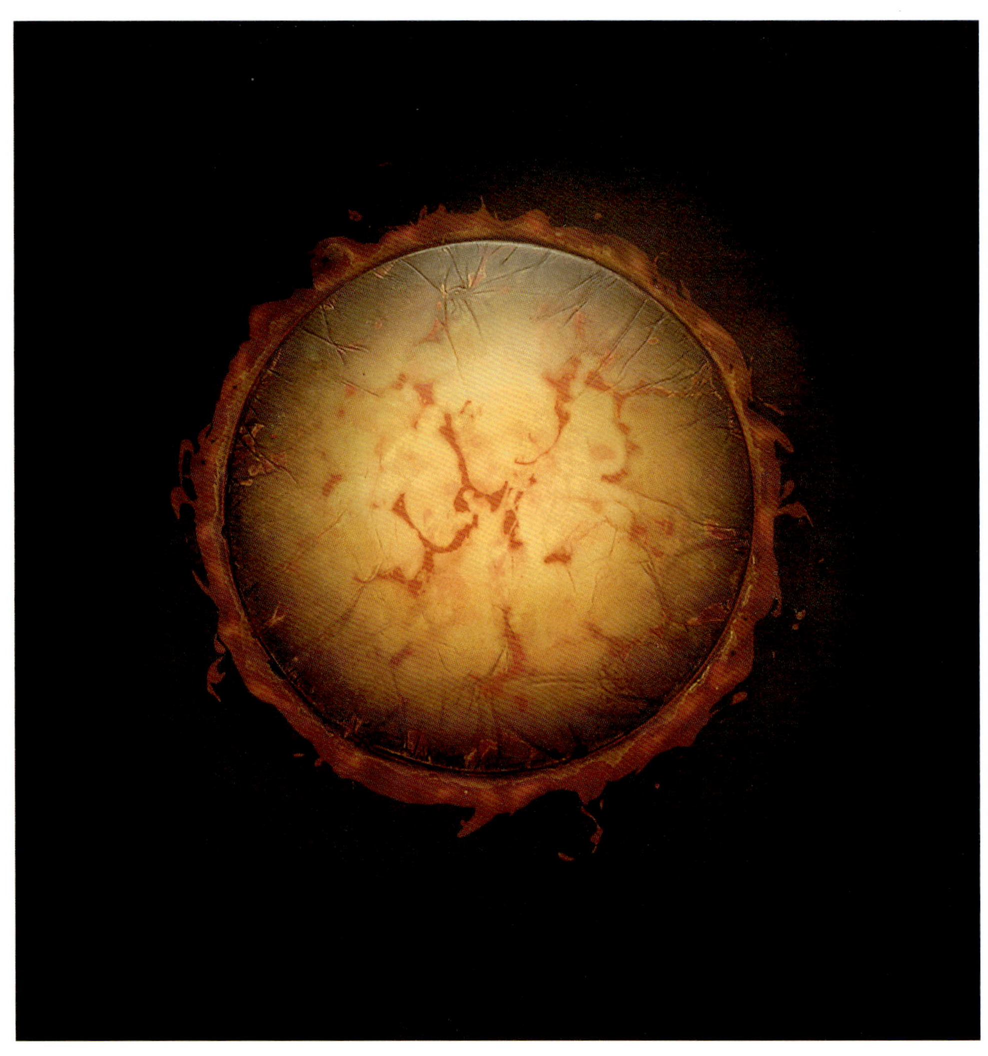

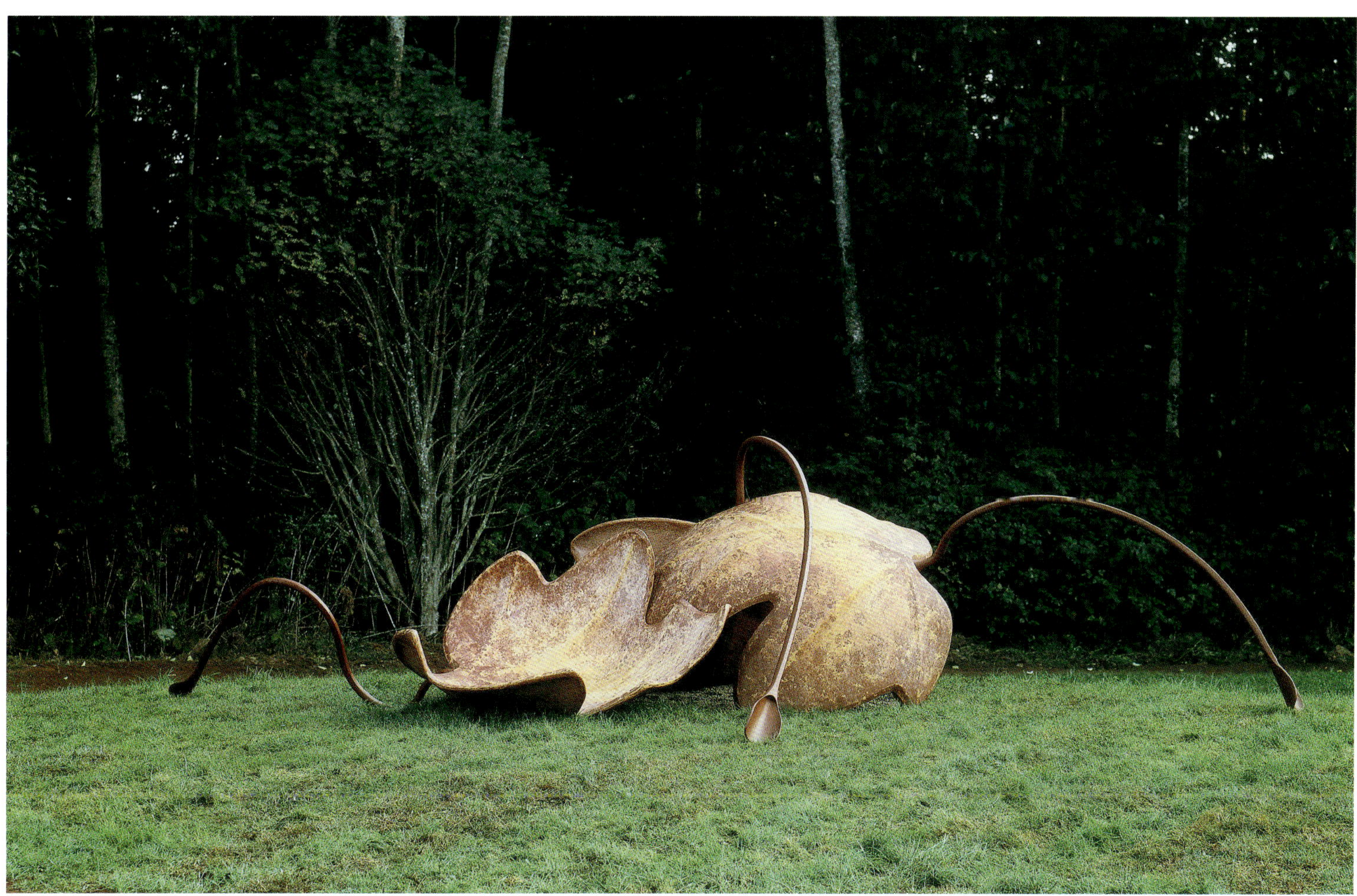

Autumn Leaves
1979
Fiberglass, concrete, and steel
58 × 261 in.
Skagit County Park, Guemes Island, Anacortes, Wash.

able to withstand both weather and human wear and tear. McCracken created a touching visual threnody, *Autumn Leaves* (1979), of fiberglass, steel, and concrete. Molds were made from full-size plaster models of three curling, fallen leaves. He coated the molds with color, then shot on a thick layer of colored concrete mixed with fiberglass, which also absorbed the color applied to the molds. The stems are forged steel with polychrome polyurethane coating.

The work is installed in the Skagit County Park on Guemes Island. The curling leaf shapes are arranged to form an informal teepee. Children are drawn to play in their shelter and swing from their stems.

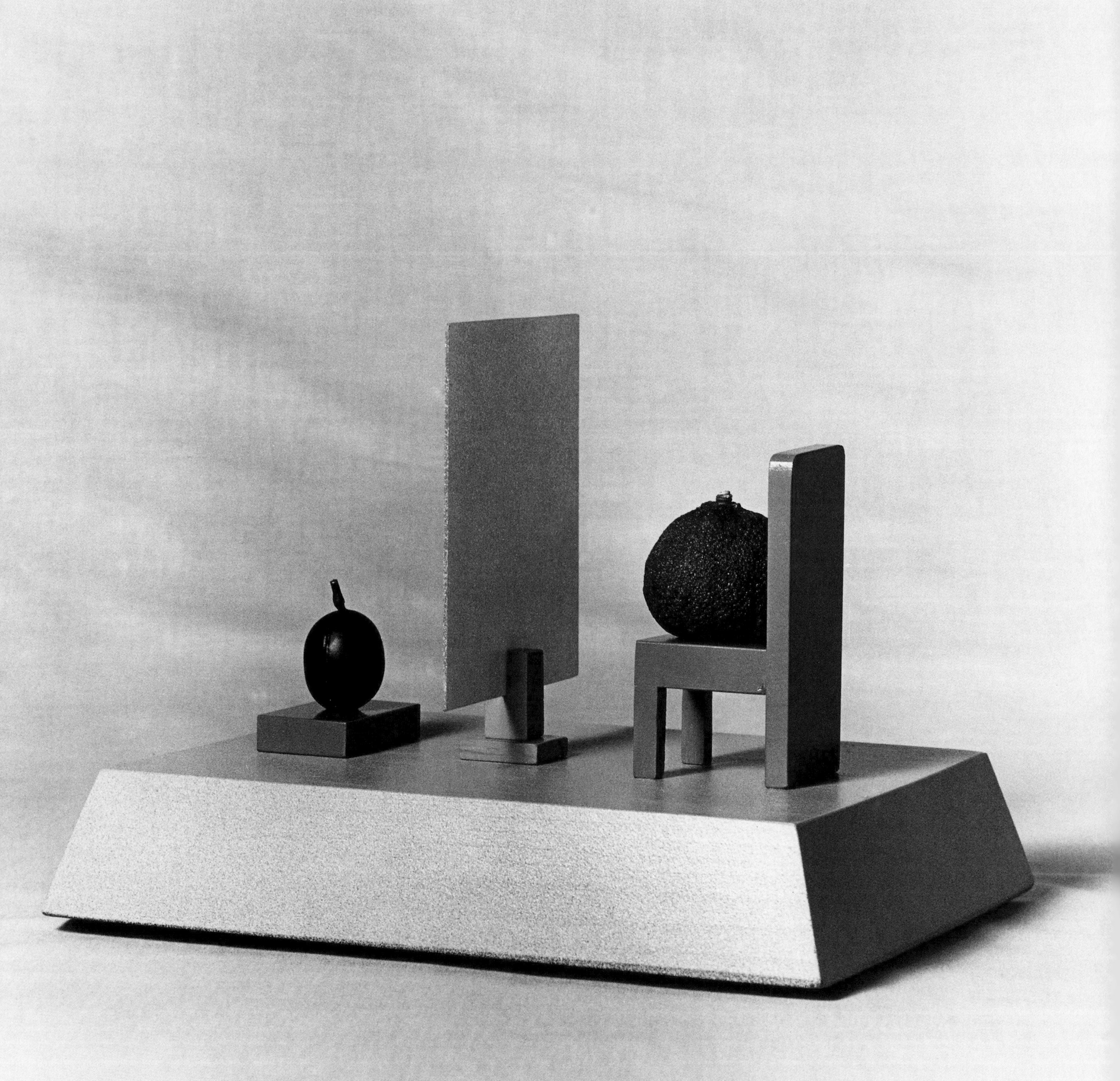

Tableaux

It is in pieces that can be read as visual puns, or three-dimensional metaphors, that one comes nearest to comprehending the importance of language in Philip McCracken's life, and to appreciating his wit. Pieces in the Tableaux series were all completed in 1977.

After he completed *Spring* in 1972—a commission that occupied almost a full year from its conception to its installation—McCracken took a break from sculpture in order to build a new house for his family. The building process consumed two years, and during the second year, in 1974, he began to work with plaster and fresco painting, producing pieces such as *Pyramids and Seascape.* New materials always suggest new forms, sending his imagination into overdrive.

While he was working with plaster, his mind became so attuned to nuances of form that the spent brushes in his studio began to suggest imaginary scenarios in which they took on greater meanings. In 1977, in the spirit of Dada, he organized such readymade objects into tableaux that suggested scenes from a drama, with inanimate objects cast as the actors.

"Some of the ideas in this series flashed into my mind during the course of using tools such as brushes and trowels," he said. "At other times it was a slow awakening of an idea. I laughed often while doing these small tableaux, but occasionally the laughter was interrupted by a wince of recognition, sometimes sadness. At other times it was reversed. An idea I thought was so serious came out sad-funny, or combinations of these things—laughing with a side ache." Such a piece was *Confession* (1977), in which he arranged a wizened orange on a miniature straight-backed chair facing a tall, blank screen. Behind it, a lone plastic grape sits on a low platform, presumably "confessing" to the larger, and presumably wiser, fruit behind the obscuring screen. "I'm the little grape," McCracken said, recalling a Catholic boyhood.

He was standing in line at a large chain store during the Christmas season when he glanced into the trash can alongside the line and espied a mannequin's pink, detached hand that had been thrown away. He rescued it and took it back to his studio, where he laid it with its elegantly curved fingers in the palm of a man's rough work glove, conveying

Confession
1977
Wood, plastic grape, and dried orange
H. 6¼ in.
Collection of the artist

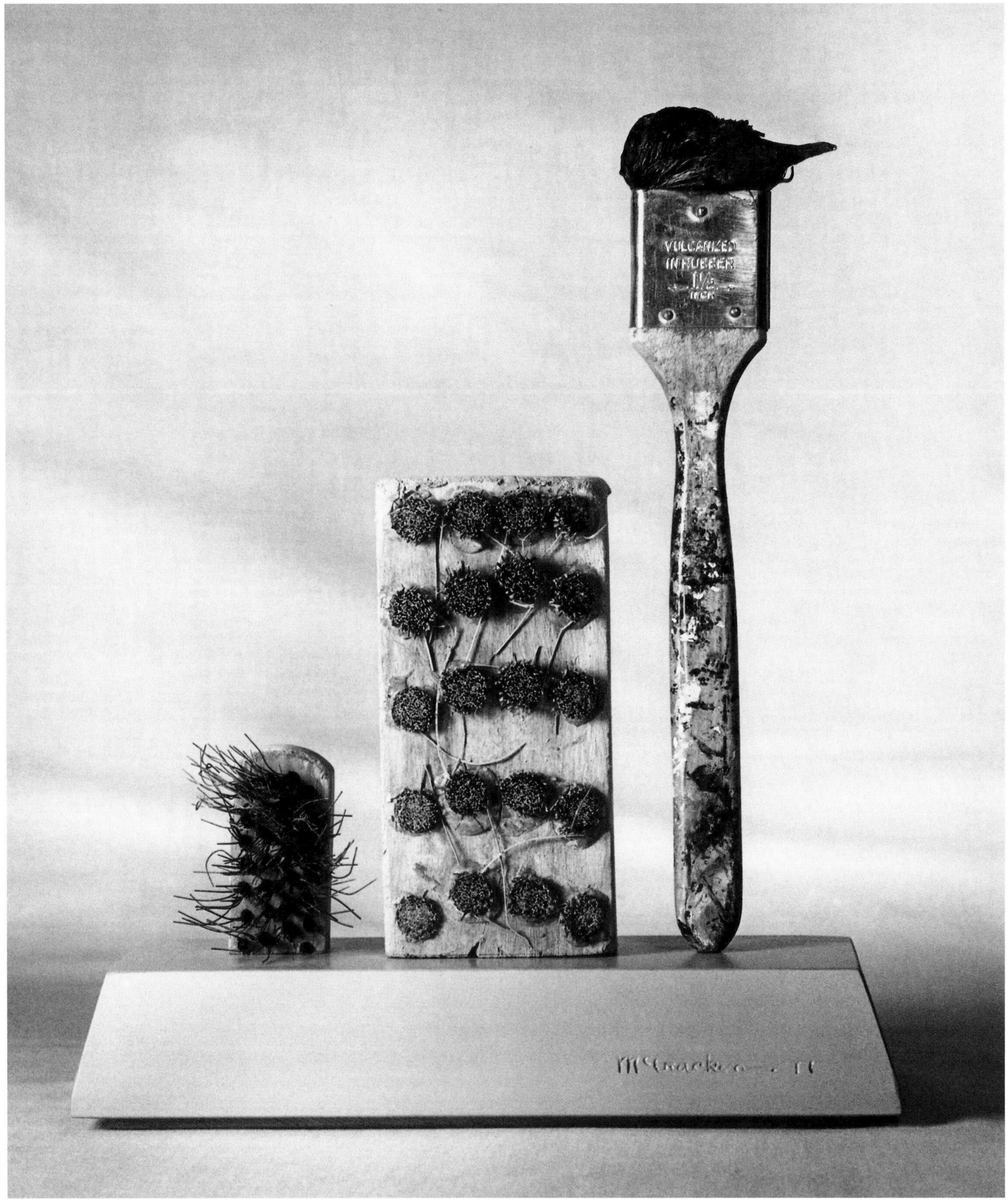

Family Group
1977
Brushes
H. 11 in.
Museum of Northwest Art,
Gift of Marshall and Helen Hatch

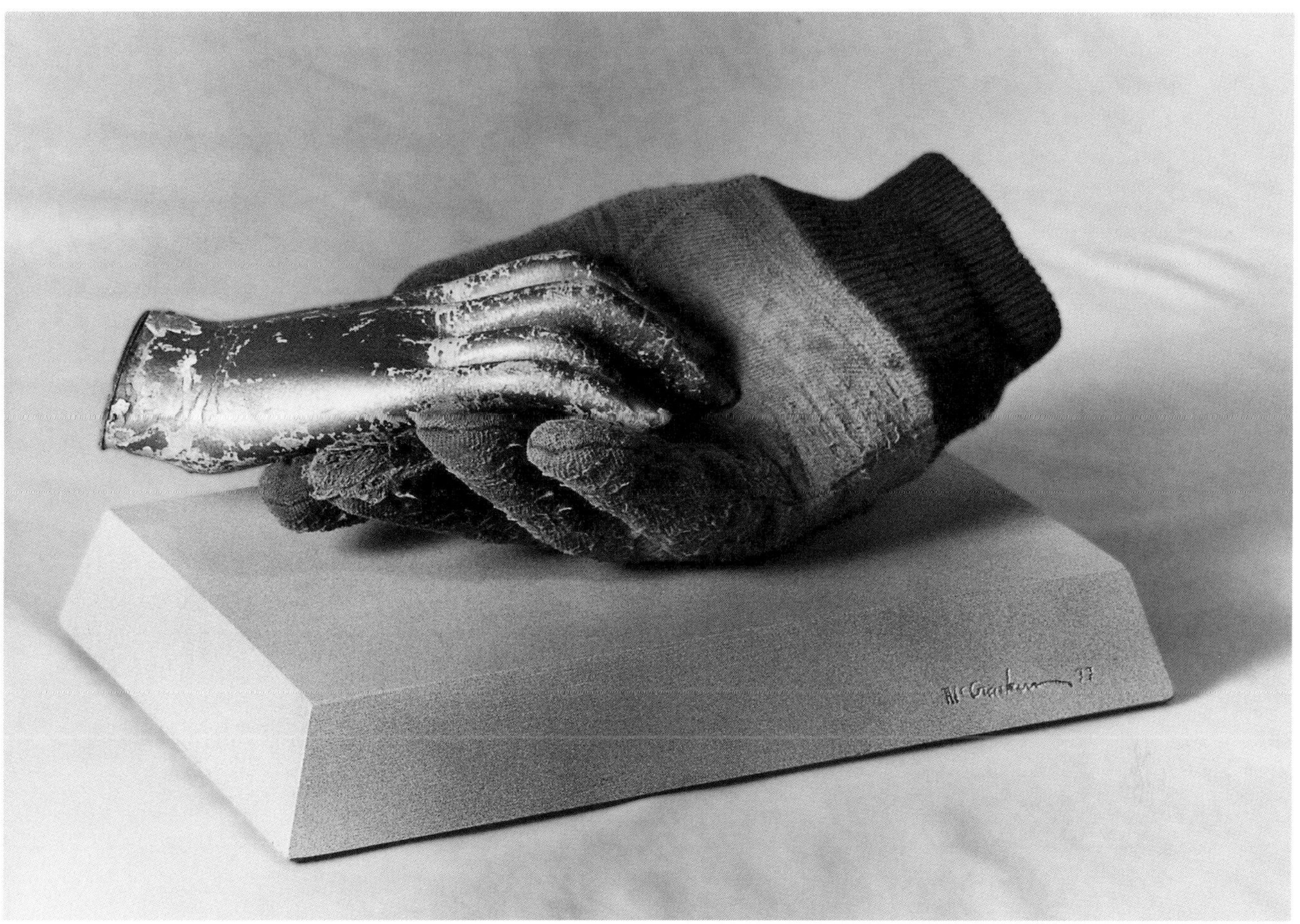

Hands
1977
Plastic, cloth, and plaster
H. 5¼ in.
Collection of Jon Dahle

the essence of a sophisticated woman hand in hand with a working stiff in the piece titled *Hands* (1977).

In yet another tableau, worn brushes take on the personae of its title, *Family Group* (1977). McCracken saw a wide, worn-out scrub brush as the mother; a tall, narrow paintbrush matted and caked with dried paint as the father; and a small scrub brush with prickly, unkempt bristles as the mischievous kid.

The arch, tongue-in-cheek new series bewildered McCracken's admirers, who had grown to expect lyrical, nature-based work, when it was shown in Seattle at the Kiku Gallery. True, the art world was paying homage and top dollar for images of soup cans and cigarette butts, but McCracken had never shown any sign of being *that* kind of artist. The disconnect in approach was hard for his fans to process. That is ironic, because had the same pieces been signed by some hot young artist with a fresh Master of Fine Arts degree, they would almost certainly have received serious critical attention. Nearly everyone had underestimated McCracken and his radical originality.

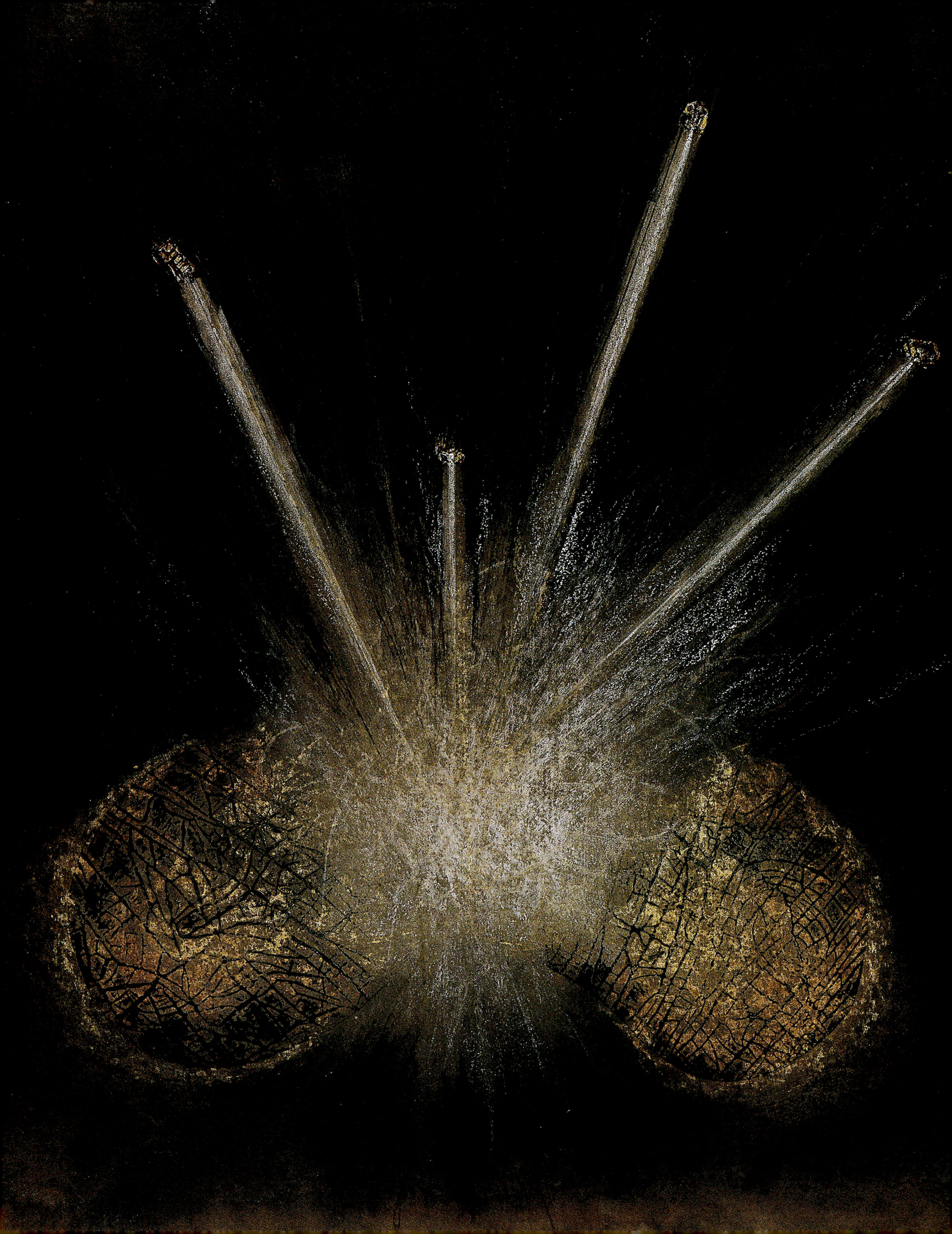

From the Potato Patch

Theodore F. Wolff wrote that "the genius of art lies in the ability to transform the ordinary into the extraordinary; to take the most everyday subject and turn it into a thing of beauty." Wolff wrote these words as art critic for the *Christian Science Monitor,* lauding McCracken's series From the Potato Patch.[1]

McCracken began to give form to his intuitions about the energies at work in the lives of plants, and especially of potatoes, in 1983. His insights about the way plants communicate with each other and with their surroundings are in concord with a decade of findings by scientists in Britain and Germany. He began drawing and painting images that suggested an emotional component to potatoes, usually regarded as the ultimate in plainness and simplicity. McCracken imbued potatoes and other root vegetables with unsuspected rich experiences, occasionally verging into visual metaphor with pieces such as *Old Sage and Disciples.*

"Much of my work in the past has been in the form of creatures of the air," he said of his leap from sky to earth. "These works are the antithesis of the airborne, yet they spring from the same source. Crooked carrots, winking potato eyes, parsnip twins; tuber and root forms are often humorous as well as good to eat. However, they are also conscious, message-bearing energy states of dancing molecules, deeply expressive of the wisdom of the earth."

At the time the From the Potato Patch series was produced, the notion of message-bearing energies in plants had been dismissed by skeptics. But recent research at Edinburgh University confirms McCracken's intuitions. Researcher Anthony Trewavas found that "plant functions are amazingly complex and elegant. . . . They use changes in voltage across their cell membranes to send electrical signals from one region to another. . . . They can assimilate information, calculate outcomes and respond using a series of molecular pathways that are remarkably like our brains."[2]

In his thoughtful book *The Botany of Desire,* Michael Pollan links vegetal intelligence to evolution:

Exploding Potato (detail)
1983 (see p. 65)

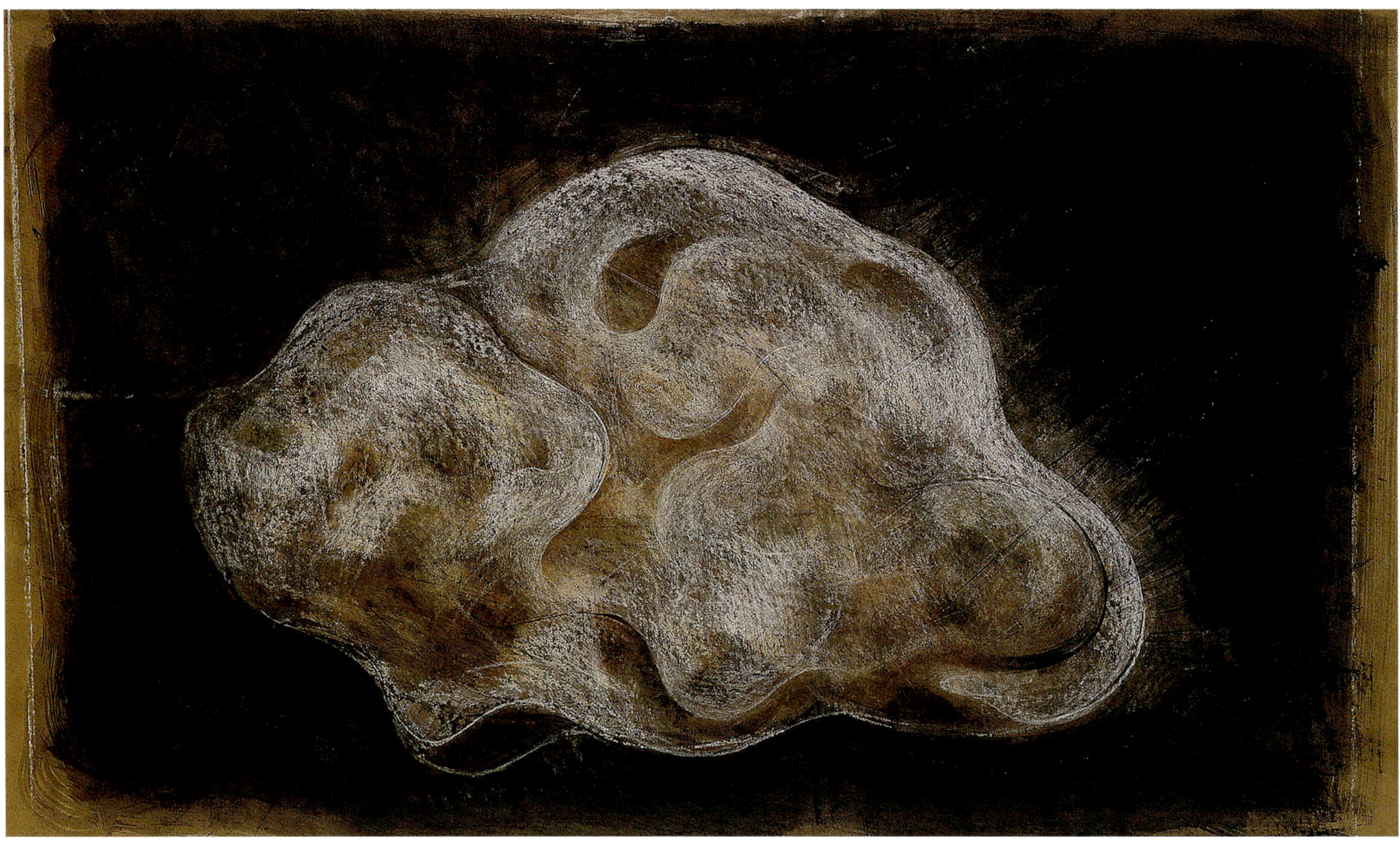

> Plants are nature's alchemists, expert at transforming water, soil, and sunlight into an array of precious substances, many of them beyond the ability of human beings to conceive, much less manufacture. While we were nailing down consciousness and learning to walk on two feet, they were, by the same process of natural selection, inventing photosynthesis (the astonishing trick of converting sunlight into food) and perfecting organic chemistry. . . . From plants come chemical compounds that nourish and heal and poison and delight the senses, others that rouse and put to sleep and intoxicate, and a few with the astounding power to alter consciousness—even to plant dreams in the brains of awake humans.[3]

Living close to the earth, McCracken gained an appreciation of plants as he did of native animals. In 1983, without any particular course of action in mind, he created a mixed-media drawing of a knotty form that curled in on itself, leaving small concavities, that could have been a study for a form in bronze. It is titled simply *Potato.* In this more than any other piece of its period, McCracken shows Henry Moore's influence, with the soft-stained surface, on which every line is contour, and every shading jumps with volume.

It led quickly to a series. These creations, McCracken noted, "came in a rush. They weren't planned or calculated—they just arose. I tend to trust that kind of intuitive energy."

Earth energies are visible in *New Potatoes,* which shows the growth of young potatoes as nodes surrounded by auras of light. Some years ago, researchers at the University of Washington studying fertility made the startling discovery that at the instant an egg is inseminated by a sperm, the egg emits a flash of light.[4] It is something like that flash of life energy that surrounds these tiny new potatoes, joined by umbilici of nourishing roots. There is something touching about seeing these young as a family descended from the same slender rhizome that joins them as an electric red line (the color of blood if not its substance). Each of the new potatoes looks as if it could be an organ, veined with light and dark cells.

A potato so large that it blots out the sky as it fills the picture plane is titled *Darkening Form.* The dusky shape seems a shadow of the hidden energies of the magnetic earth. Life

Potato (above)
1983
Wax crayon, pencil, and ink wash on paper
31⅜ × 47½ in.
Collection of Tim and Mardy McCracken

New Potatoes (opposite, top)
1983
Print, pencil, and ink wash on paper
19 × 24½ in.
Collection of Tim and Gail Bruce

Darkening Form (opposite, bottom)
1983
Wax crayon and ink wash on paper
31⅜ × 41¾ in.
Private collection

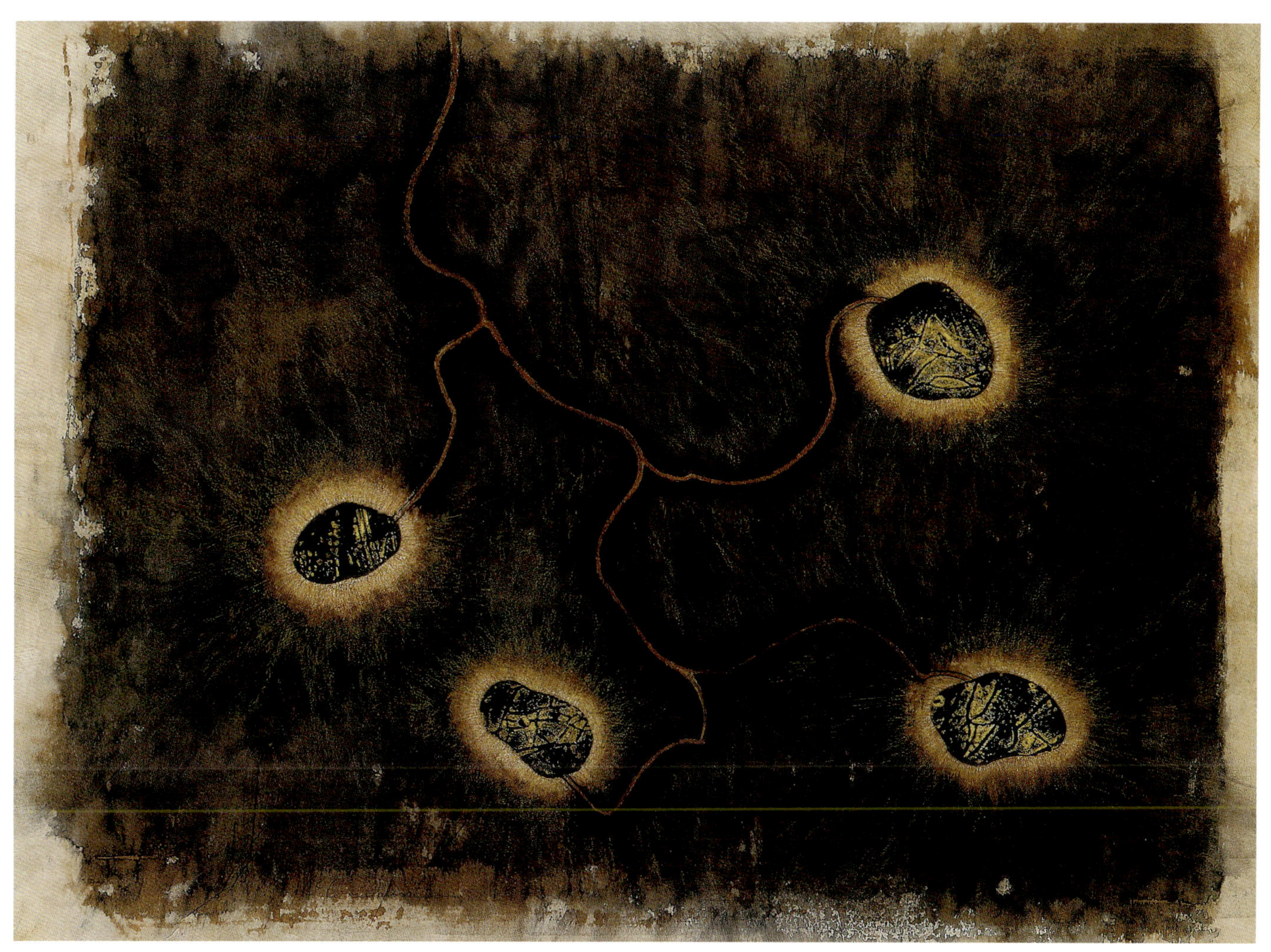

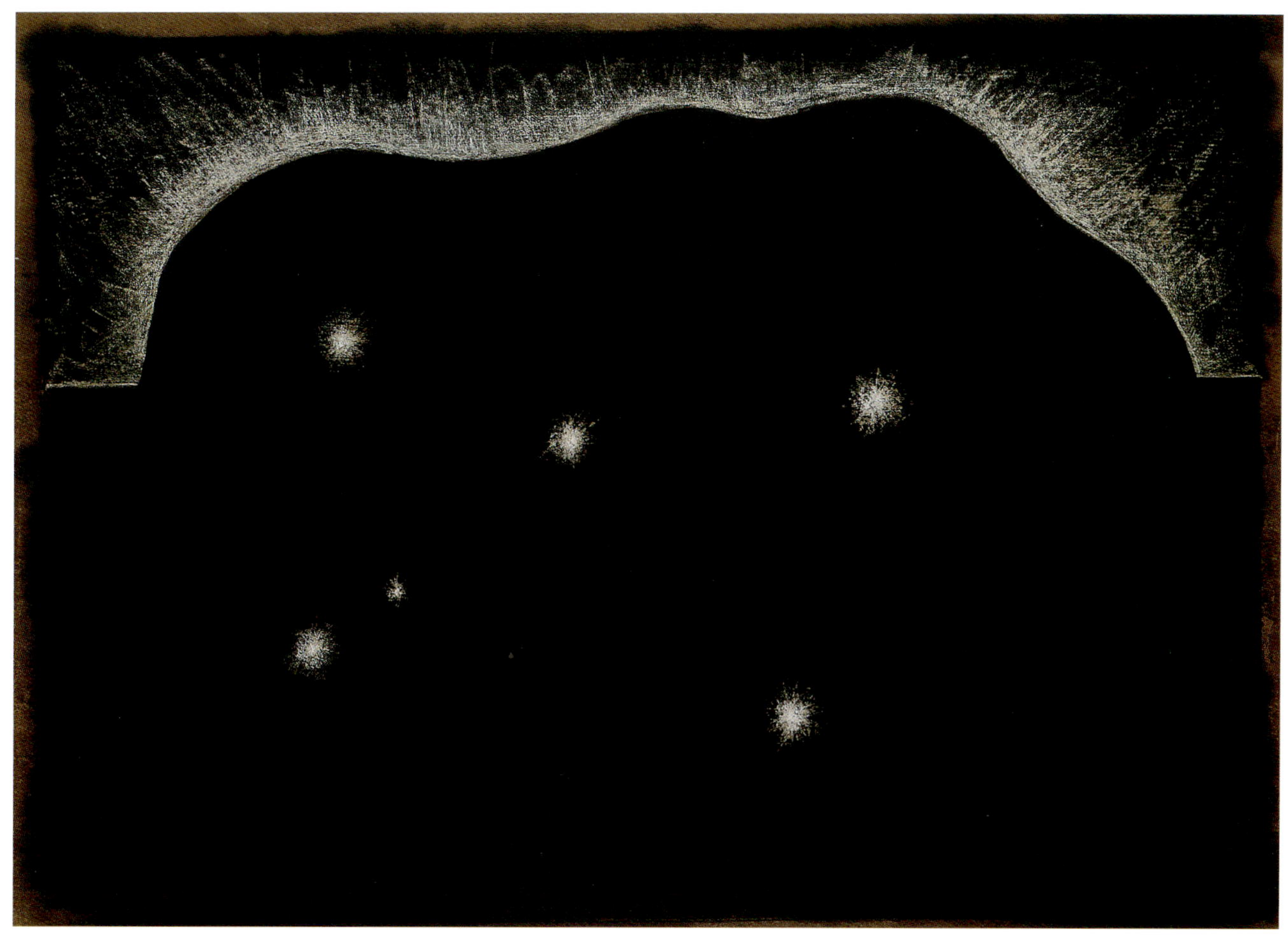

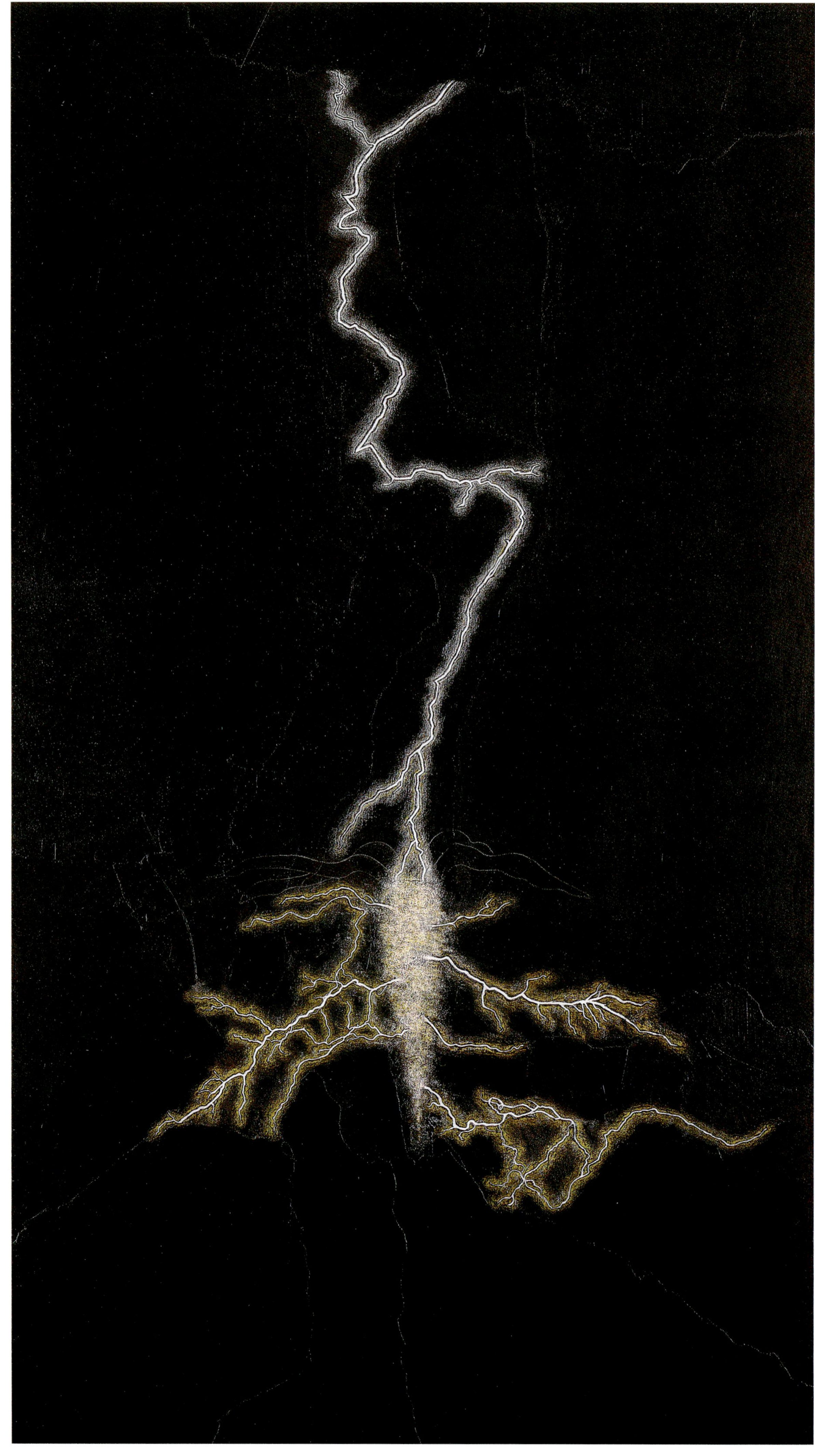

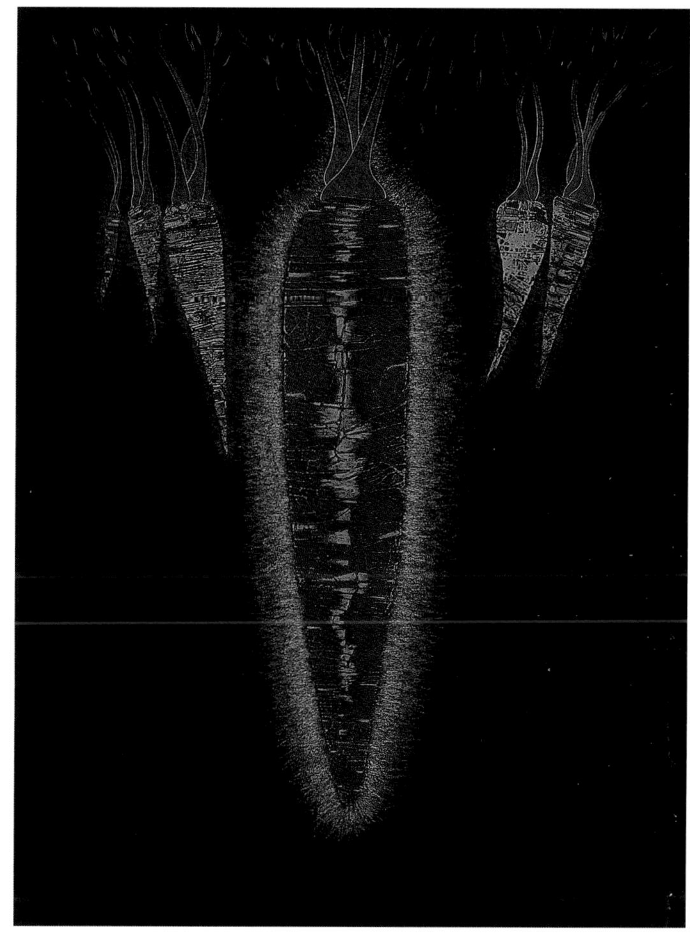

energy shines as a visible halo around it, while germinating "eyes" evoke the luminescence of stars in a night sky. The flesh of the potato may darken and rot, the painting seems to say, but the eyes are already in motion to sprout new life.

It was not solely potatoes whose energies fascinated McCracken. He drew a mandrake still in the earth, its roots flashing as with lightning. Faint crackles of light suggest energy converging from adventitious roots. Unlike the potato, which is a synonym for the plain and ordinary, the mandrake comes with a history of witchcraft and rumors of magic. Because the mandrake often grows with forked roots that suggest the torso and legs of a man, ancient superstition claimed that an uprooted mandrake was capable of screaming.[5] McCracken's painting suggests a secret energy filling it (and presumably its consumers) with great power. Mandrake roots once were—and perhaps still are—used in "witches' potions" to induce the sensation of flying. McCracken's painting gives the mandrake its due.

McCracken also showed radiant energy emanating from a large, perfect carrot, a queen among carrots, still surrounded with black earth, flanked by smaller ones whose color and "carrotness" are still developing. He titled it *Carrot with Attendants,* as if we were looking at an underground beauty pageant. The carrots in particular impressed McCracken's old friend Morris Graves. When McCracken sent him a catalogue of an exhibition of the series, Graves responded: "Living 'above ground' turned quietly to thoughts of life 'under ground' when I saw your *Carrot with Attendants* & your acknowledgement/celebration of the potato's psyche. I love to think of how many other lives, urban & rural, will be enhanced by your concepts & great artistry & the depth & breadth of your awareness."[6]

Carrots, however, did not hold McCracken's attention. It was potatoes, those nutritional nuggets the English used to call "bread root" that most fired his imagination. Potato forms in his drawings grew more and more extraordinary.

The rot visible in *Bad Potato* takes a peculiarly bloody form—as if the potato had spurted its life energy up into the surrounding air. At the center of that poisonous effluvium hang twin dark forms suggestive of giant spermatozoa wrapped in haloes of light. The brushstrokes that compose the body of the potato carry a vitality that suggests the opposite of rot. Indeed, this *Bad Potato* has an in-your-face vivacity that

Mandrake Root (opposite)
1983
Print, collage, pencil,
and ink wash on wood panel
46½ × 23¾ in.
Private collection

Carrot with Attendants (above)
1983
Print, pencil, and ink wash on paper
26¼ × 20¼ in.
Collection of Tim and Gail Bruce

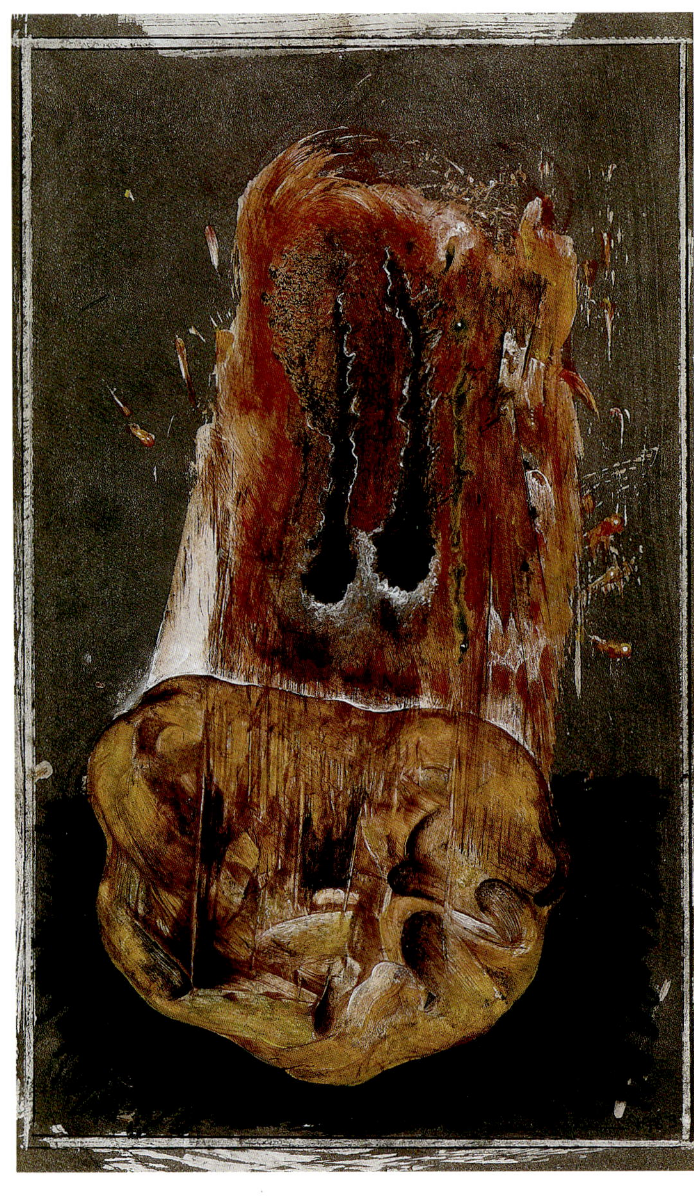

Bad Potato
1983
Epoxy, pencil, and oil on paper
13½ × 8½ in.
Collection of the artist

suggests a construction of "bad" that is rather more devilish than decaying. That is, in fact, a historically accurate view of the early European opinion of potatoes.

Pollan writes that "even after people recognized that this peculiar new plant could produce more food on less land than any other crop, most of European culture remained inhospitable to the potato. Why? Europeans hadn't eaten tubers before; the potato was a member of the nightshade family (along with the equally disreputable tomato); potatoes were thought to cause leprosy and immorality; potatoes were mentioned nowhere in the Bible; potatoes came from America, where they were a staple of an uncivilized and conquered race."[7]

The wind was in McCracken's sails, and more strange potatoes surfaced. *Exploding Potato,* shown at the instant of bursting, releasing so much energy that fragments fly from it like missiles, could be seen as a result of carrying the life energy to an extreme that could no longer be contained within the white interior. Of course it could, with equal plausibility, be the product of a potato left for too long in a microwave oven set on high.

A similar waggish humor is visible in *Patriot,* a potato whose cellular energy is depicted in living red, white, and blue colors. Here, as in *Exploding Potato,* the humorous aspect is secondary to aesthetics. The patriot's cellular divisions create a compact internal pattern of great complexity, to which the assigning of color seems almost an afterthought. The piece shows an affinity to the work of the Swiss artist Paul Klee in its synthesis of abstract and representational elements, and its delicate, sensitive, and rather wry handling of its organic subject.

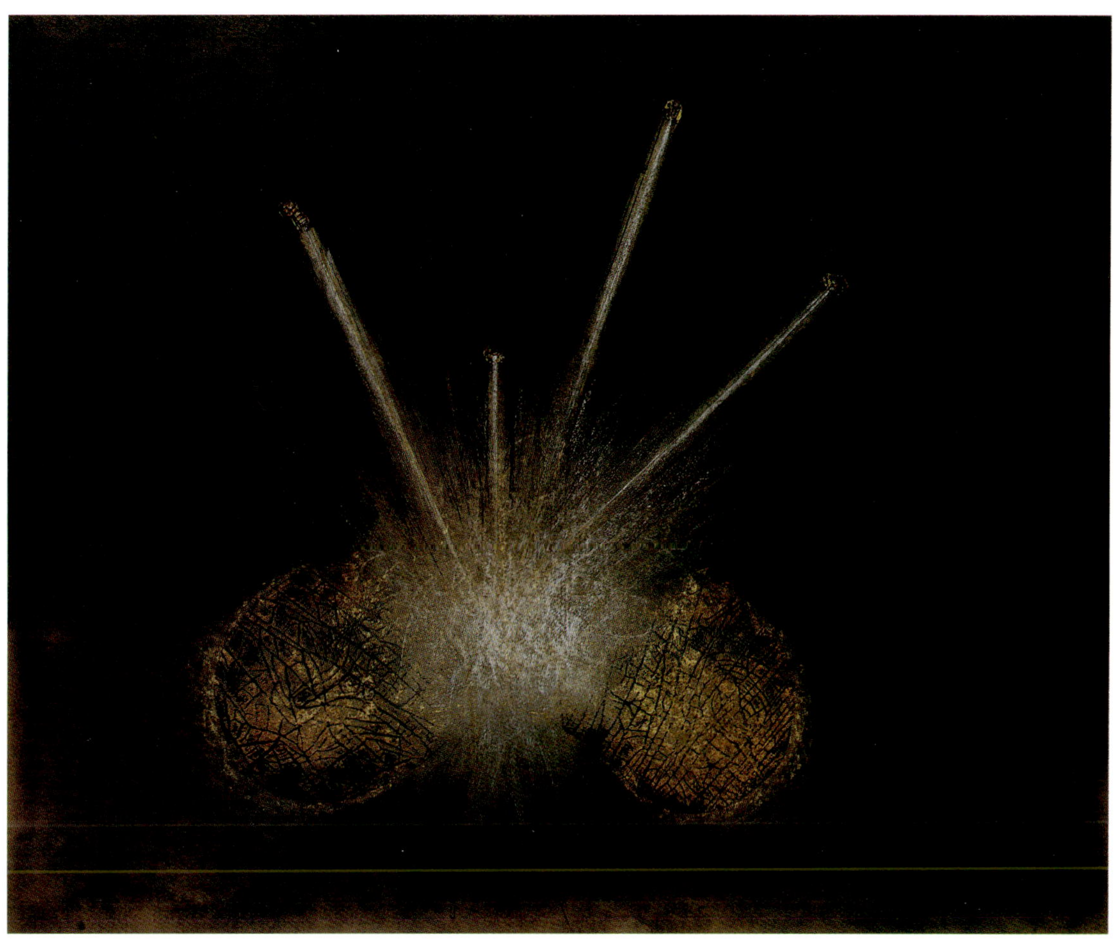

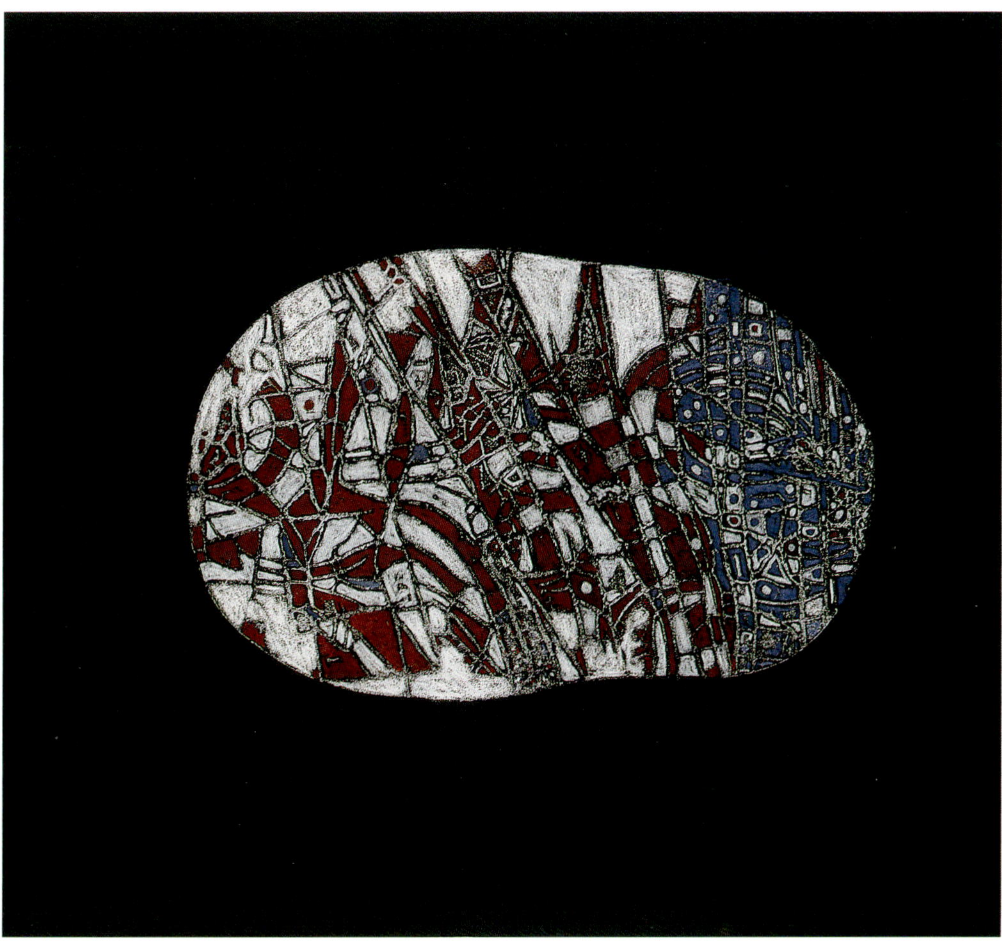

Exploding Potato
1983
Print, wax crayon, and ink wash on paper
25⅜ × 30⅜ in.
Private collection

Patriot
1983
Print, pencil, and ink wash on paper
12½ × 13½ in.
Private collection

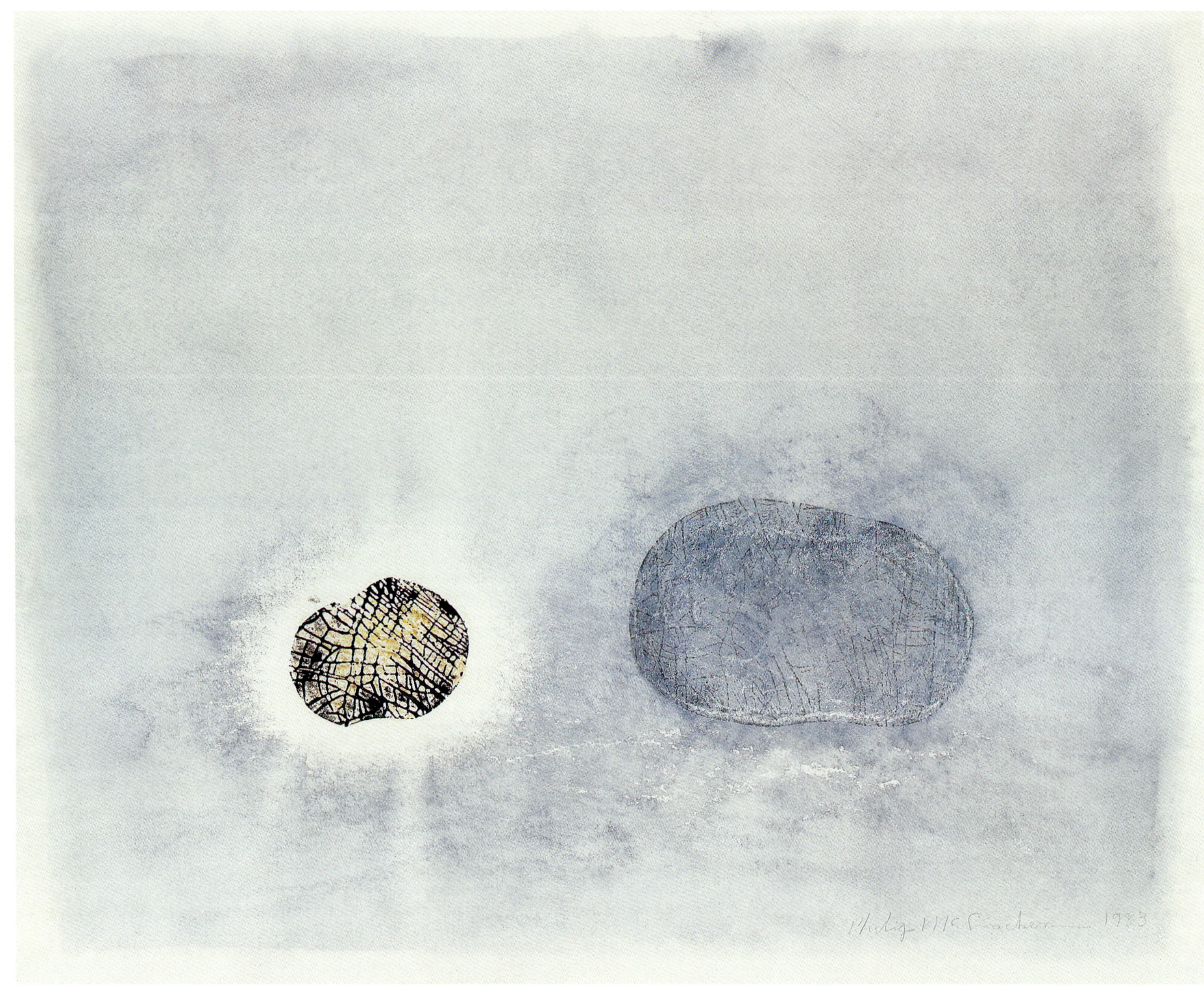

Enlightened Disciple
1983
Print, pencil, and ink wash on paper
25½ × 30½ in.
Collection of Steve Conners

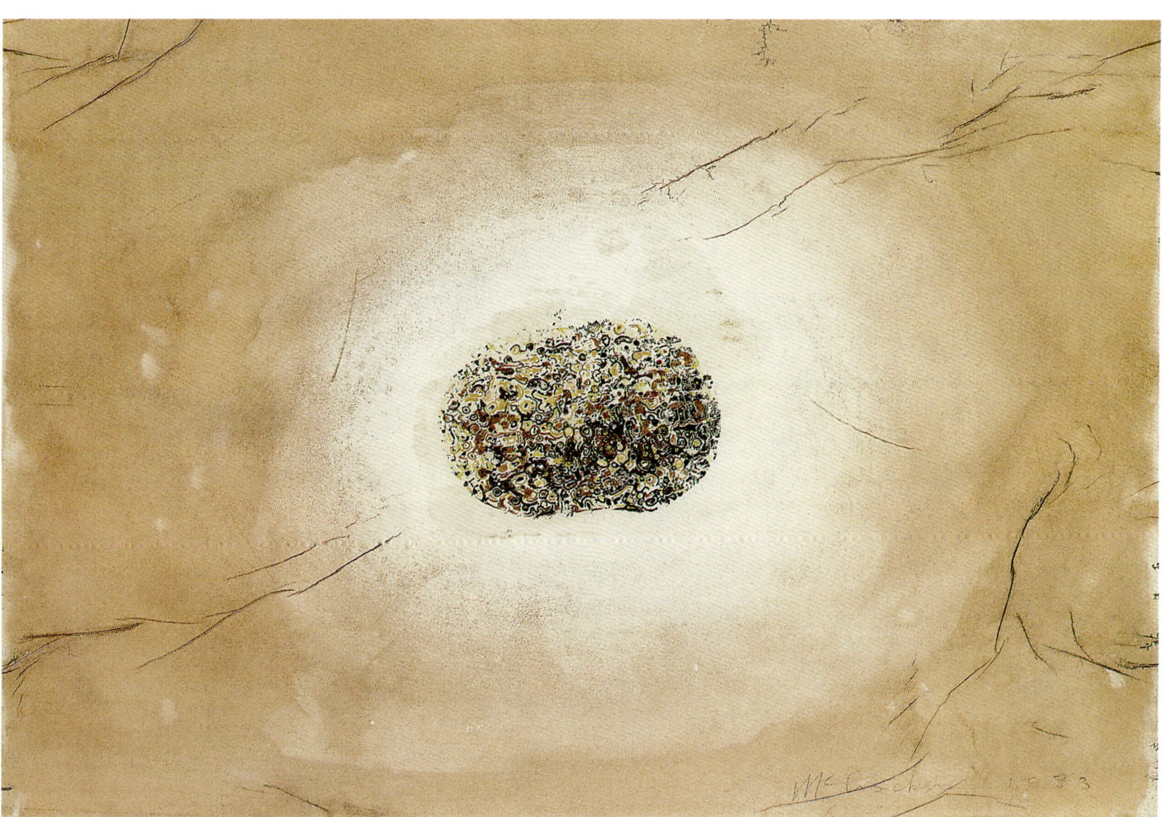

Transformation
1983
Print, pencil, and ink wash on paper
14⅛ × 19 in.
Private collection

McCracken's wit is always near the surface. Taking as his models a large potato and a far smaller new potato, he drew a piece titled *Enlightened Disciple*—as if the older potato, now growing dim, had modeled a pattern of growth for the smaller one, with its crisply drawn, crisscrossed cells of growth. The idea is reprised in *Old Sage and Disciples,* except that in it the large potato still emits a powerful field of radiant energy, while the small tubers that surround it glow with lesser lights.

There is a clear link between some of McCracken's plant motifs and microscope images of cellular structures. Those cellular divisions render a potato as an aggregate community of living cells, rather than a dusky, inert brown lump. The focus is on the energy of the cycle of growth and decay in a drawing titled *Transformation,* which renders a potato as a tight group of swarming, growing cells without the boundary of an exterior skin. In another drawing, *Earth Rhythms,* he shows earth energy as rippling layers of hot red and yellow, rising in shaggy channels to growing potatoes radiant in the midst of dark earth. The subject is so abstracted that no sign of roots or rhizomes remains—only shimmering energy signatures.

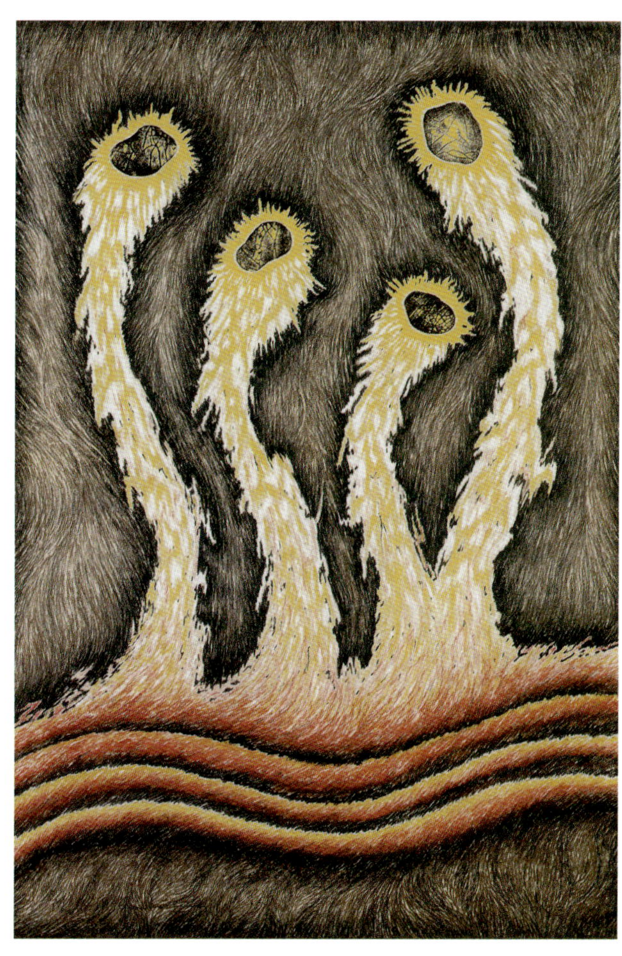

Earth Rhythms
1983
Colored pencil on paper
36 × 24¼ in.
Collection of Jean Wharton

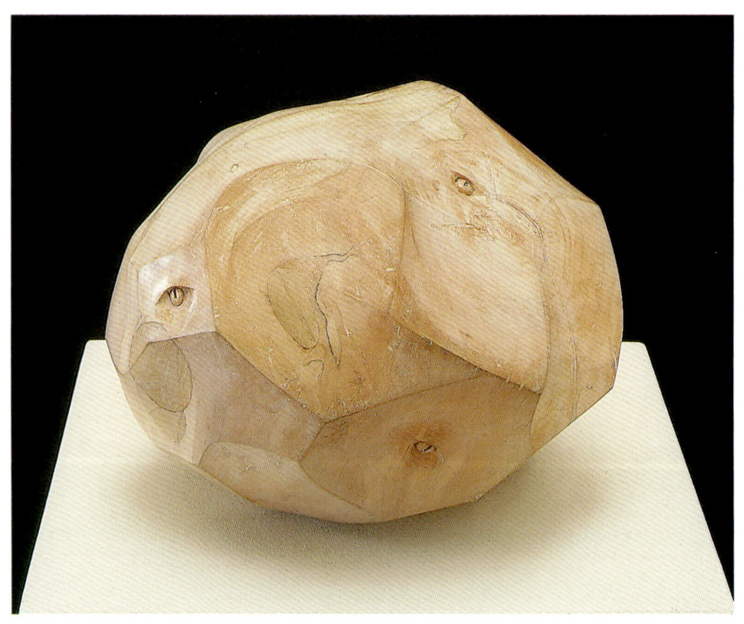

Potato with Eyes I
1984
Cherry wood
H. 8½ in.
Potato Museum, Albuquerque, New Mexico

Earth/Prism
1983
Wax crayon and ink wash on paper
25½ × 30½ in.
Collection of Lance and J.P. Brigham

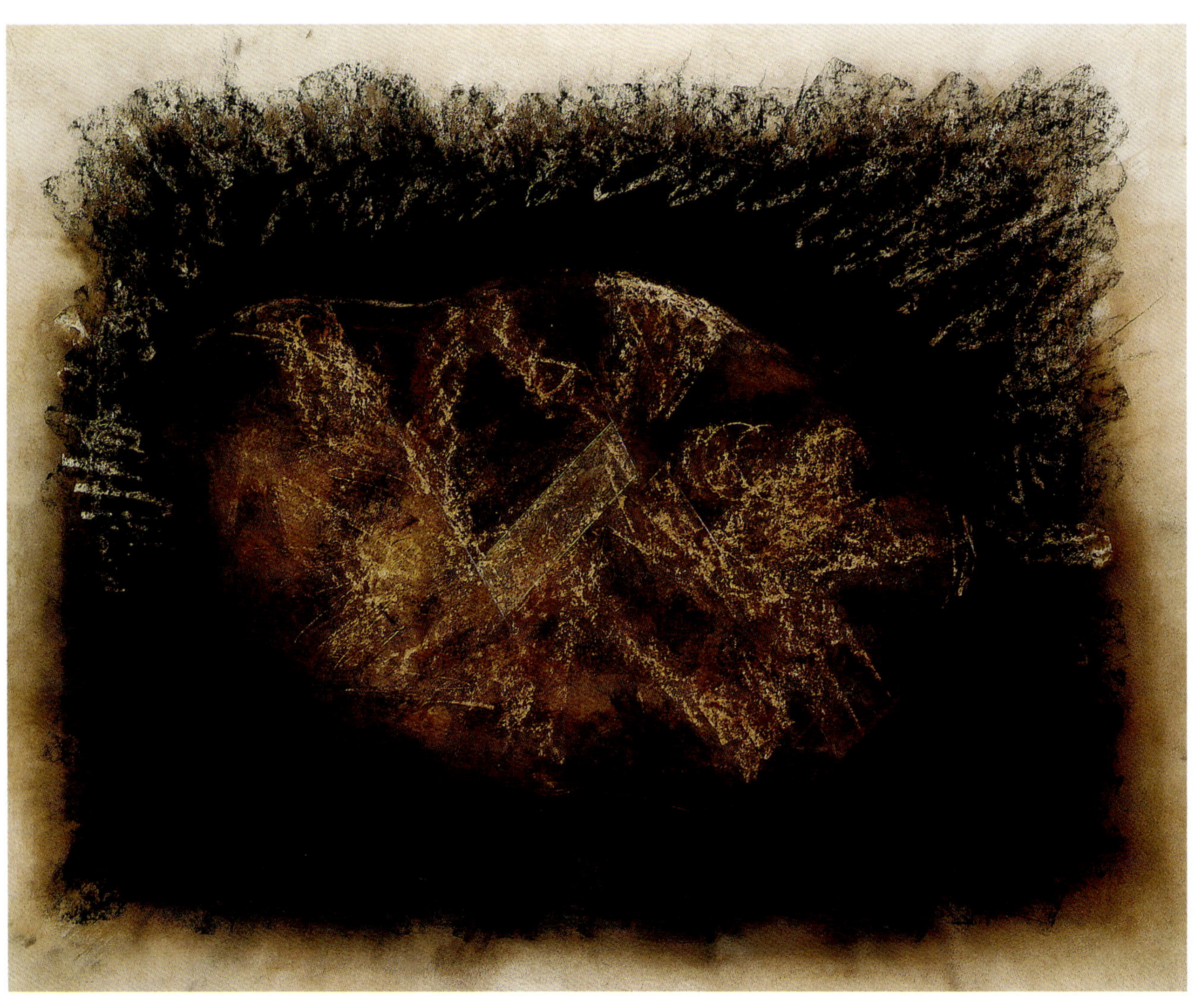

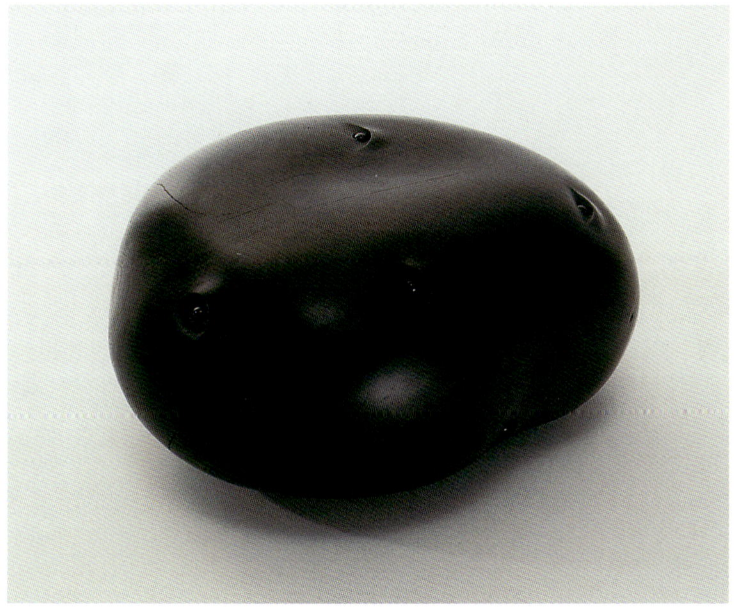

Potato with Eyes II
1986
Juniper and onyx
H. 4½ in.
Collection of Lynn McAllister

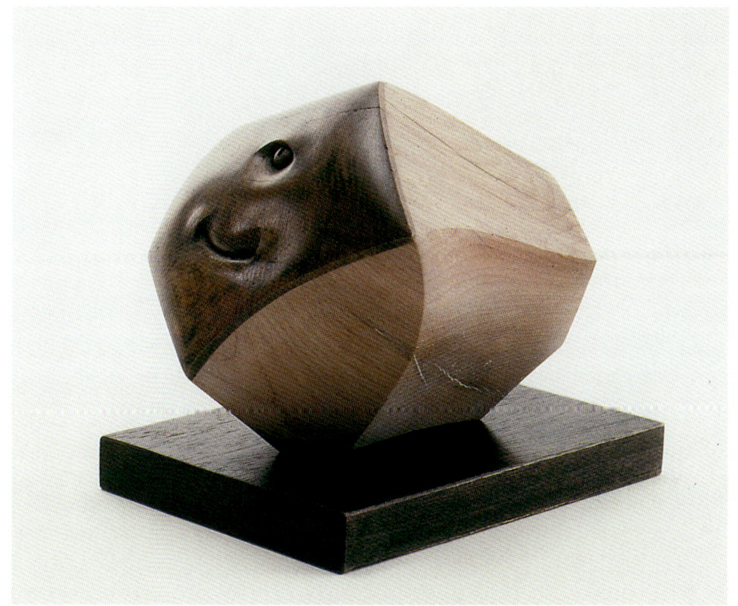

Potato with Wandering Eye
1986
Juniper
H. 6 in.
Private collection

By 1984, McCracken was ready to express the energy inherent in potatoes in sculpture. If his potato drawings stressed the dynamics of molecular activity, his sculptures appeared to have absorbed sufficient wisdom to contemplate the world with deeply knowing eyes.

Potato with Eyes I, Potato with Eyes II, and *Potato with Wandering Eye* are carved of wood. They vary from faceted to smooth-skinned, polished approximations of some Platonic ideal of "potatoness." In all of them, the most remarkable aspect is their eyes. Lightly hooded, gifted with a central "lens," they appear to gaze back at the viewer with appreciable, unsettling intelligence. Indeed, *Potato with Wandering Eye* has a rakish air, wearing what appears to be a gash of a smirk below his single eye, as he perches on a narrow face of his faceted surface. He has the air of one who knows secrets he is itching to divulge.

McCracken is doubtless in agreement with Pollan in his assessment that "the qualities of a potato—as of any domesticated plant or animal—are a fair reflection of the values of the people who grow and eat it." Wild potatoes are too bitter and toxic to eat. "We are partners in a co-evolutionary relationship, as indeed we have been ever since the birth of agriculture more than ten thousand years ago." Pollan notes, "So the question arose in my mind . . . Did I choose to plant these potatoes, or did the potato make me do it?" McCracken might, with equal curiosity, ask, Did I choose to draw the potato, or did the potato make me do it? And reach the same conclusion as Pollan: in fact, both statements are true.[8]

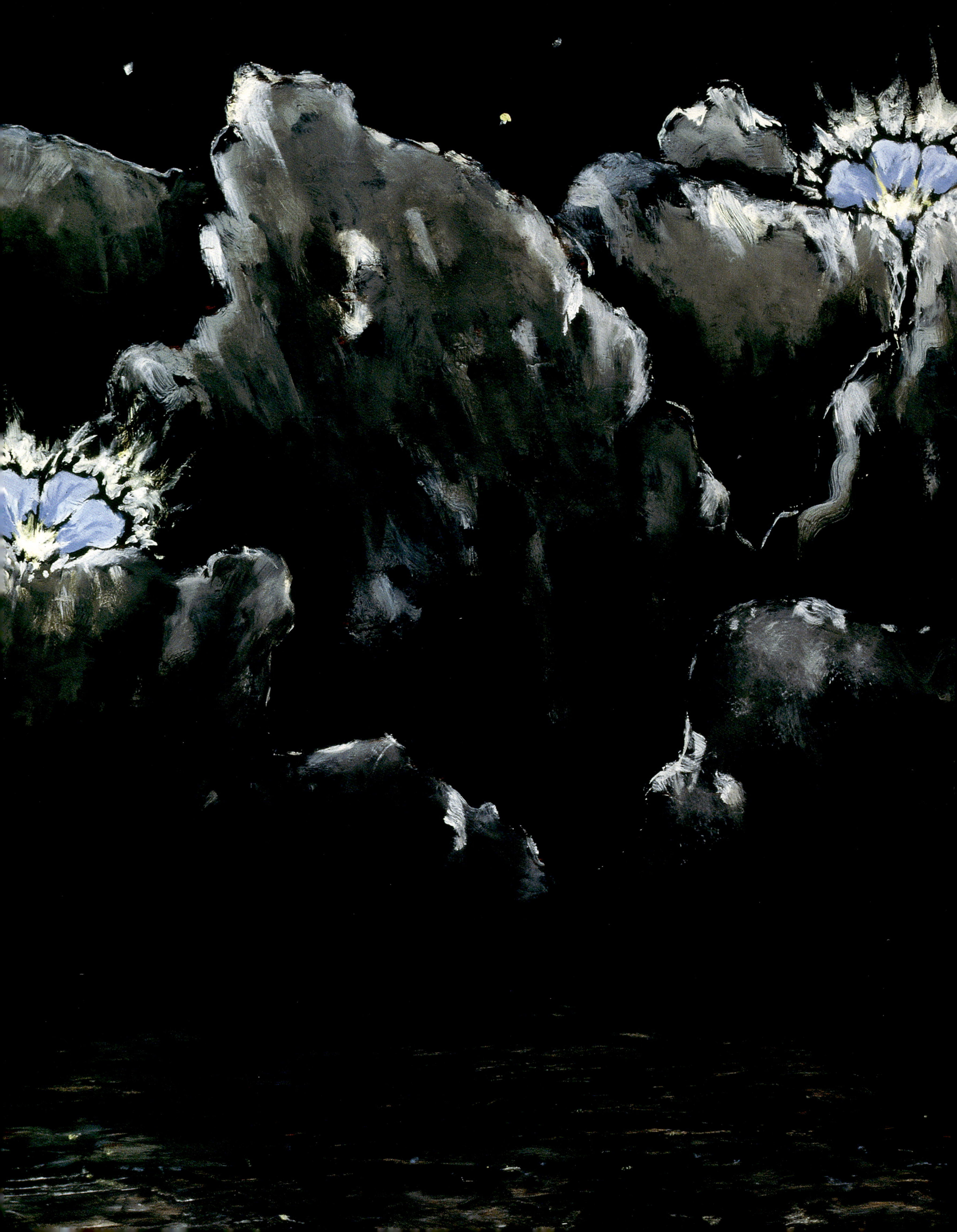

Fragments of Night Sky

Albert Einstein once said, "The most beautiful thing we can experience is the mysterious." True artists never lose a sense of wonder. They remain open each day to a fresh vision of mundane things that most of us take for granted. In 1989, McCracken experienced a change in his awareness of the nature of flowers—particularly purple pansies. It triggered a series of paintings of Flowers and Night Sky.

"I had thought of pansies before as pleasant little flowers, but something happened similar to the turning of the end of a kaleidoscope. The basic elements that make up the image are the same, but there is a rapid rearranging of them, revealing a surprising new order. In place of the tiny pansy, I was seeing a monumental macrocosmic element in the landscape, loaded with power and energy, deeply poignant, and full of mystery."

Night Flowers and the Sea: Fog Bank, Lummi Island (detail)
1989 (see p. 76)

Night Flowers
1989
Oil on wood panel
24 × 48 in.
Collection of the artist

Blue pansies so large they become elements of landscape fill the lower half of Night Flowers. *These are a sculptor's flowers; the petals appear solidly volumetric, with little modulation between deep black shadows and petal highlights that jump into foreground. They are placed before a sky of no ordinary night. A window in the darkness shows a daylight vignette of snow-capped mountains and green foothills, as if the night sky had been superimposed over a scene of bright daylight. Sheets of pale color descend through the darkness like the lights of the aurora borealis. It is the sky of a volcanic eruption that brings dark at midday, with gusts of blowing ash.*

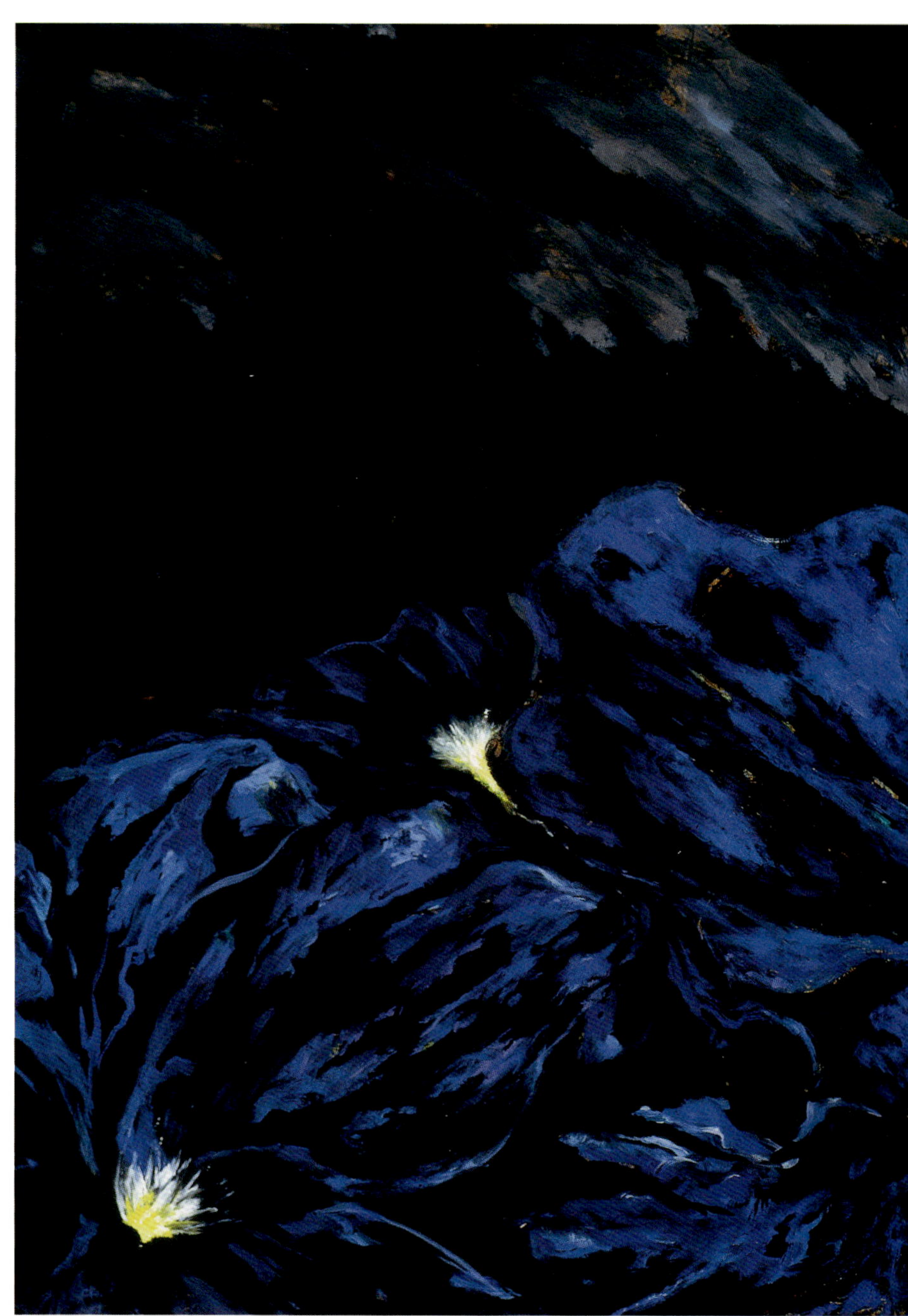

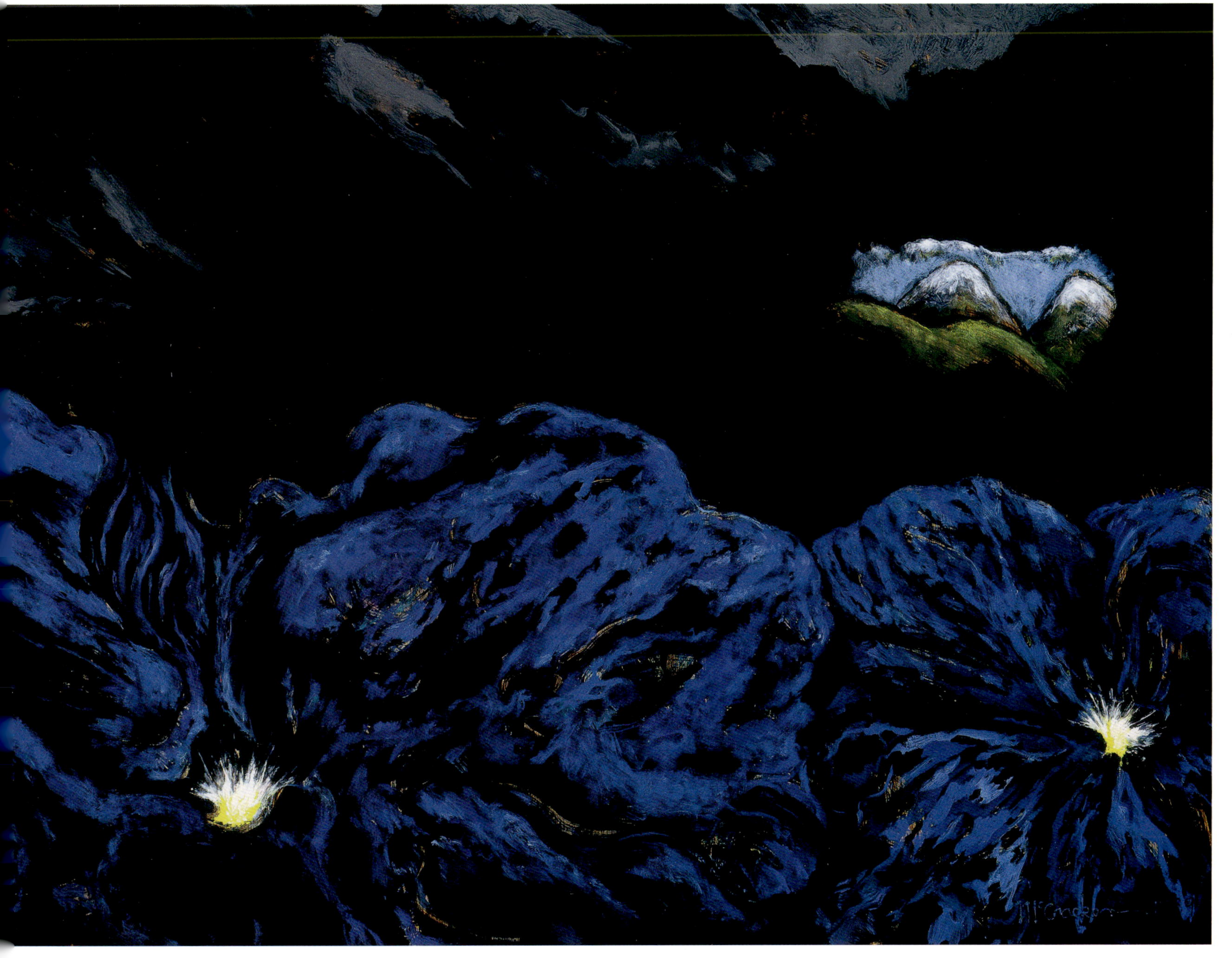

Landscape/Seascape
1989
Oil on wood panel
36 × 48 in.
Collection of Dick and Candy Garvey

A giant blue pansy dominates the landscape, its lower half disappearing below the painting's bottom edge, suggesting that it is too large to be contained within a single field of vision. Solid volumes of petal suggest this flower is anything but delicate. The title proposes a link between the swirling currents of blue paint that form the flower and the motion of the sea.

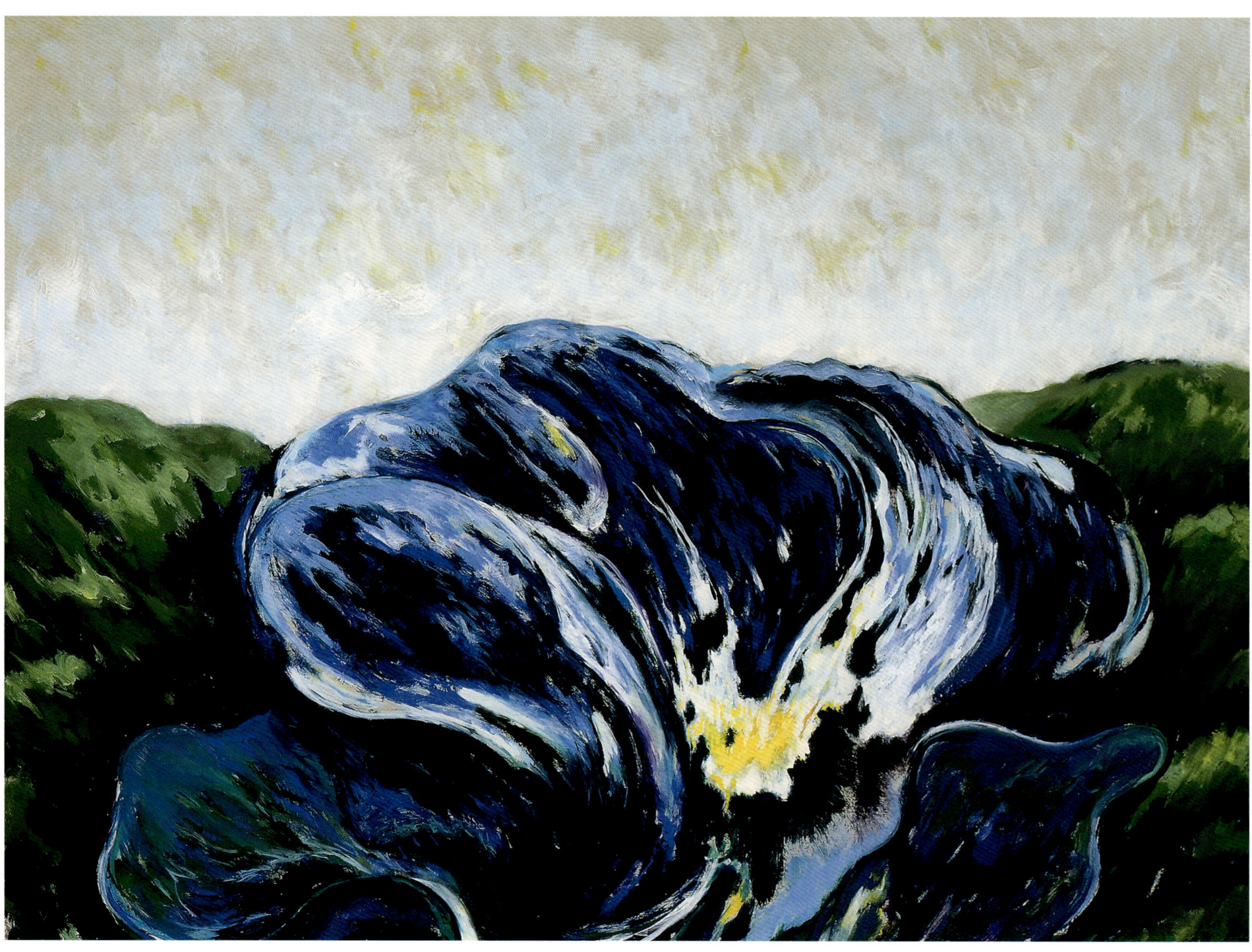

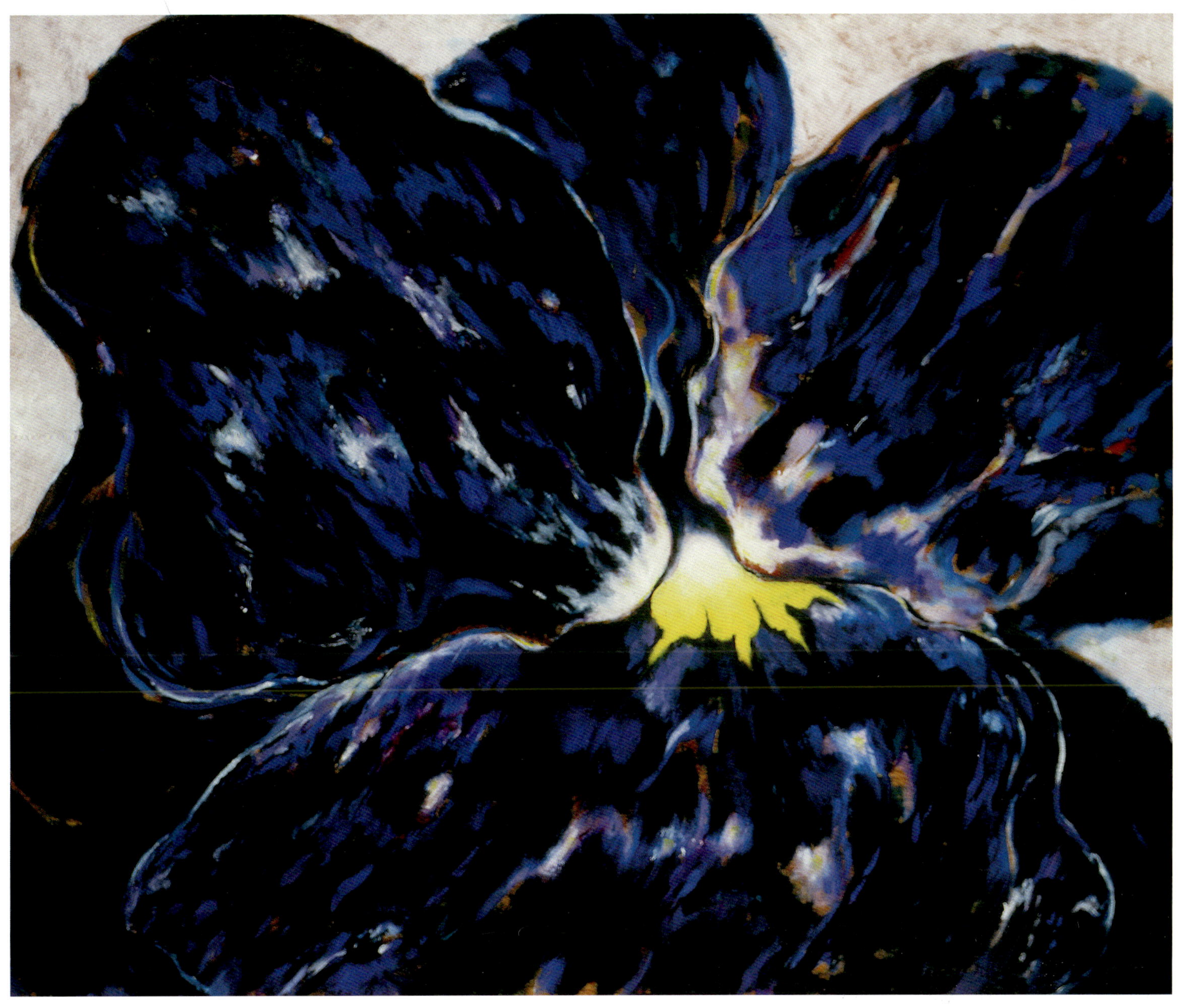

Purple Pansy
1989
Oil on wood panel
26¼ × 31 in.
Collection of the artist

A massive blossom swells to fill the picture plane, with a palpable density that denies the organic fragility usually associated with flowers. The fleshy petals lie in place as if arranged by a sculptor's hand.

Night Flowers and the Sea: Fog Bank, Lummi Island
1989
Oil on wood panel
22¾ × 66¾ in.
Collection of the artist

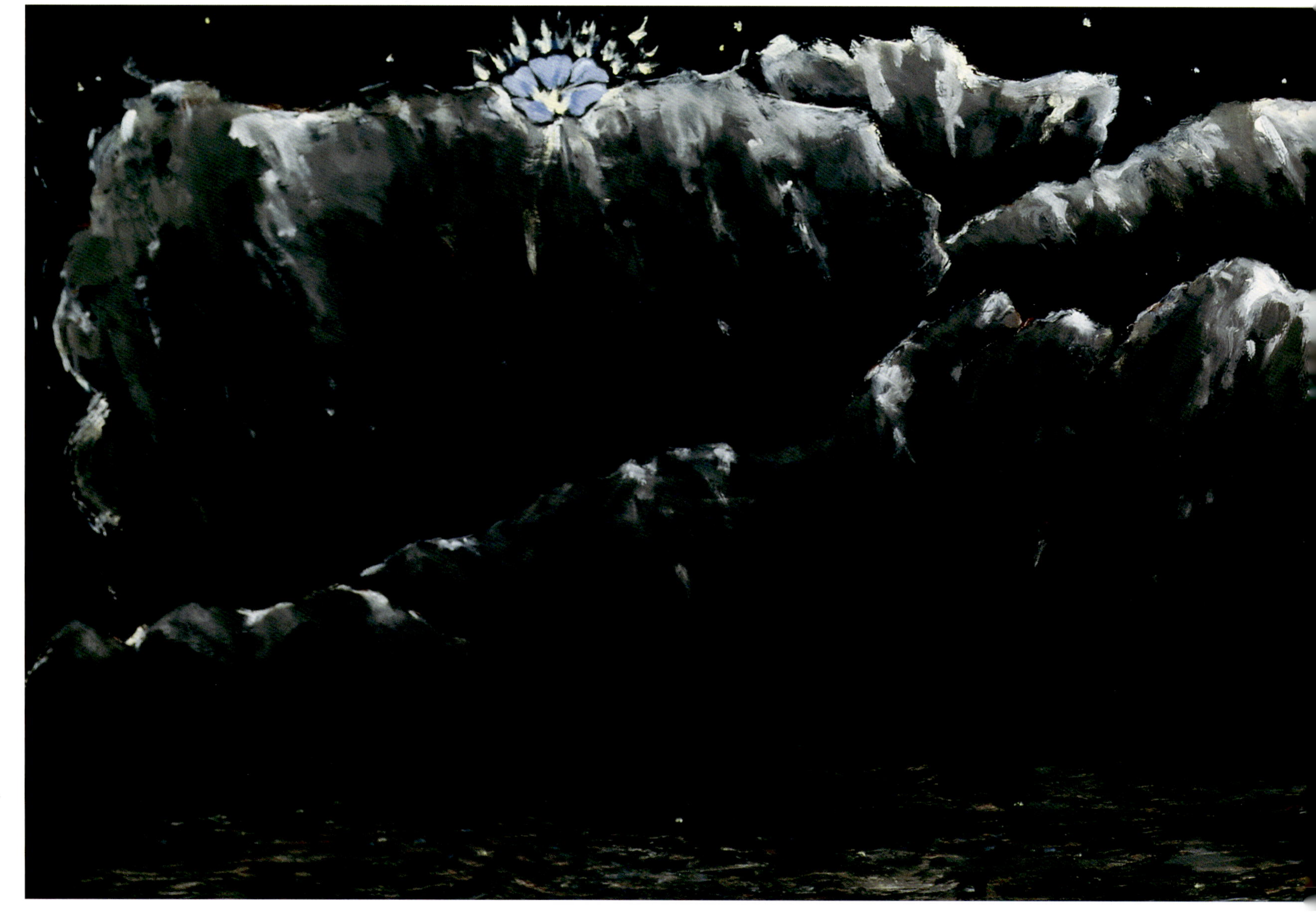

The image comes from an experience McCracken endured one night on the water near Lummi Island, when he was commercial fishing on his gillnetter, The Salish Moon. *Gillnetting on Puget Sound, by law, can be done only at night. The fog was thick when his nylon net became caught in the boat's propeller, and froze the shaft, stopping the engine. When he tried to radio for help, he discovered the radio was dead. The tide was running out, and the boat was swept on a strong current toward the Strait of Juan de Fuca, and the open ocean beyond. "I was on my way to Yokohama," McCracken said. Ultimately, he was towed in by another fishing boat. The painting arose from his memory of looking back toward Lummi Island, with banks of fog against the night sky. Perhaps because the experience occurred while he was in the midst of the* Flowers and Night Sky *series, the fog suggested flower petals. In the painting, blue pansies gleam through from behind the fog.*

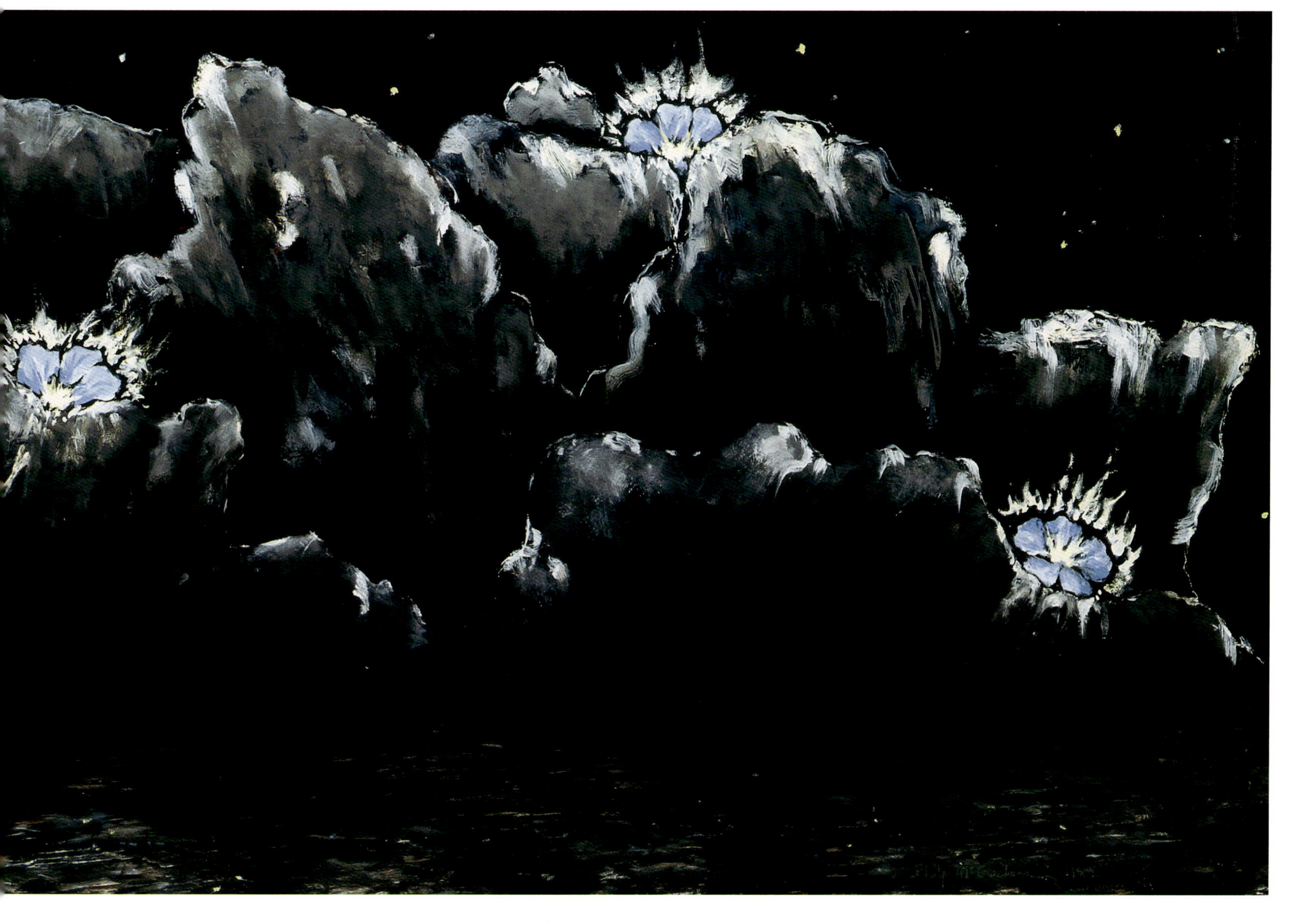

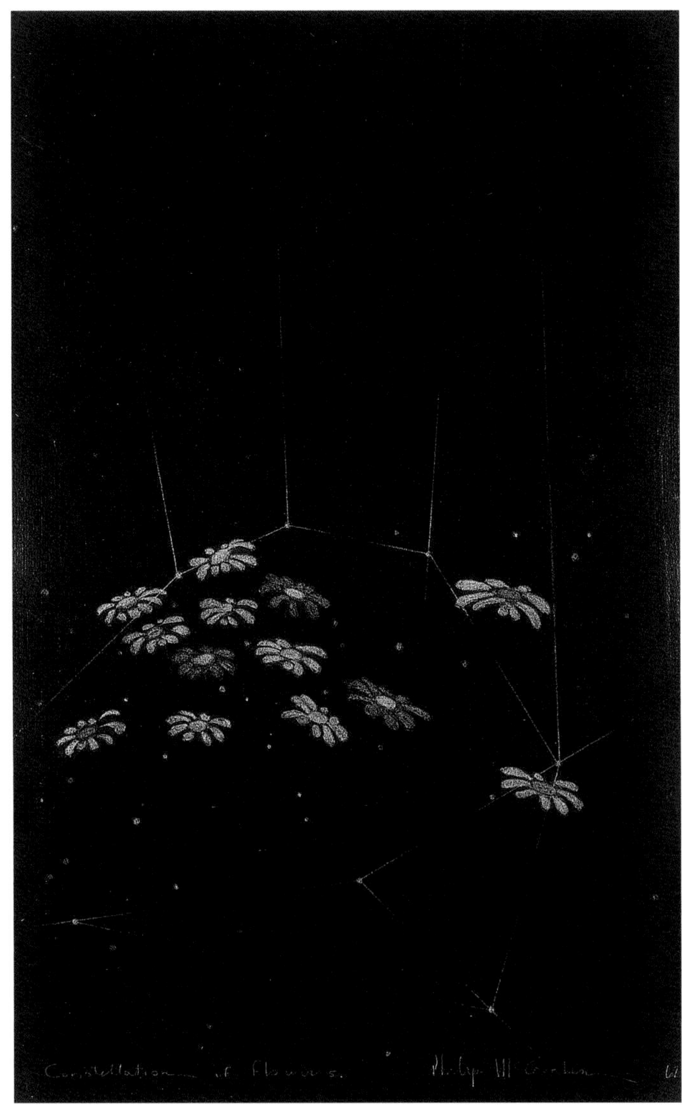

Constellation of Flowers
1989
Crayon and ink wash on paper
42½ × 26 in.
Collection of the artist

In times past, desert people who studied the heavens imagined shapes formed by invisible lines linking stars. McCracken's stargazing vision of a field of white flowers as a constellation was a forerunner of a sculpture series that carved fresh tracks by tackling an unprecedented field: sculptures of the night sky.

When McCracken conceived of sculptures of the night sky, he had to address two staggering problems: first, of method—how to approach an infinite subject in finite, three-dimensional form—and second, of material—what medium could suffice to mimic the heavens? After an early, unsatisfying experiment with stone, he turned to wood, the material he knows best. But this time, it was not perfect, straight-grained pieces he sought. Instead, he looked for "ornery" wood: the gnarled and knotty wood of fruit trees, which dries with checks and voids. McCracken shaped the pieces into polygons that resonate to mathematics—the only system of thought that can approach an apprehension of the enormity of space.[1]

Occasionally, in a conflagration of clarity, an artist expresses something no one has ever before imagined possible. More often than not, such art is a distant early warning of a movement in the collective thinking of the society around him. Visionary art alerts us that a conceptual shift is occurring in the way we experience the world. As art critic John Russell put it, "There is in art a clairvoyance for which we have not yet found a name, and still less an explanation."[2]

McCracken's Fragments of Night Sky series was such a leap. It introduced the concept of space as integral to matter. Only one sculptor had previously done such a thing. Henry Moore, McCracken's mentor, understood that the boundary between the mass of an object and the negative space around it was an illusion. He expressed this difficult idea with massive, smooth-flowing figurative pieces that incorporate voids, so that space pours into the mass, and conversely, mass surrounds empty space, blurring the distinction between inside mass and outside space. Moore invited the viewer to entertain the notion that space and mass are not necessarily opposites; each affects and informs the other. Einstein reached much the same conclusion.

Einstein's special theory of relativity, expressed in the equation $E=mc^2$, says that the energy stored within a grain of matter is equal to its mass times 186,000 miles per second raised to the second power. The explosive force of the conversion of matter into energy is the source of our sun's outpoured energy. If the equation is reversed, and energy were converted into mass, then we must accept that pure energy can wring matter from the void. Elemental particles could literally appear out of nowhere, making incorporeal fields of energy the progenitors of mass.

McCracken said, "In this [Fragments of Night Sky] series I explored time in terms of the speed of light, gauging the distance between stars." It is probable that in the long history of sculpture, no such attempt has ever before been made. Yet the history of art is filled with similar leaps of perception. Leonardo da Vinci was the first to make the all-important surmise that light travels through space and time as a wave. Throughout history, artists have intuited ideas that, in retrospect, prove to have been an avant-garde for the thought patterns of a scientific age not yet born.

McCracken produced the series from imagined shapes. "The sculptures grew out of experiences I had as a child," he said, "sleeping out of doors under the stars, creating forms in my mind by connecting the stars in various combinations, visualizing three-dimensional forms expressed as the enclosed space of light years between the stars. In this new area of sculpture the scale changes from the immensity of the universe to the hand-held object—macrocosmic to microcosmic—in these fragments of night sky."

He added, "With this series I am bringing to bear more empirical and theoretical information beginning with 'facts' such as the speed of light, gravity, time, a host of things which I questioned as a child and which have never been answered to my satisfaction. It has been encouraging to learn that most of the major figures in contemporary physics, astronomy, and cosmology admit, in the end, that they do not have definitive answers for the deepest questions."

In the works, polygons set boundaries, as if the artist had excised a piece of the night sky, revealing a cross section of the firmament—a swirling nebula, or the incendiary speed of a meteor shower. Star death, warped space-time, black holes—all of these achingly beautiful and profoundly awesome phenomena are represented.

The great Renaissance sculptor Benvenuto Cellini boasted in his autobiography, "The art of sculpture is eight times as great as any other art based on drawing, because a statue has eight views and they must all be equally good." What might he have thought of sculpture that speaks of solar winds and swirling galaxies in the microcosm of the grain of wood?

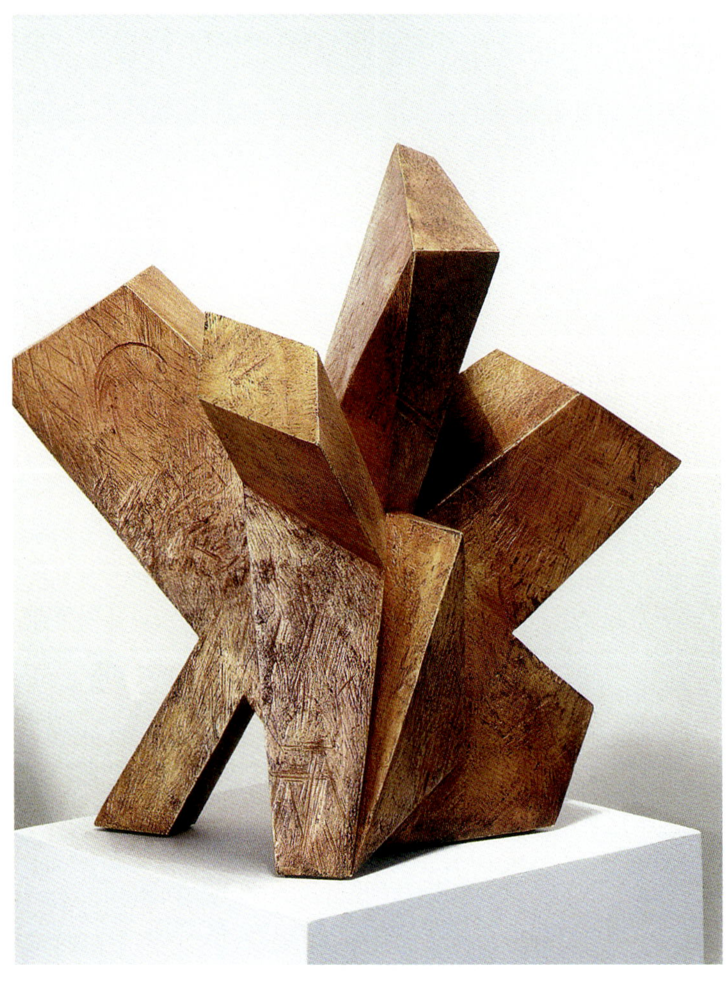

Alpha
1990
Polychromed cedar and gold
H. 26 in.
Collection of Dorothea and Murray Adaskin

Alpha is the beginning; the Big Bang, with segments hurtled outward in every direction. Yet even in explosive expulsion, some order reigns. Geometry and mathematics still dictate motion and aggregate form. The massive timbers that fly out from a dense center are gouged and scratched with stress. And still, even with each segment thrusting in its own direction, we are aware of a harmonious sense of balance not usually associated with massive explosion.

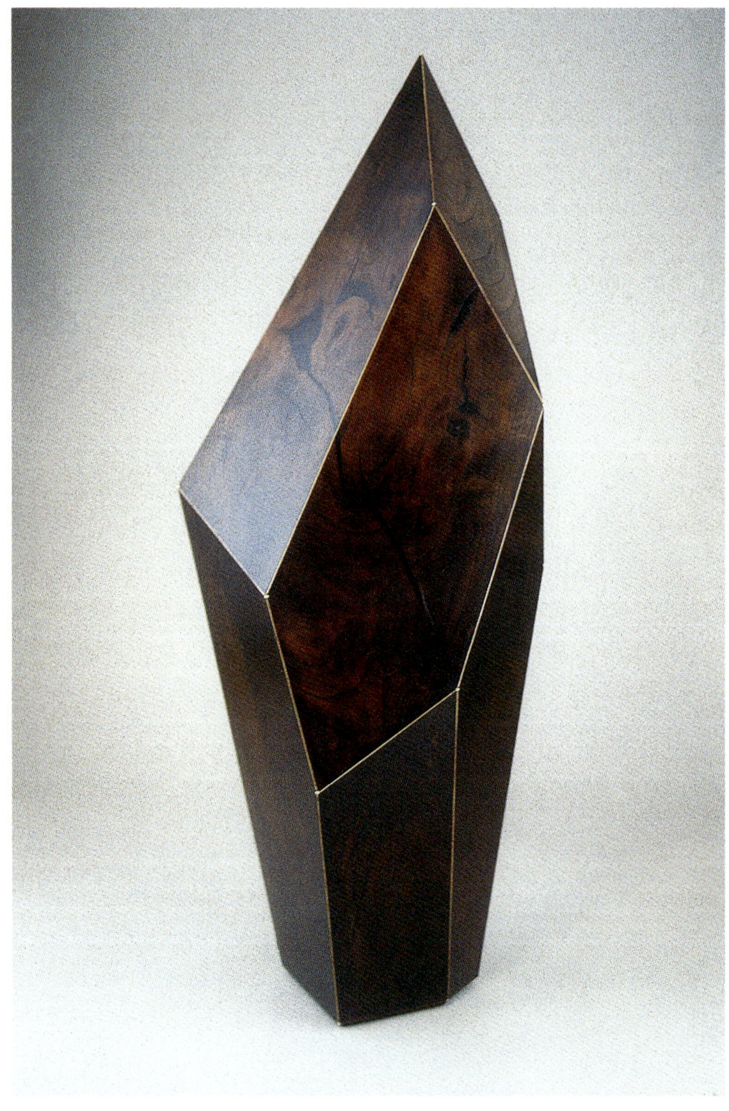

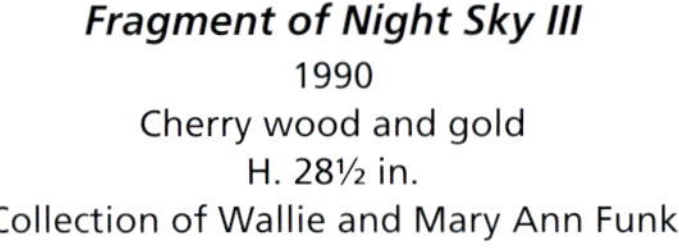

Fragment of Night Sky III
1990
Cherry wood and gold
H. 28½ in.
Collection of Wallie and Mary Ann Funk

The irregular polygons of this chunk excised from the night sky shine with a slender line of gold at each juncture, as if the piece were filled with captured light visible only at the boundaries of each plane. McCracken was feeling his way into his subject, allowing the grain and burls to be a microcosm of the swirling galaxies and streaming clouds of gaseous matter of the macrocosm of the heavens.

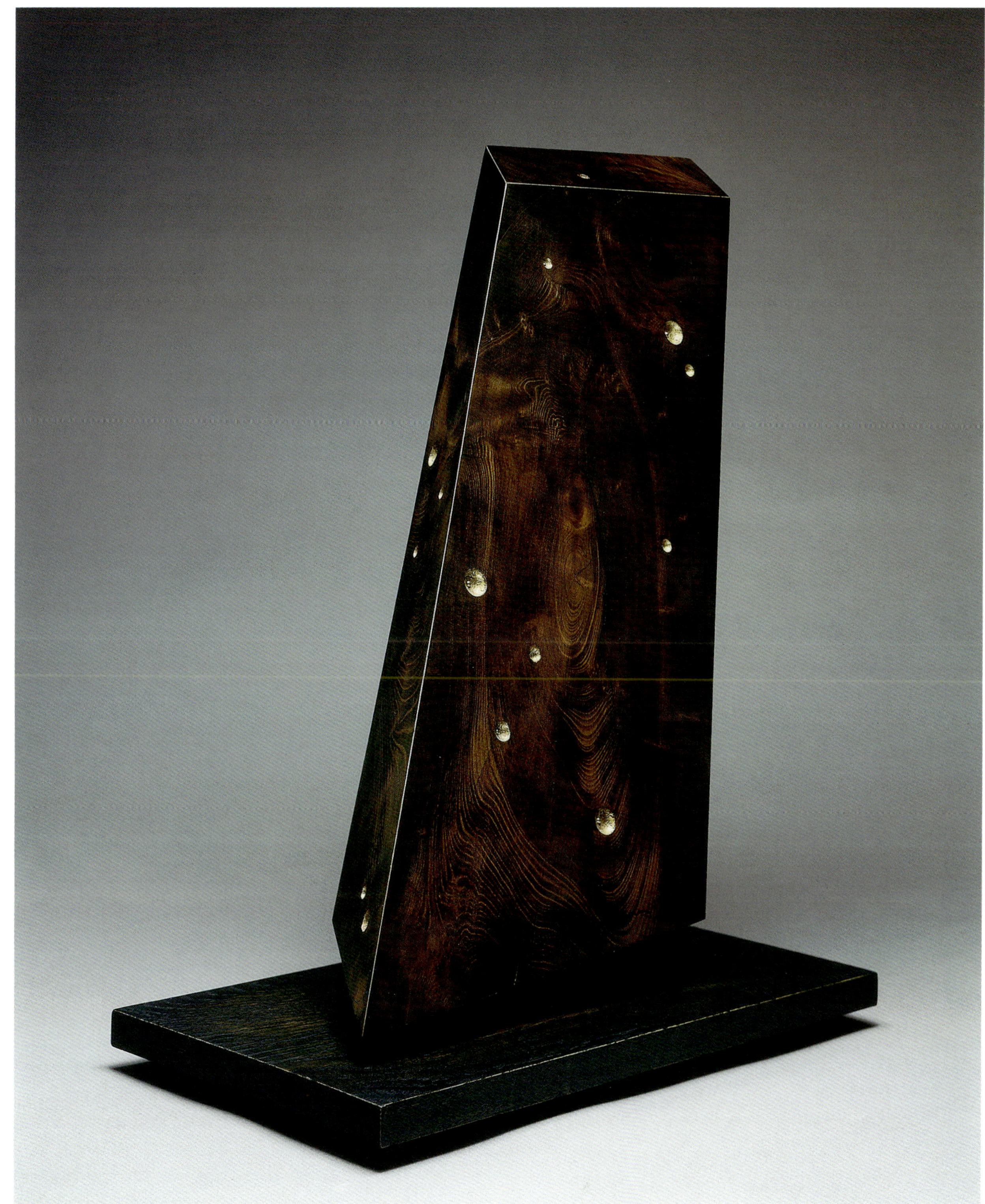

Hexahedron
1991
Redwood, acrylic, and gold leaf
H. 21 in.
Collection of Chris and Amy Gulick

Hexahedron *casts the amorphous and ethereal nature of space outside the solar system into a geometric shape, rather like the astronomical equivalent of a geological core sample. Tapered holes, shining with gold, evoke glowing stars which catch enough light to stand vibrant against a dusky sweep that can be seen as interstellar dust. McCracken attached the sculpture to a base of a different material, as if providing a viewing platform for the heavens.*

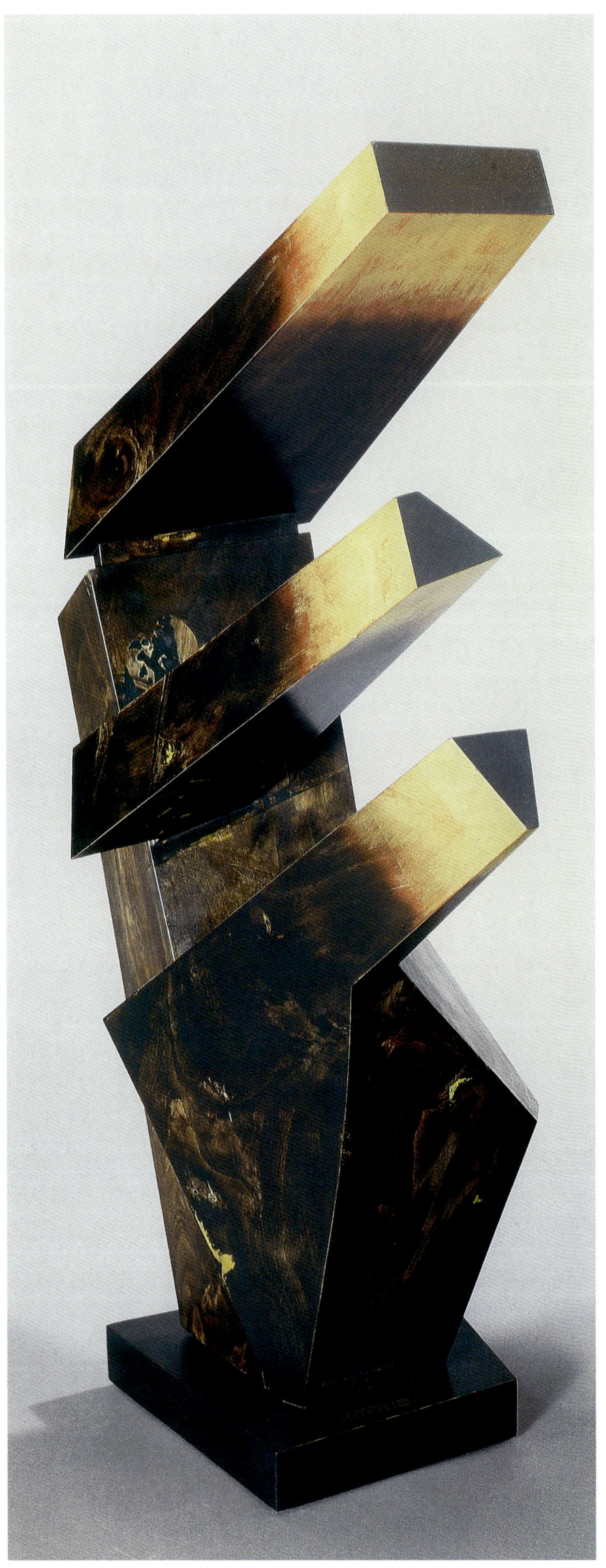

Night Scanner
1991
Alder and gold leaf
H. 28 in.
Collection of Dorothea and Murray Adaskin

Of all the Fragments of Night Sky sculptures, Night Scanner *most resembles something conceived by an alien race in the outer reaches of space. Three forms reach like beacons—metamorphosing from dark to bright gold at the outer reaches—from a shaft that leans to balance the thrusting arms. Whether this is some otherworldly instrument to monitor the movements of the stars, or a continuation of the outfall from the Big Bang, we cannot distinguish. We only know that outer space is stranger than we conceive, and probably stranger than we* can *conceive.*

Decahedron (opposite)
1992
Cherry wood and epoxy
H. 17 in.
Collection of Anne McCracken

Like Night Sky *before it,* Decahedron *shows McCracken's inspired technique for optimizing the splits and gnarls of dry wood. White resin was poured into the voids of the surface. After the resin dried, the piece was sanded and polished to a gloss, so that the checks and patterns of the openings in the surface glow with the pattern of a starburst. To the unaided eye few things are more serene than the night sky, yet space telescopes bring us images of cataclysmic explosions. The surfaces of* Decahedron *are strewn with the visualized wreckage of exploding stars.*

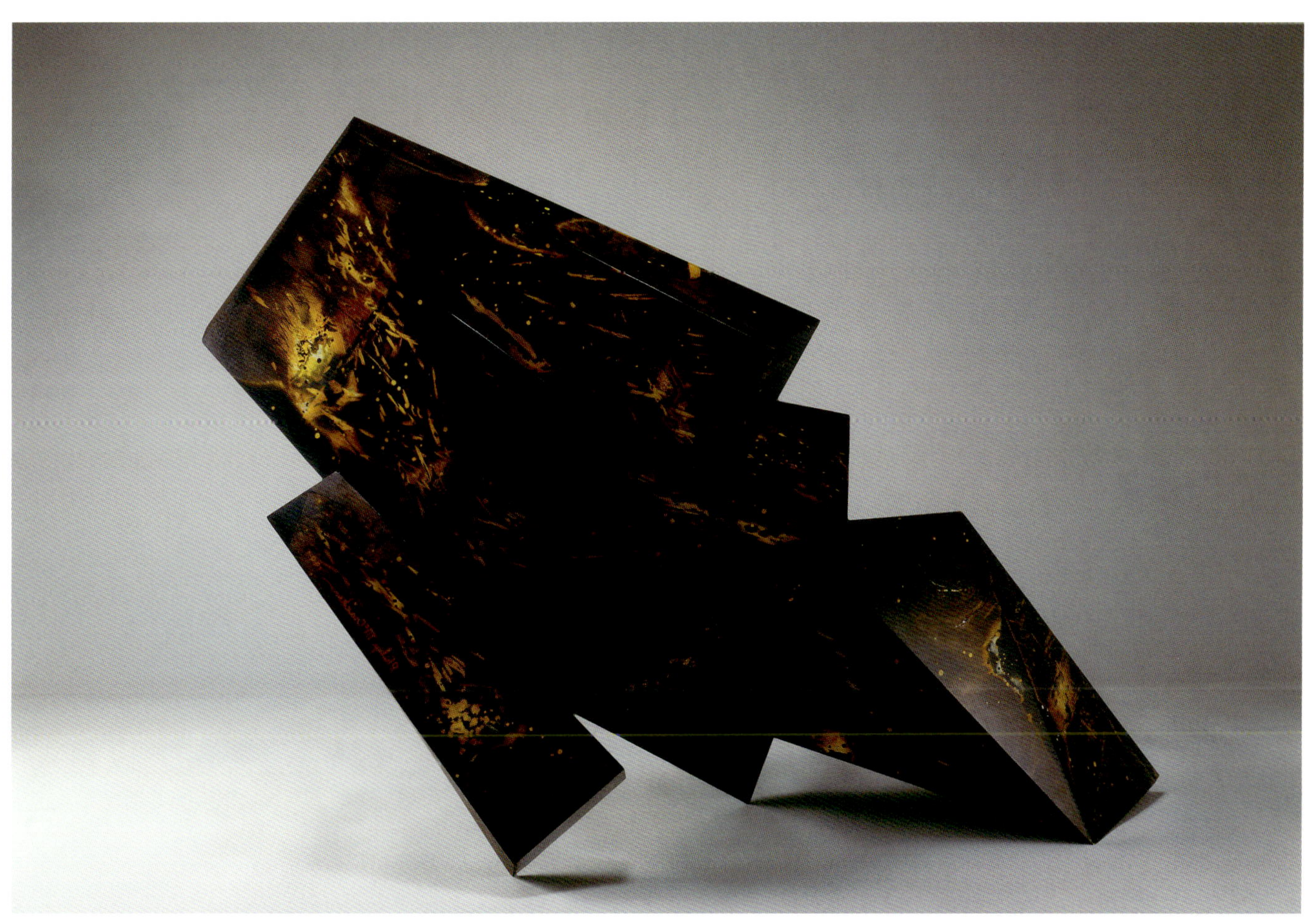

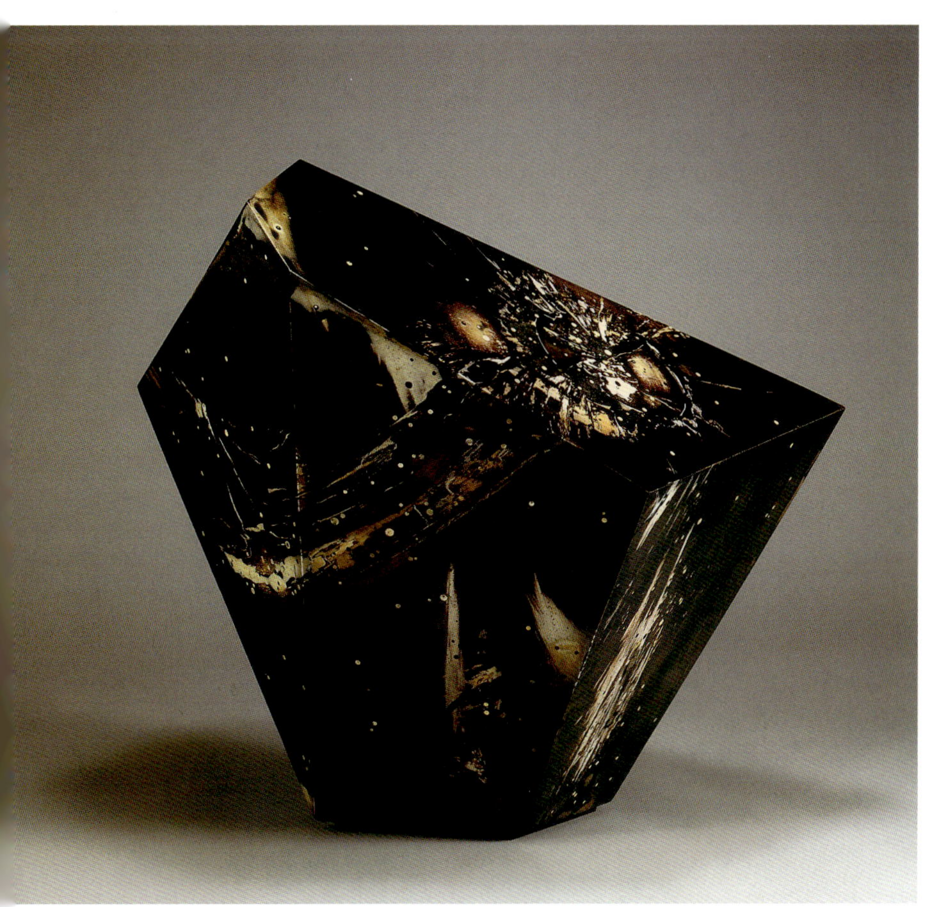

Night Sky
1991
Maple and epoxy
H. 28 in.
Collection of the artist

Poised like a cubistic interstellar ship aimed toward the stars, chunks of dark space carved out by an extraterrestrial civilization stand balanced, filled with the roiling fire of ionized gas clouds, powered to cross light years of distance. Night Sky *is space itself, with galaxies, crab nebulae, hot gases, and cold black voids.*

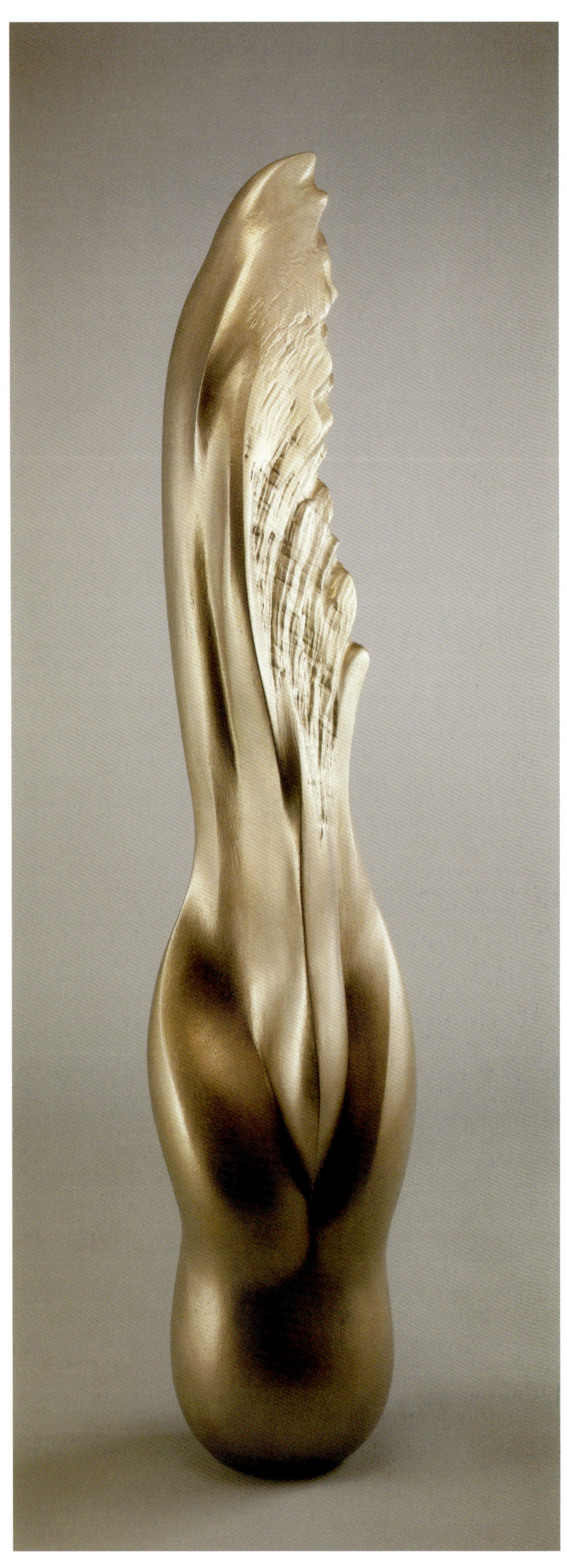

Comet
1992
Polychromed cedar
H. 31 in.
Collection of Mrs. William H. Bryant

Comet *is among McCracken's most sensuous pieces. The effect is achieved with a tapering and swelling body as organic as a human torso, with a sweeping head that could be the abstract shape of uplifted arms that taper into a feathered wing.* Comet *can be seen as a contemporary version of the Winged Victory of Samothrace, as well as an impression of a comet with its gaseous tail metamorphosed into feathering wood.*

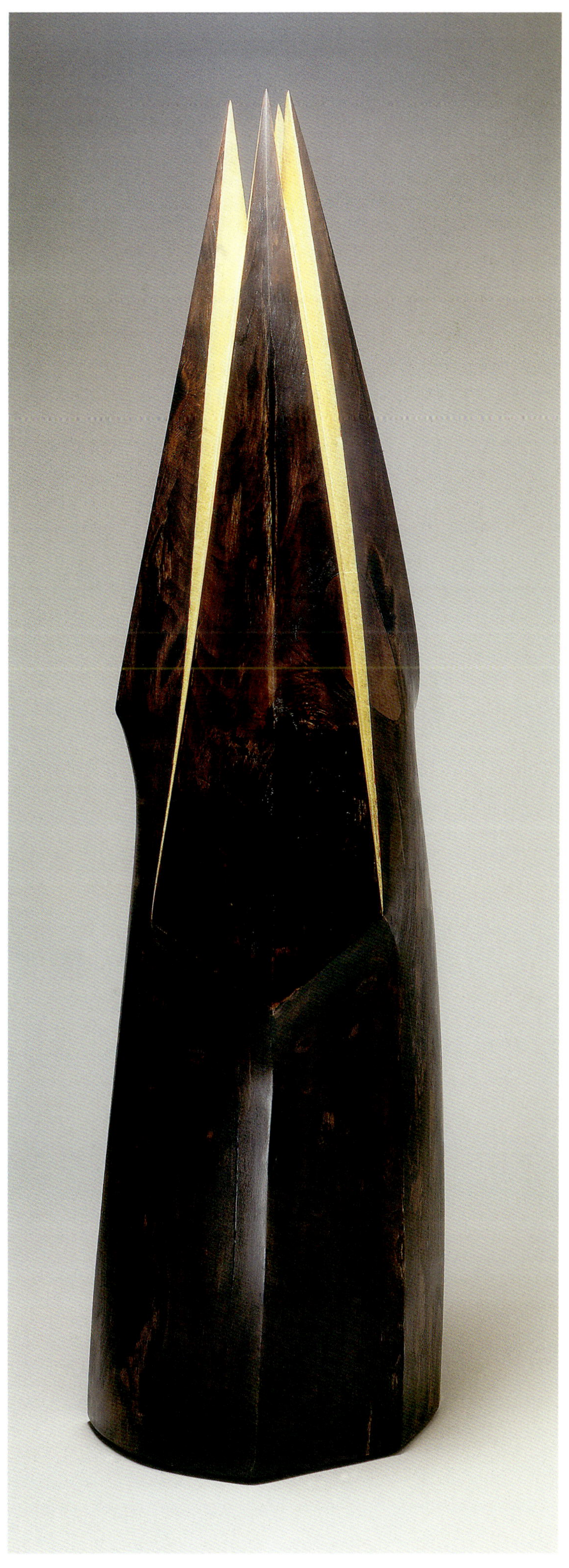

Spires
1992
Cherry wood and gold leaf
H. 38½ in.
Collection of the artist

McCracken conceived a contrast to the explosive forms of the Fragments of Night Sky with the formal symmetry of Spires. *Sharp Gothic peaks have begun to separate like petals of a geometric flower. The suggestion of inner treasure is present in the gilded interior.*

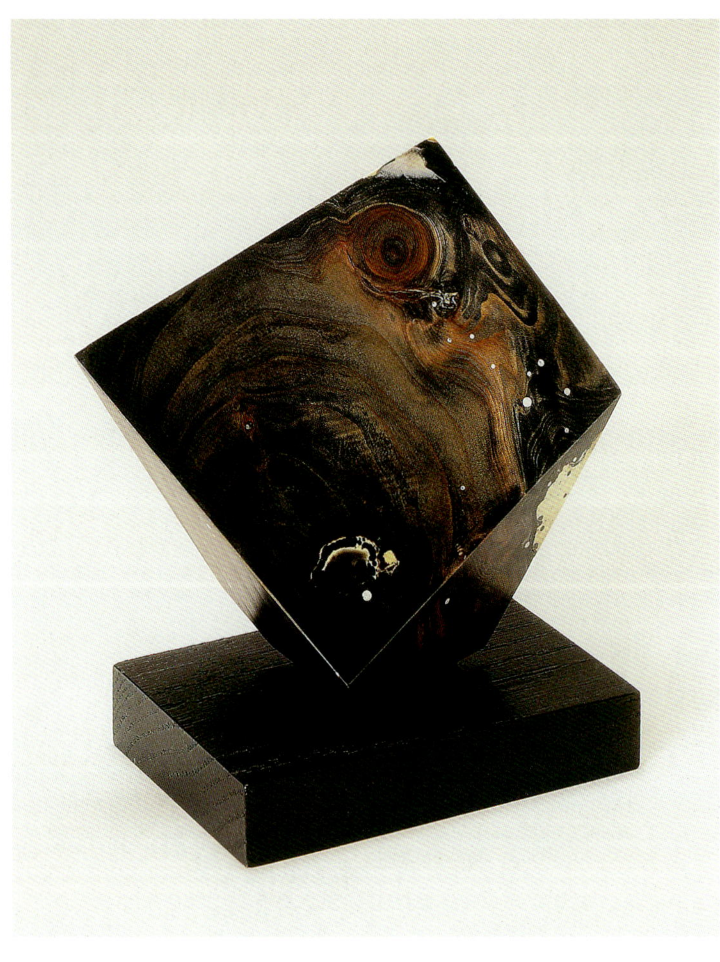

Vault of Heaven
1993
Cedar and epoxy
H. 6¼ in.
Collection of Jim and Susan Rupp

Pinpoints identifiable as stars imply that the scene is set in the same galaxy as our own solar system. Faint background clouds symbolize the white-hot cosmic dust of the Milky Way.

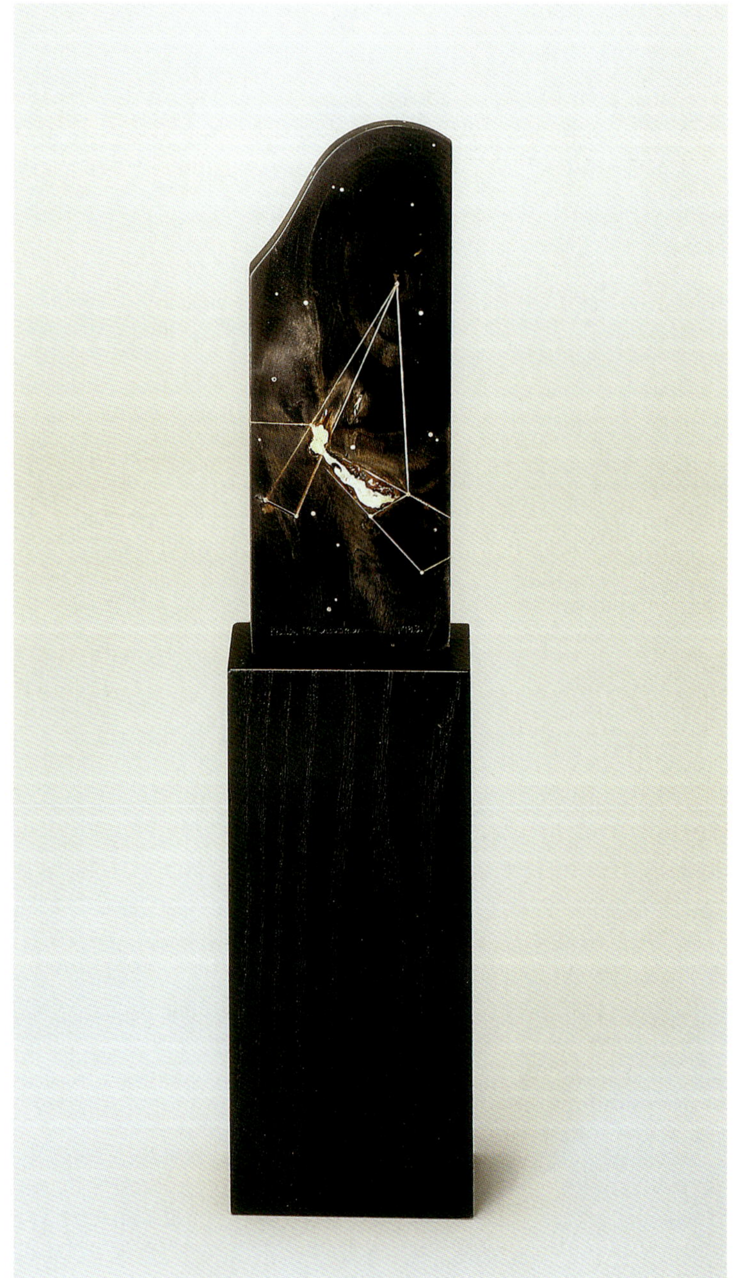

Euclid's World
1993
Apple wood and epoxy
H. 15 in.
Collection of Marshall and Helen Hatch

"Euclid alone has looked on Beauty bare," the poet Edna St. Vincent Millay once wrote, in acknowledgement of the beauty of mathematics and geometry.[3] When Philip McCracken was growing up, he often lay awake at night gazing at the stars, drawing mental lines between them as star charts identify constellations and formations such as the Big Dipper. Euclid's World *is a response to his intuition that certain interconnections would have had meaning for Euclid, the Greek mathematician called the father of geometry. Shown in epoxy, a right triangle forms one side of a complex solid whose side and bottom thrust into elongated planes that disappear from sight. The linear axioms of Euclid did not allow for the possibility of curved space. In his system, a straight line continued into infinity.*

Magnetic Fields
1993
Apple wood and epoxy
H. 5½ in.
Private collection

The kind of patterned alignment iron filings make in the presence of a magnetic field is visible in the light inclusions of this piece. The white points of "stars" stand apart from force fields like those of a magnetar, a neutron star with a super-strong magnetic field a thousand trillion times stronger than Earth's. This field slows the rotation of the star and causes starquakes that send flashes of energy into the surrounding gases, which emit soft bursts of gamma radiation. Scientists say our galaxy may include a few hundred million undiscovered magnetars.[4] *One such phenomenon is suggested by this piece. Tipped slightly off center, balanced on a point rather than standing on one of its planes, this chunk of space seems kept in place by the strong invisible force of a magnetic field.*

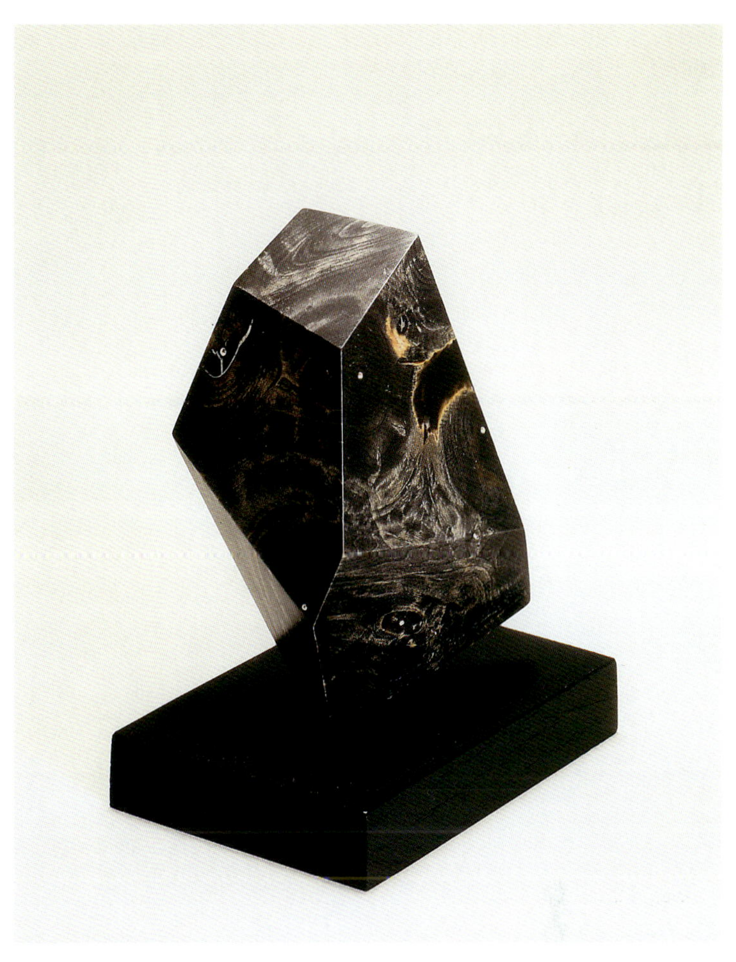

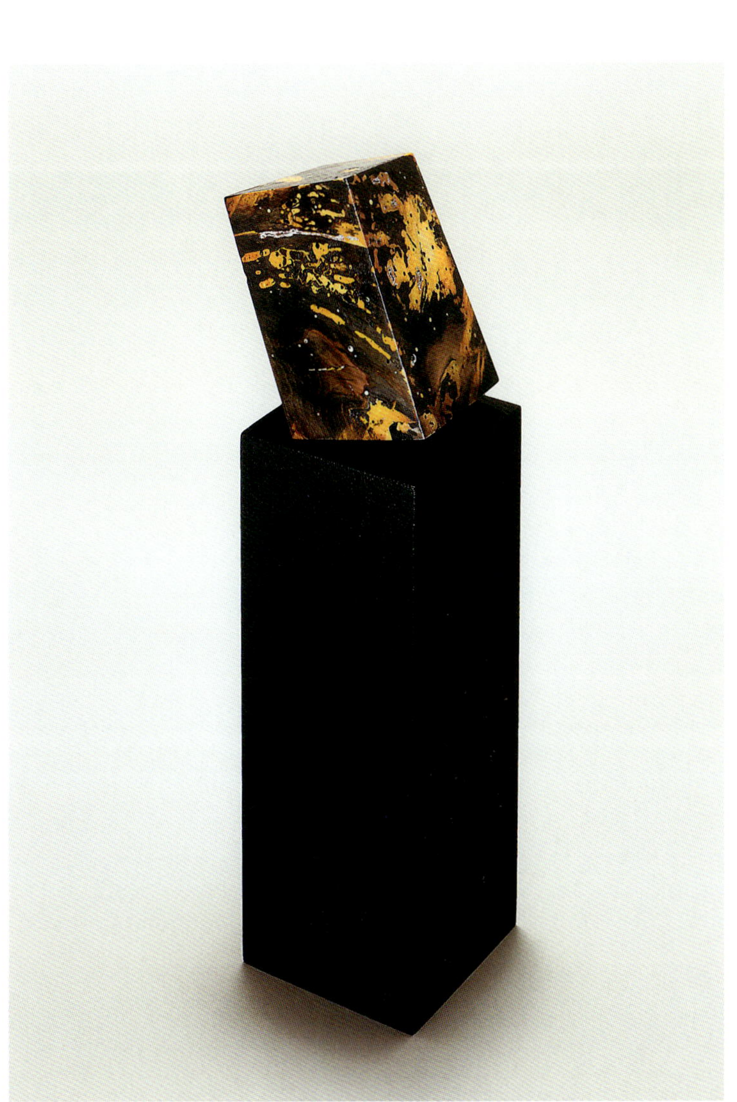

Embers
1993
Maple and epoxy
H. 14¾ in.
Schneider Museum of Art,
Southern Oregon University, Ashland

Internal fire, like that which sometimes glows from a fire log, lights this piece. Yet it is not a burn-scarred husk; to the contrary, it appears to be set in motion, as the outer shell seems barely to contain the light of its great interior conflagration. It is tipped to one side, threatening to fall rather than settle back into equilibrium.

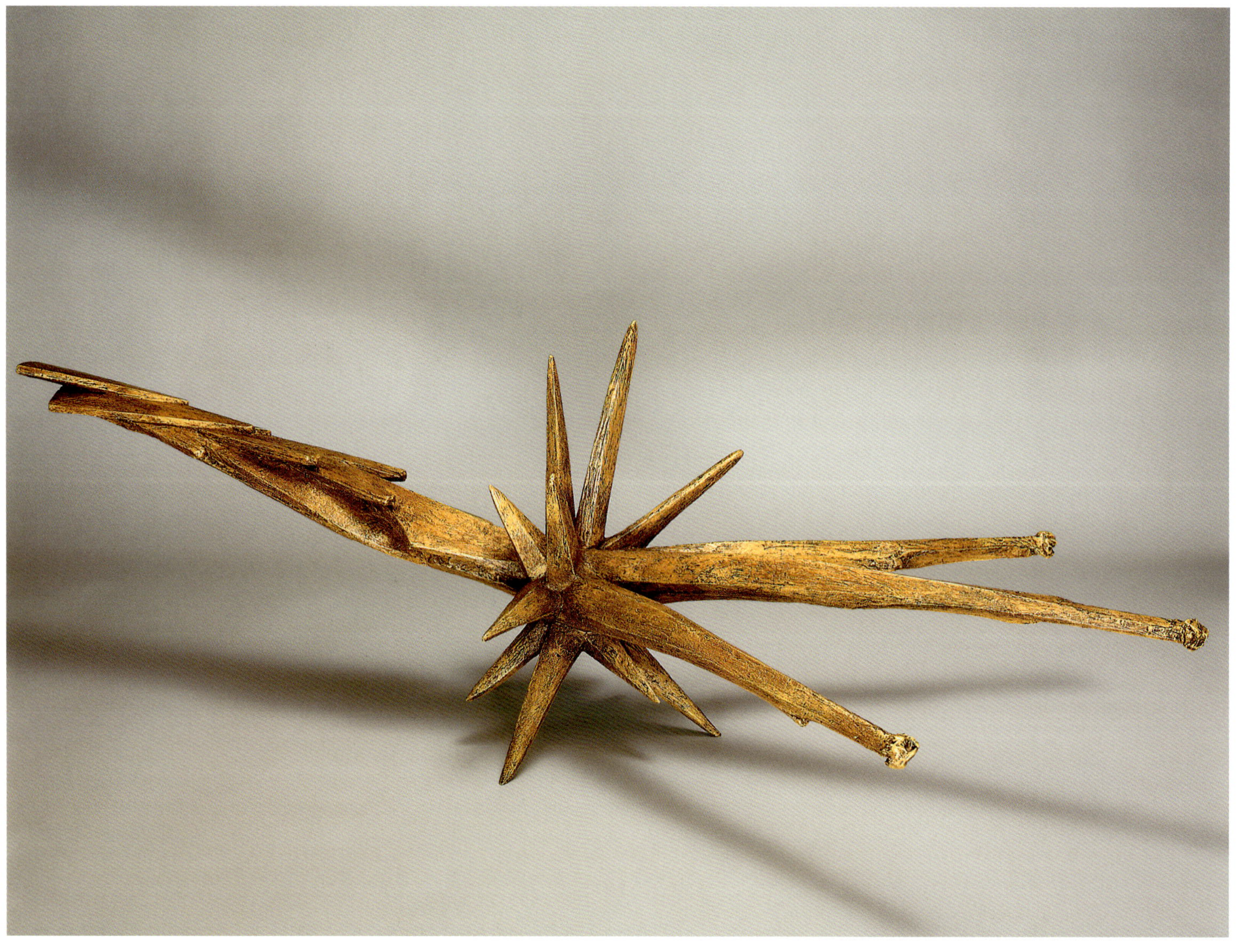

Meteor Burst
1993
Polychrome plaster for bronze
H. 17½ in.
Collection of the artist

McCracken freezes in golden form the explosive instant when the speed of a falling meteor causes enough friction in the atmosphere to ignite in a burst of self-immolating fire. Silent spikes of energy are discharged from a fisted core. It bears an eerie resemblance to the explosion of the space shuttle Columbia, *which occurred ten years after this piece was created.*

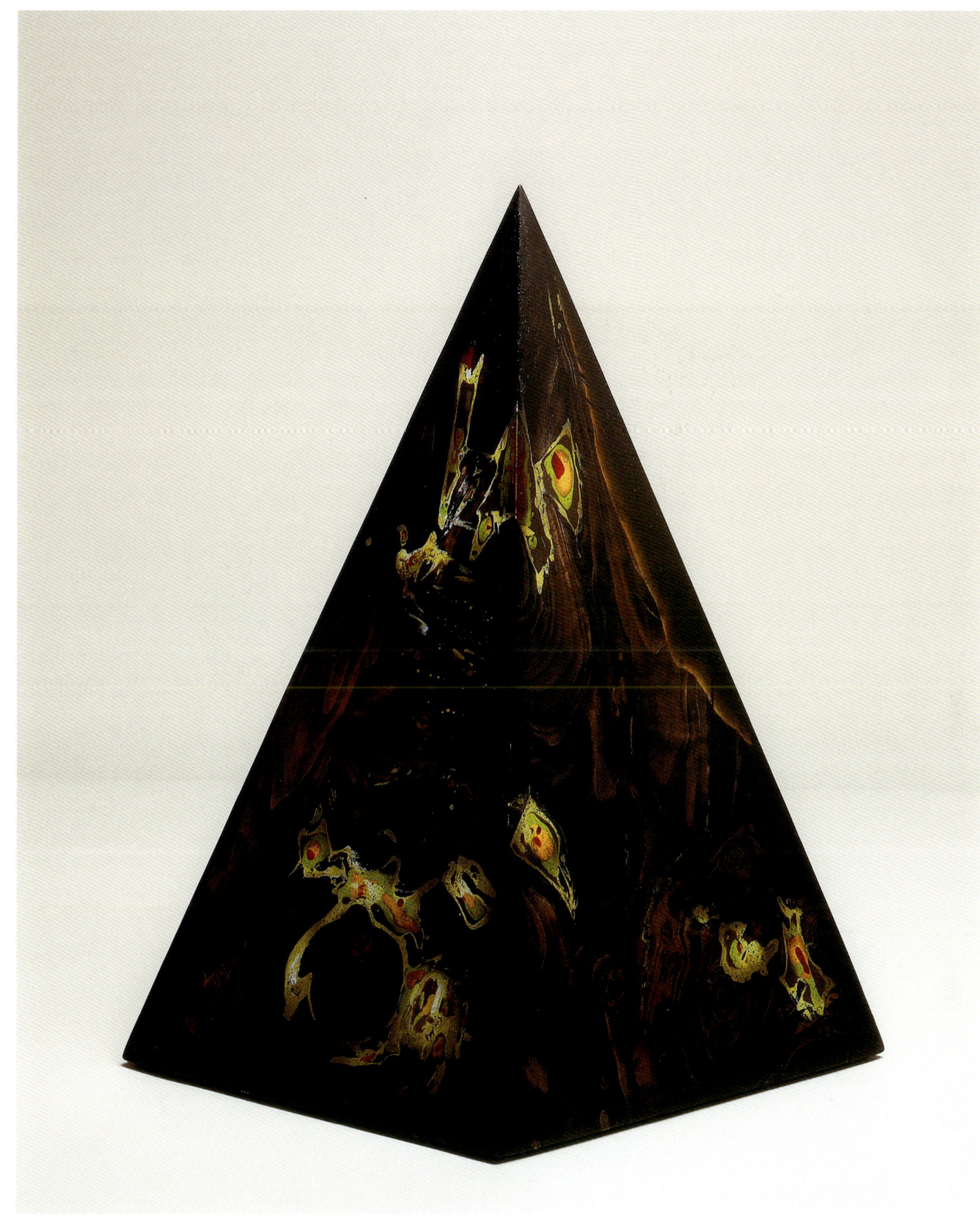

Pyramid II
1994
Cedar and epoxy
H. 18½ in.
Collection of Roger and Marny Heinen

The pyramid has long been a symbol of hidden ancient knowledge—wisdom expressed in this piece as inner light. In all of its aspects, from the speed of light to the age of light from distant stars, the quintessence of man's exploration of space is light itself. It is the link connecting space, time, energy, and matter. Pyramid *is a haunting piece in the way its formations appear backlit, as if some inner star were resident deep in this pyramid of space.*

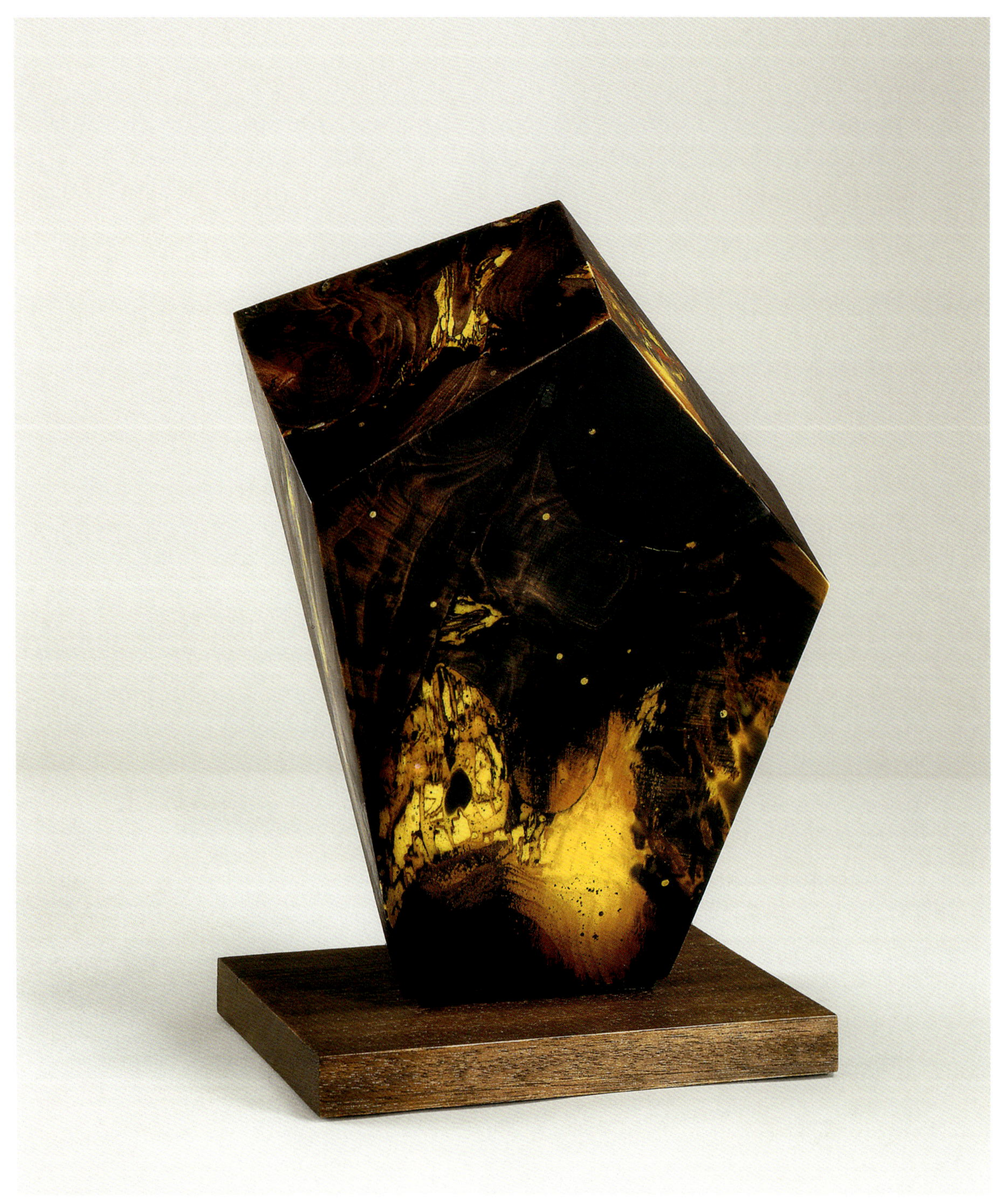

Star Embers
1994
Cedar and epoxy
H. 11½ in.
Collection of Dorothea and Murray Adaskin

In clouds of swirling plasma, star embers glow with the spilled fire of a dying star. Blackness is punctuated by distant young stars seen only as white specks, in contrast to the fiery death throes of a foreground blaze, emitted in an agony of light.

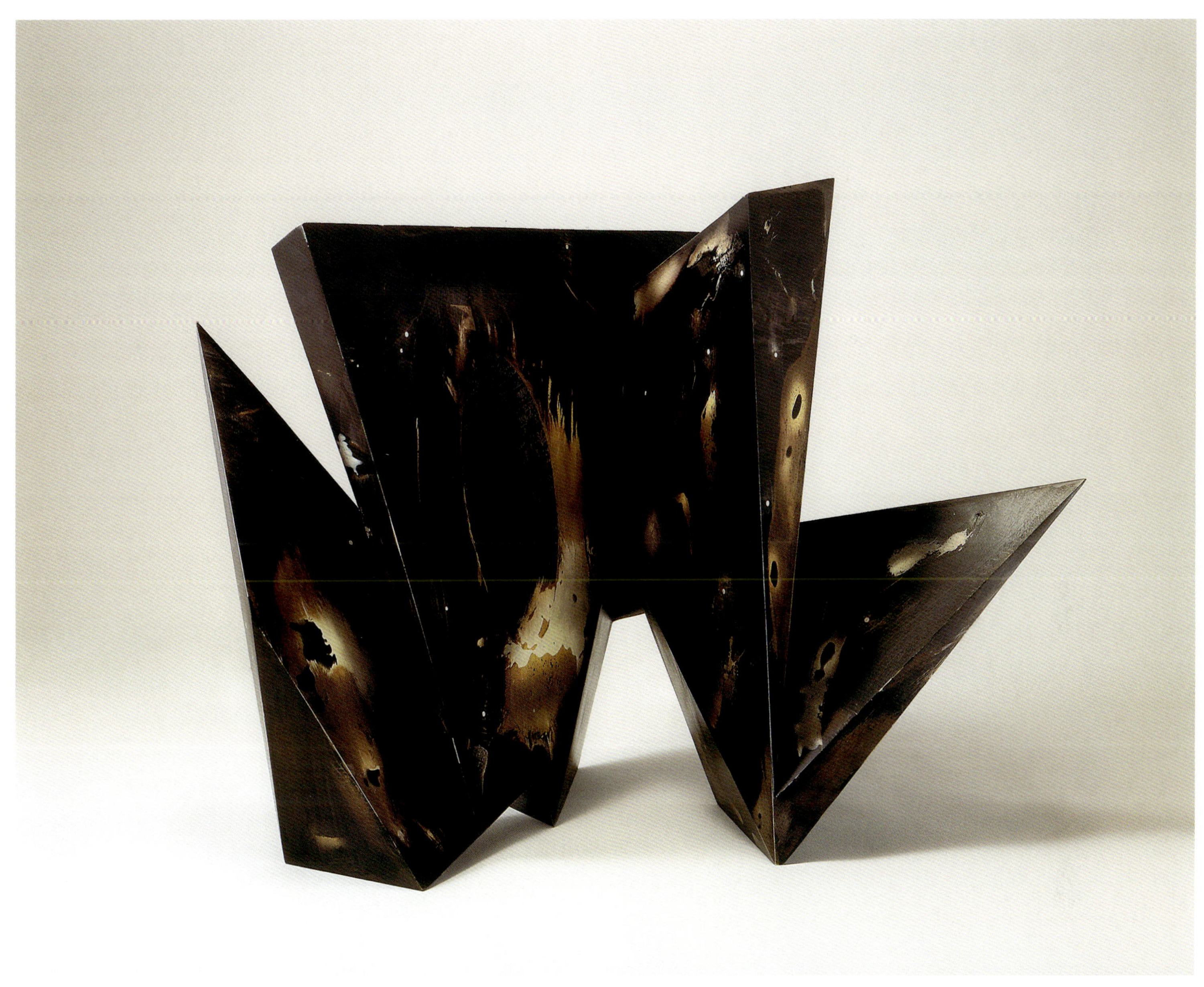

Beyond the Sun
1994
Maple and epoxy
H. 19 in.
Collection of the artist

Beyond the Sun, *in its stunning angularity, reminds us that past the reach of our best telescopes and deepest space probes still lies infinity. Most astronomers believe that the universe is expanding. Something of the violent expansionary energy on a cosmic scale is suggested by this powerful structure. Everything is in flux. Clouds of matter and wisps of gas career through galaxies. The centers of galaxies are widely suspected of harboring black holes, some of which, in elliptical form, are suggested here.*

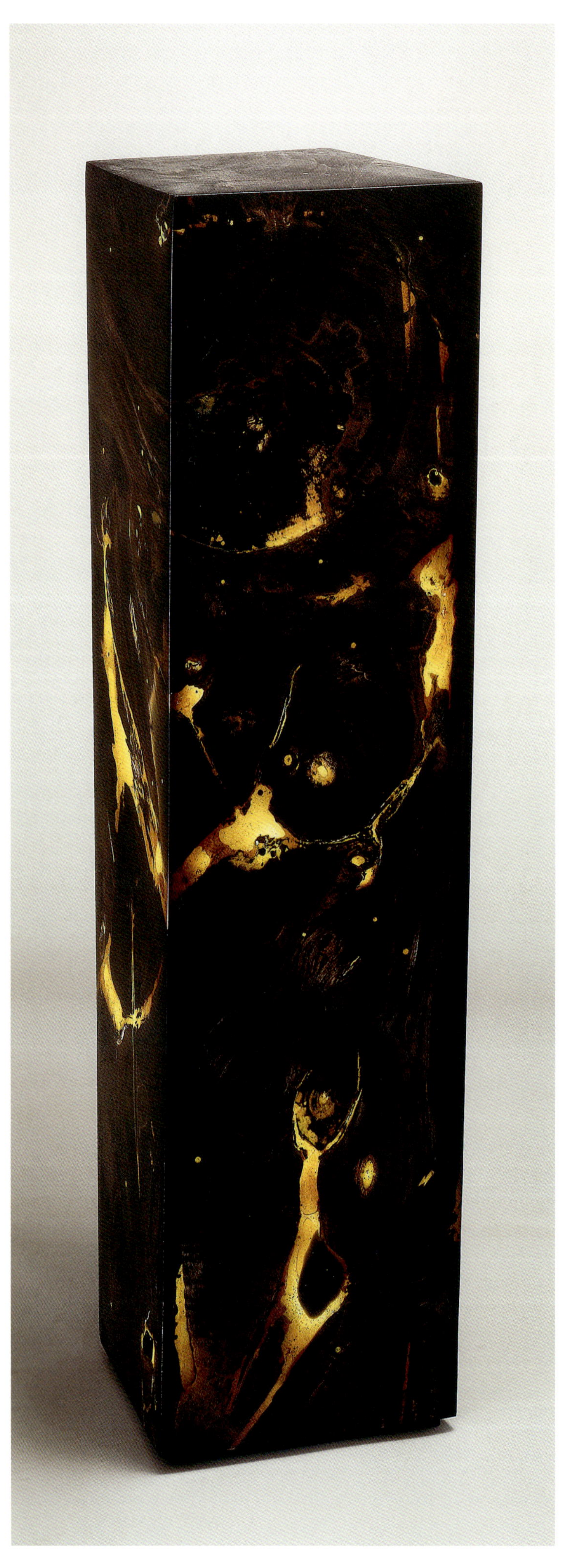

Column of Night Sky
1994
Maple and epoxy
H. 25¼ in.
Collection of Edward G.S. Miller

Of all the works in this series, this rectilinear piece has the simplest form. But within it are brooding forces and hurtling spheres. The brush of a celestial calligrapher seems to be at work, creating shapes that suggest some cosmic dance. Each plane of the column can be seen both as part of an orchestrated whole and as an abstract painting in its own right. Overall it has a presence that conjures the monolith in the Stanley Kubrick film 2001: A Space Odyssey.

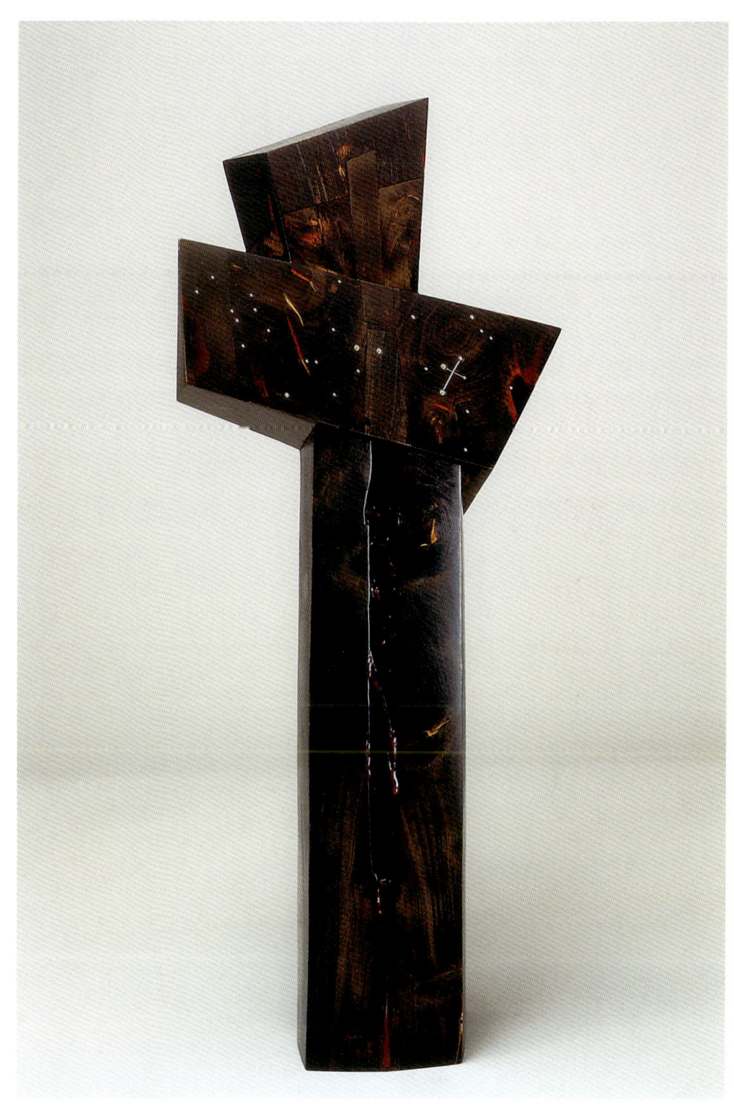

Southern Cross
1994
Apple wood, gold, and epoxy
H. 23 in.
Collection of Marshall and Helen Hatch

As the Big Dipper is the best-known constellation in the northern hemisphere, the Southern Cross is the most recognizable in the southern hemisphere. But more is intended here than the depiction of a constellation. One cannot long dwell on the subject of space without a growing sense of naked insignificance. Southern Cross *is a fulcrum piece. It pulls into one dynamic form the cold, indifferent perfection of the universe juxtaposed with the ultimate Western symbol of the frailty and suffering of humanity. The yawning check in the base of the cross speaks to the imperfection of a race that can speculate on the magnitude of the heavens without escaping its own pettiness and brutality.*

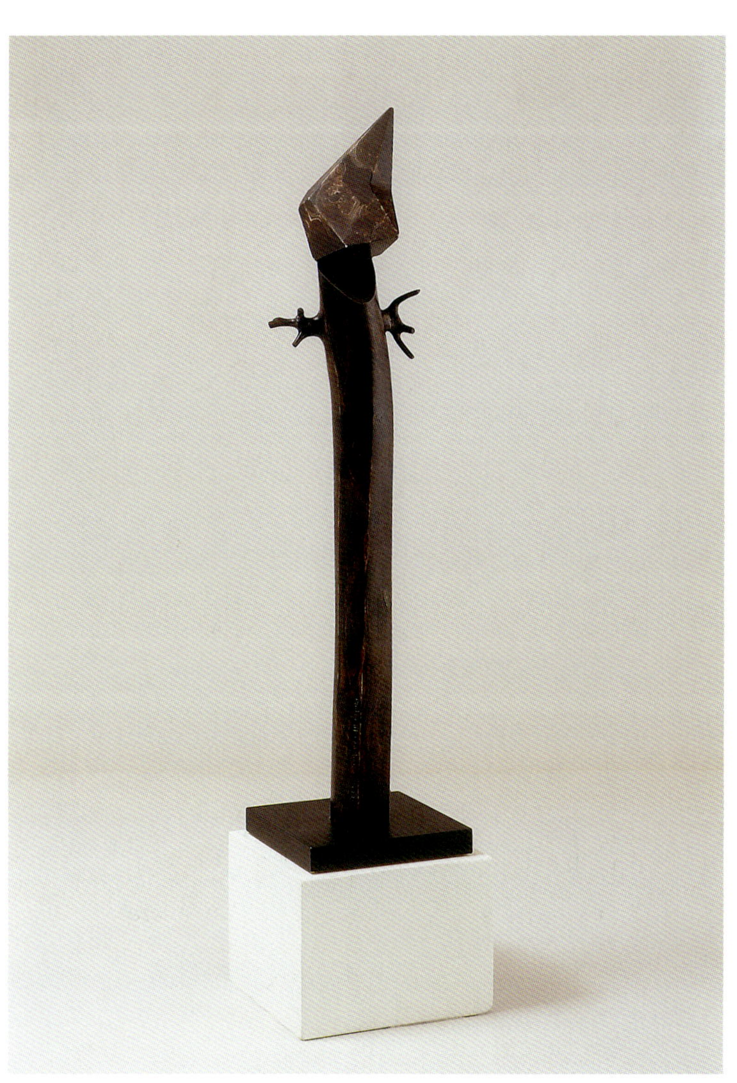

The Astronomer
1996
Apple wood and gold
H. 19¾ in.
Collection of Colin and Sylvia Graham

Like the stick figure of a man with a head pointed at the stars, filled to bursting with visions of the heavens, The Astronomer *stands straight, armless, with shrunken hands incapable of any effectual work. For McCracken, this was less a comment on the abilities of astronomers than a recognition of man's smallness in the universe.*

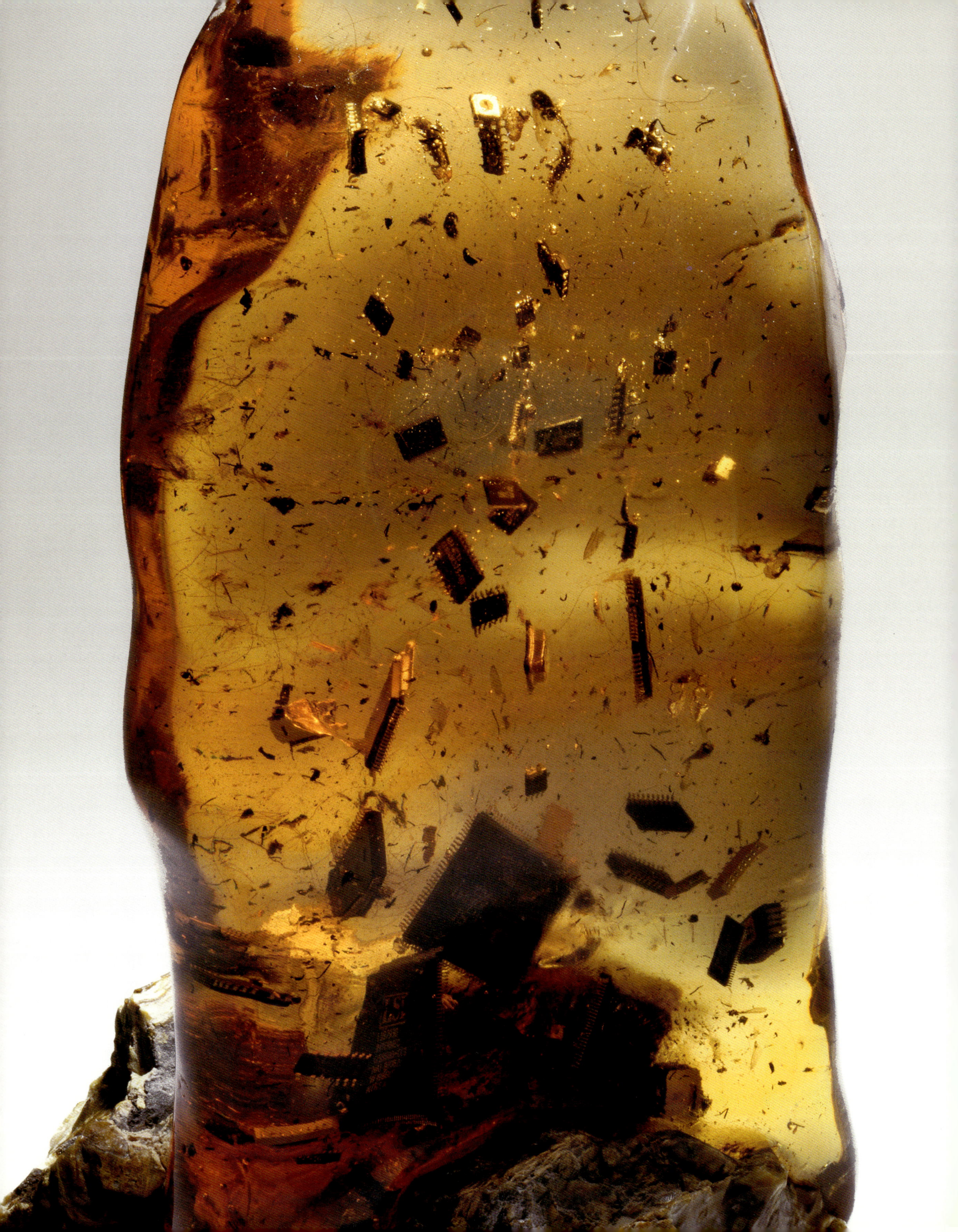

The Future Past

> An Eastern monarch once charged his wise men to invent him a sentence to be ever in view, and which should be true and appropriate in all times and situations. They presented him the words "And this, too, shall pass away."[1]

As time on a cosmic scale occupied McCracken's creative energy during the early 1990s, by the end of the decade he had begun to think of time on a geological scale. What, he wondered, would happen in the new millennium, and how might society be different? What would last? How might archaeologists of some distant future interpret today's detritus? With some amusement, he began to imagine what artifacts might be found, and to speculate on how they could be construed.[2]

He invited friends to bring him things they thought might be remembered as contemporary icons. He received a wide assortment of objects, including a crack vial. Two of the items he chose to encase in bubbles of amber—a golf tee and a used Band-Aid—were lost, not by the passage of eons, but broken in an accident that occurred during the opening of their first exhibition. Other equally poignant pieces remain.

"The forms in this series are icons of contemporary life, as well as expressions of wonder at the nature of time," he said. "I have visualized finding at some point, millions of years in the future, fossil forms representing objects from our contemporary culture. Although the work is fundamentally serious, I found myself enjoying the surprises and humor inherent in many of these forms."

Dot.com (detail)
2000 (see p. 101)

Cigarette Butt
1997
Polyester resin, petrified wood, and cigarette butt
H. 4½ in.
Collection of the artist

McCracken was thinking of ancient insects preserved in amber when he began to imagine what equally trivial contemporary objects might be prized by someone in the distant future. The first thing he wanted to embed in synthetic amber was a cigarette butt. He began to make inquiries about how artificial amber was made, and promptly hit a stone wall. No one he contacted knew how.

No reference work McCracken checked described the technique. An Internet search yielded nothing. Ultimately, he had to develop his own technique for emulating amber: tinted polyester resin embedded with hair, dust, and fragments of insects. He began to experiment with it after coming across a technique in an old craft book for encasing the head of a dandelion in clear acrylic resin.

Since McCracken doesn't smoke, he had to rely on the kindness of a friend for the butt. It should be noted that this is not just any cigarette butt. Without realizing it, most of us hold an image of "cigarette butt" that consists of a straight end standing bent over a stubbed-out ash. No split paper. McCracken's "specimen" is a filter-tip Kool, trapped in a bubble of amber along with flecks of ash, attached to a matrix of petrified wood—presumably the wood of the tree that oozed the resin we know as amber when it is petrified. To complete the illusion, McCracken attached a faux museum cataloguing label, indicating the accession number and source of this fossil "find."

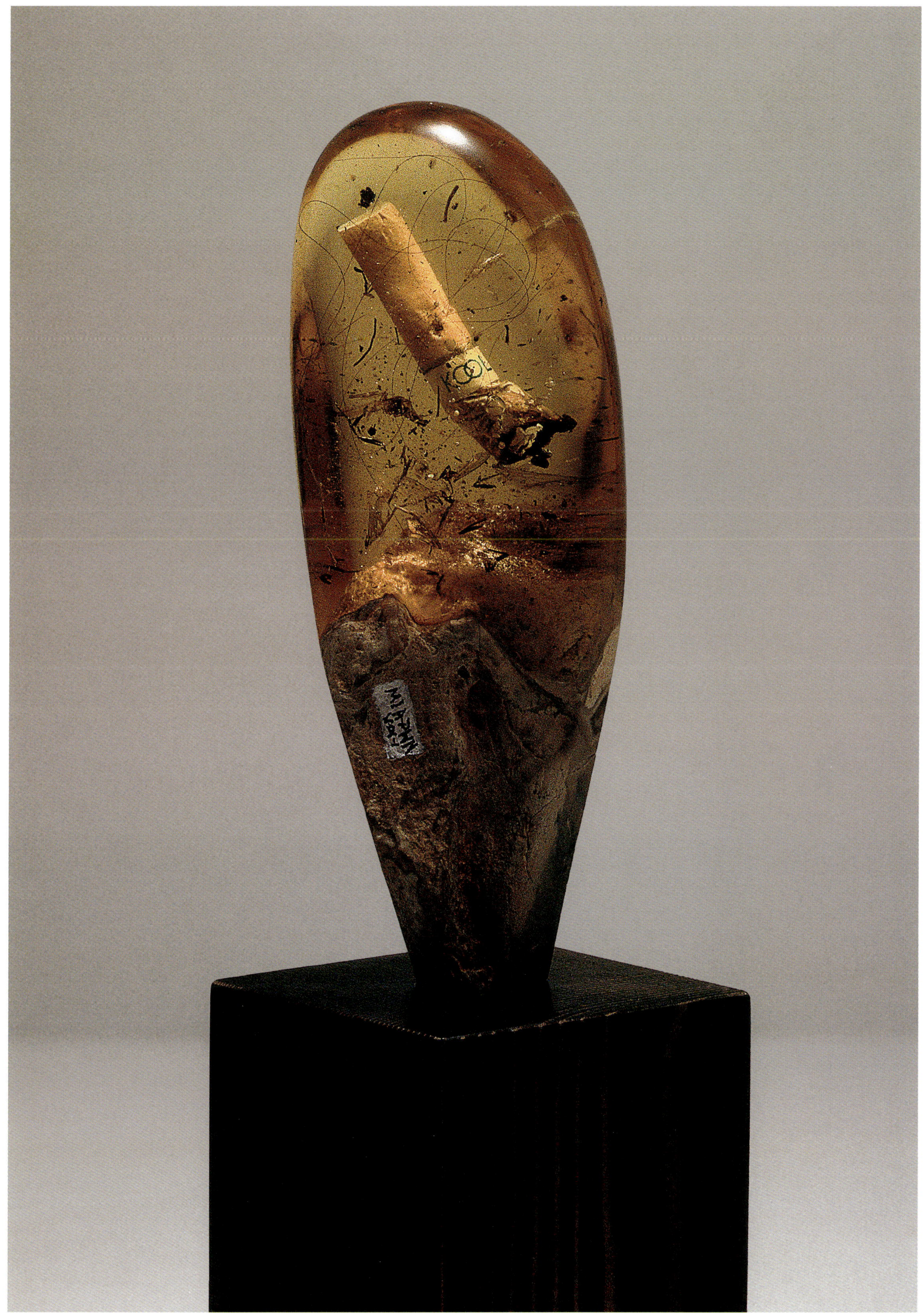
KOOL

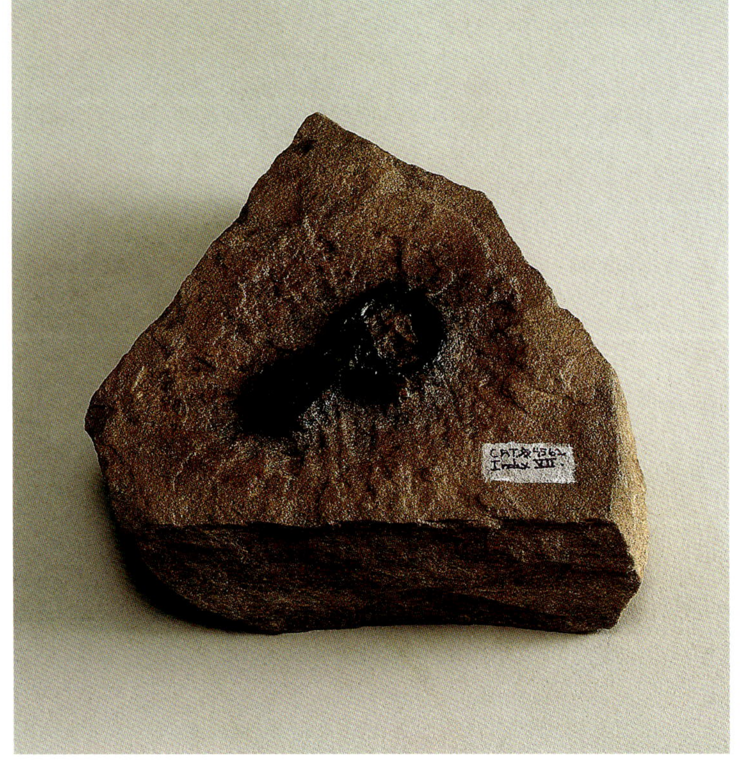

Pull Tab Fossil
1999
Sandstone, aluminum pull tab, and epoxy
1½ × 5¾ in.
Collection of the artist

The second future fossil McCracken created was a metal pull tab in a split section of sedimentary rock. The ubiquitous pull tabs that open soft drink and beer cans are among the most common throwaways on the planet, and—McCracken seems to say—among the most durable. Pull Tab Fossil *makes the unsettling suggestion that our most enduring legacy will be our trash. This "specimen" also bears a proper label listing its museum catalogue number and source—a detail that conjures the vision of people of the future clustered around a glass case featuring this small treasure from the past.*

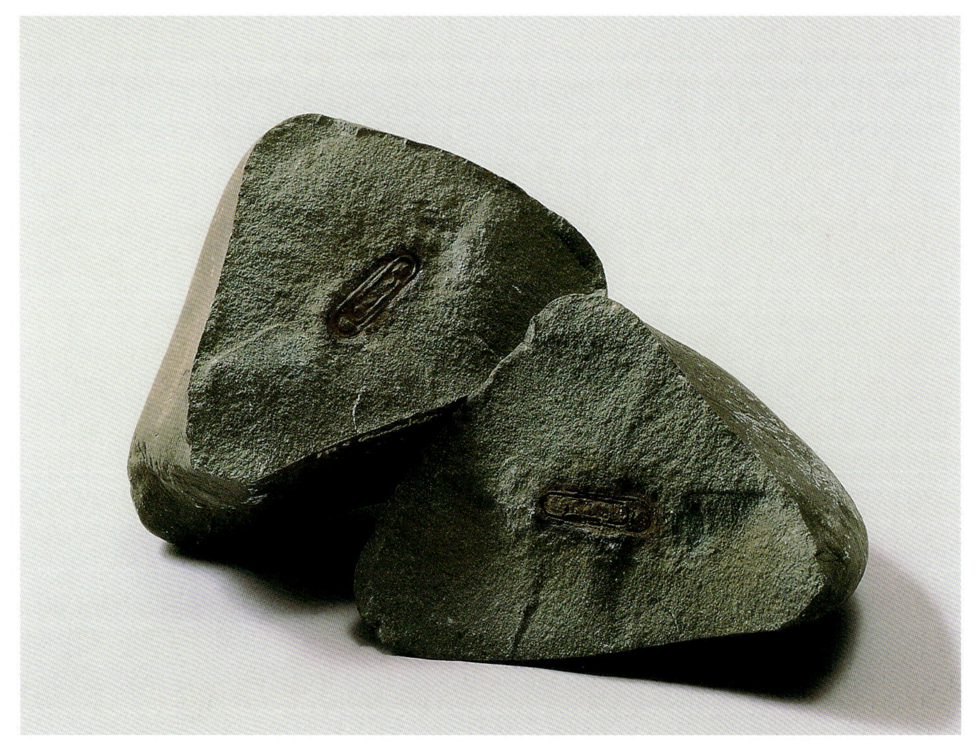

Paper Clip
2000
Fieldstone and paper clip
3 × 6¼ in.
Collection of the artist

A split sedimentary rock reveals a paper clip at its core, as if it had been discarded and caught in a mudflow that eventually, over eons, was compressed into rock. Seen as an inclusion in the stone, this commonplace item that we use routinely without really looking at it can be appreciated afresh for the simple beauty of its elongated coiling form.

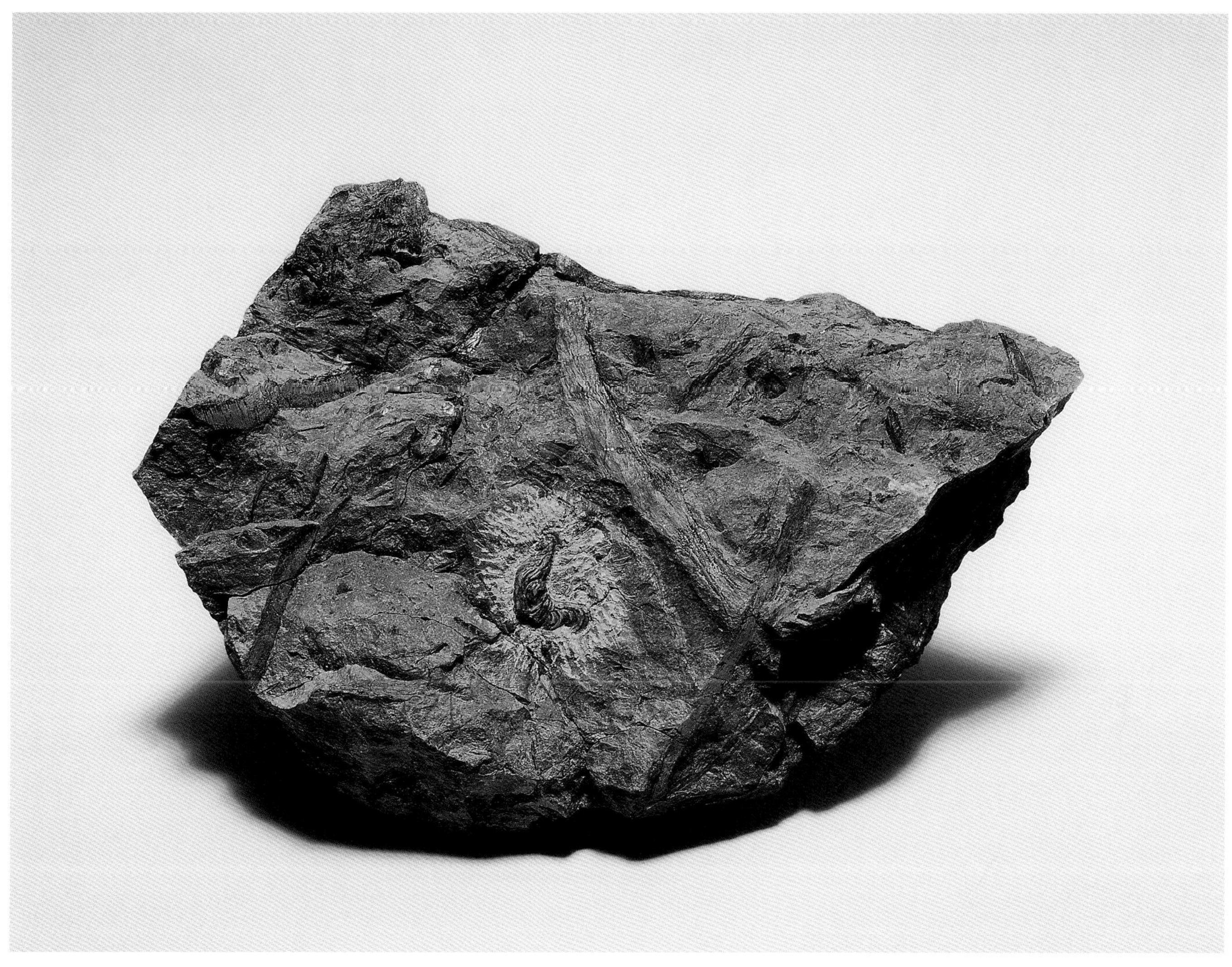

Little Chicken Fossil
2000
Mudstone and plastic
3 × 9½ in.
Collection of the artist

A chunk of rock holds the preserved impression of a perfect miniature chicken. Was it, future archeologists may wonder, an evolutionary forerunner of full-size chickens, as the small dawn horse, Eohippus, was an eight-inch-high Eocene epoch forerunner of contemporary horses? Or will a scrap of the original yellow plastic endure to tip them off that the impression was left by a cast image of a chicken? In the latter case they may be curious why we venerated the chicken enough to create images of it. Despite its small size, Little Chicken Fossil *is a heroic image, a rooster triumphant, with fine plumage; head high as if about to crow. It would be, one supposes, the way chickens would like to be remembered: not as batter-fried drumettes, but as noble creatures.*

Dot.com
2000
Polyester resin, computer chips,
and petrified wood
H. 12½ in.
Private collection

Rising from a matrix of petrified wood, an irregular bubble of artificial amber holds a scattering of computer chips. It is no small feat to have created their free-floating distribution. McCracken accomplished it with a six-section pour, with each layer carefully timed so a fresh layer would bond seamlessly with the one below it.

"Polyester resin is a very temperamental material to handle," McCracken points out. "It generates heat, and it has to be kept within a very narrow temperature range to cure properly. Doing a layered pour calls for careful timing to avoid leaving visible lines between layers. It also gives off some extremely toxic fumes. I had to work wearing a respirator and gloves." His lungs have already suffered from years of working around stone dust, wood dust, and chemical fumes from patinas laid on bronze.

Dot.com *is a tongue-in-cheek comment on the ultimate destination of innovations we greet as cutting-edge technology.*

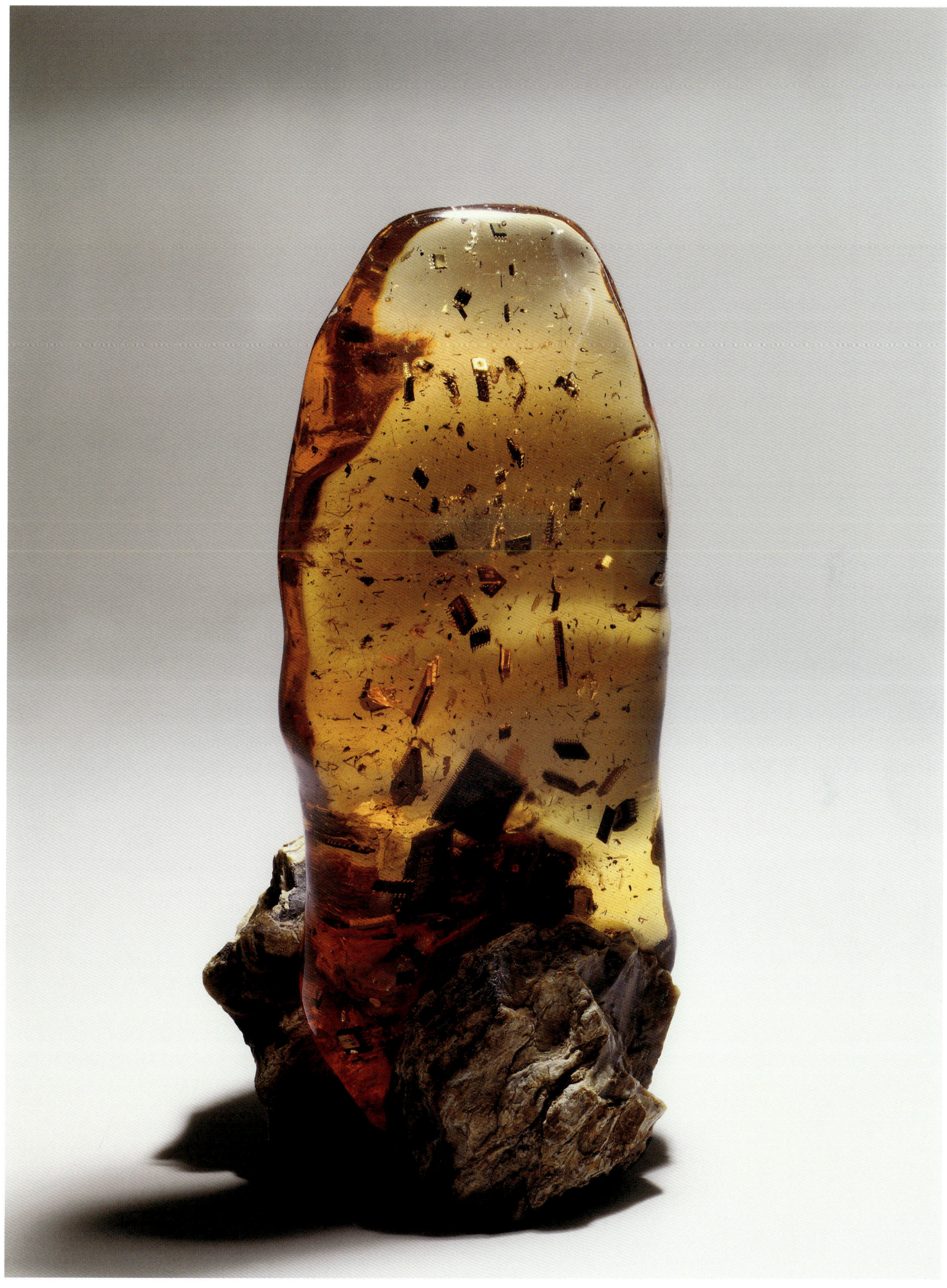

Ancient Creature
2000
Bone fragments and plaster
H. 11½ in.
Collection of the artist

The yawning jaws and snakelike fangs of this restored ancient skull suggest it belonged to a formidable creature—perhaps a gigantic serpent—in prehistory. Lower molars are still visible at the back of the mouth. The lower incisors are worn down, indicating a mature specimen. Bone fragments have been filled in to show the probable shape of missing elements.

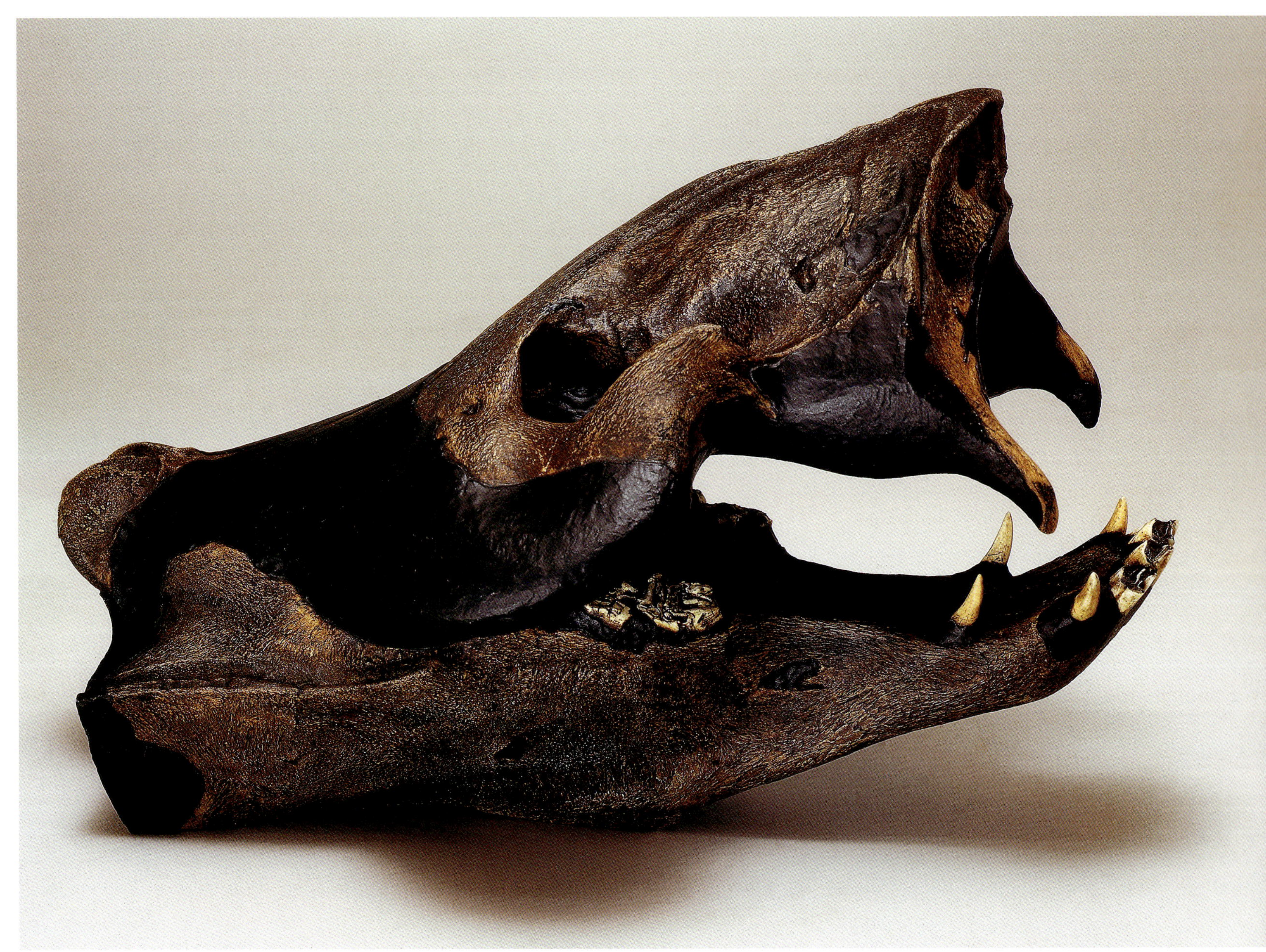

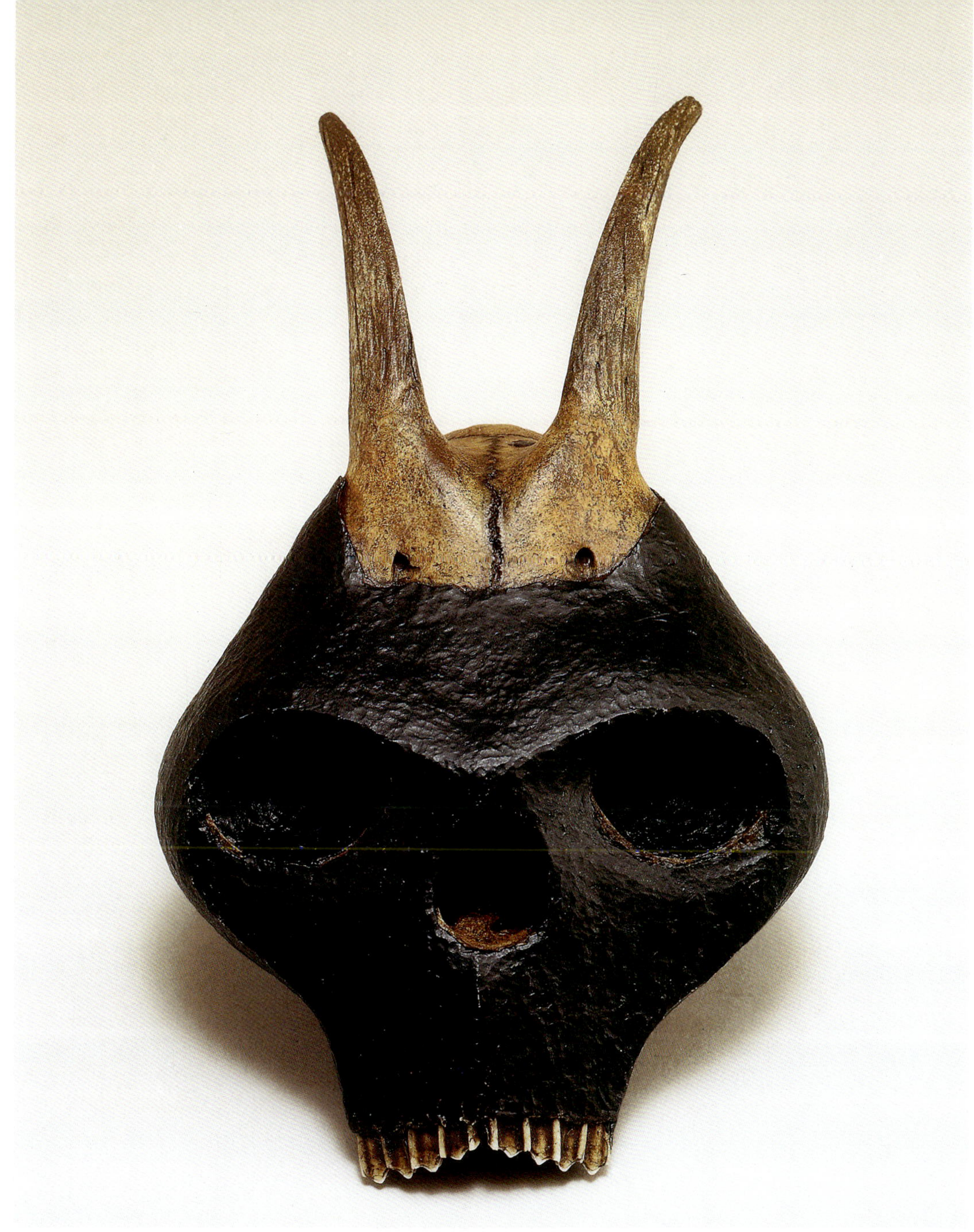

Pan
2000
Bone fragments and plaster
6¾ × 9 in.
Collection of the artist

In the year 2000, McCracken shifted from presenting commonplace objects from our own era as future relics to the creation of objects that could be unearthed any day now, such as this one.

Conceptual forms take on a frisson of meaning when they suggest something we either love or fear. The close-set horns and feral teeth of this specimen suggest something to be feared. Half man, half goat, Pan was the notoriously lusty Greek god of the woods, shepherds, and huntsmen. With the horns, beard, cloven feet, and shaggy legs of a goat, he roamed the woods playing his panpipe. It was said that he often frightened people who walked in the woods, filling them with the terror and awe we call panic. McCracken's sculpture captures this dark side of Pan's nature in the black skull with its gaping eye sockets and oddly shaped teeth. The skull appears to be that of a creature who slipped off the side of the evolutionary ladder eons ago.

Ancient Creatures
2000
Sandstone, pinecones, and fish spines
1¾ × 31½ in.
Collection of the artist

Projecting his imagination still deeper into the past, to the beginning of the Paleozoic era hundreds of millions of years ago, McCracken sculpted an eerie group of nine shaggy, sluglike creatures. An air of immense antiquity and primitiveness about these sinister little invertebrates is entirely convincing.

"I imagined a time when, in some great cataclysm, an oceanic plate was subsumed under a continental plate. A great mudslide would cover these creatures, trapping them in position, all aimed into the current, as sea creatures do," McCracken said.

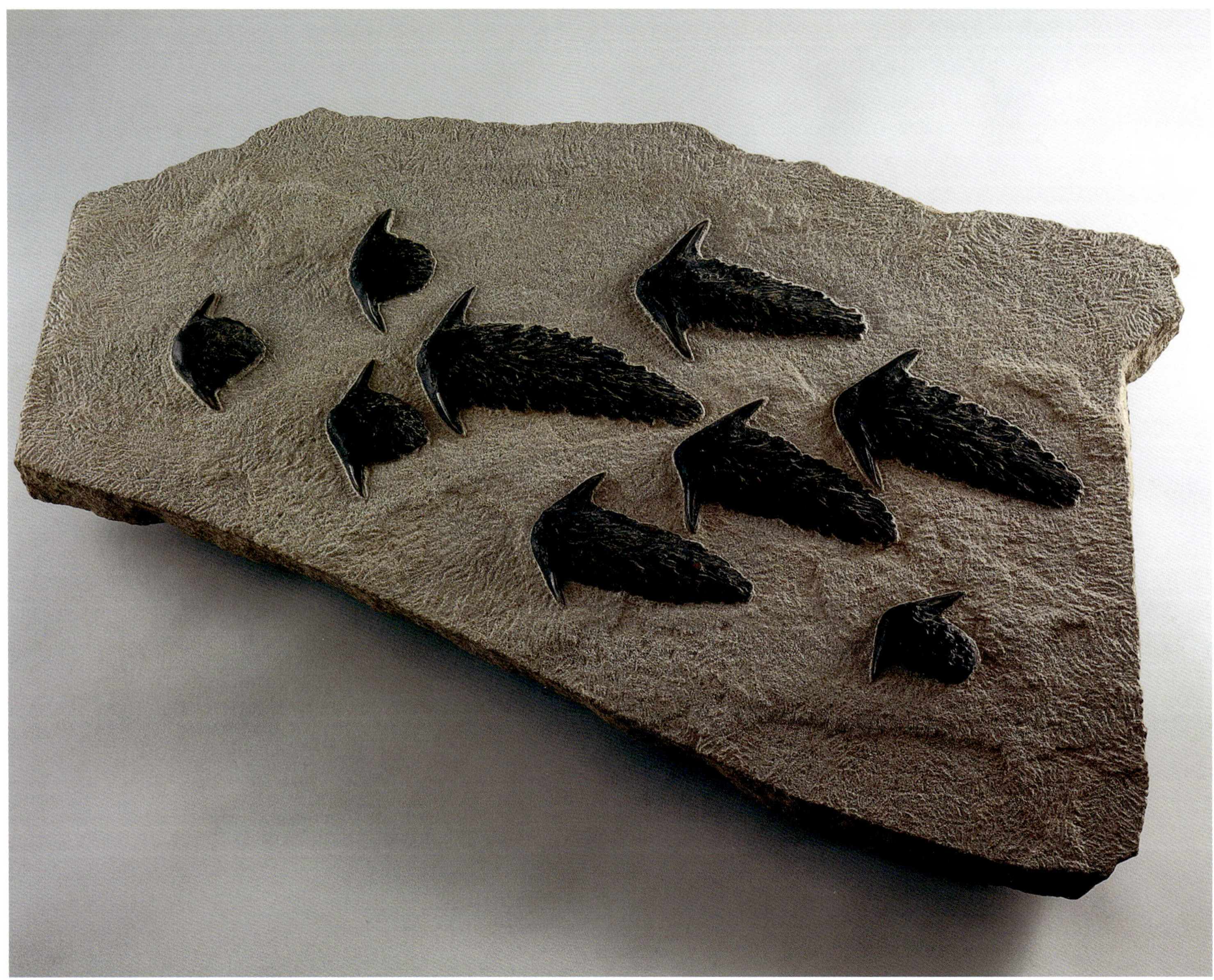

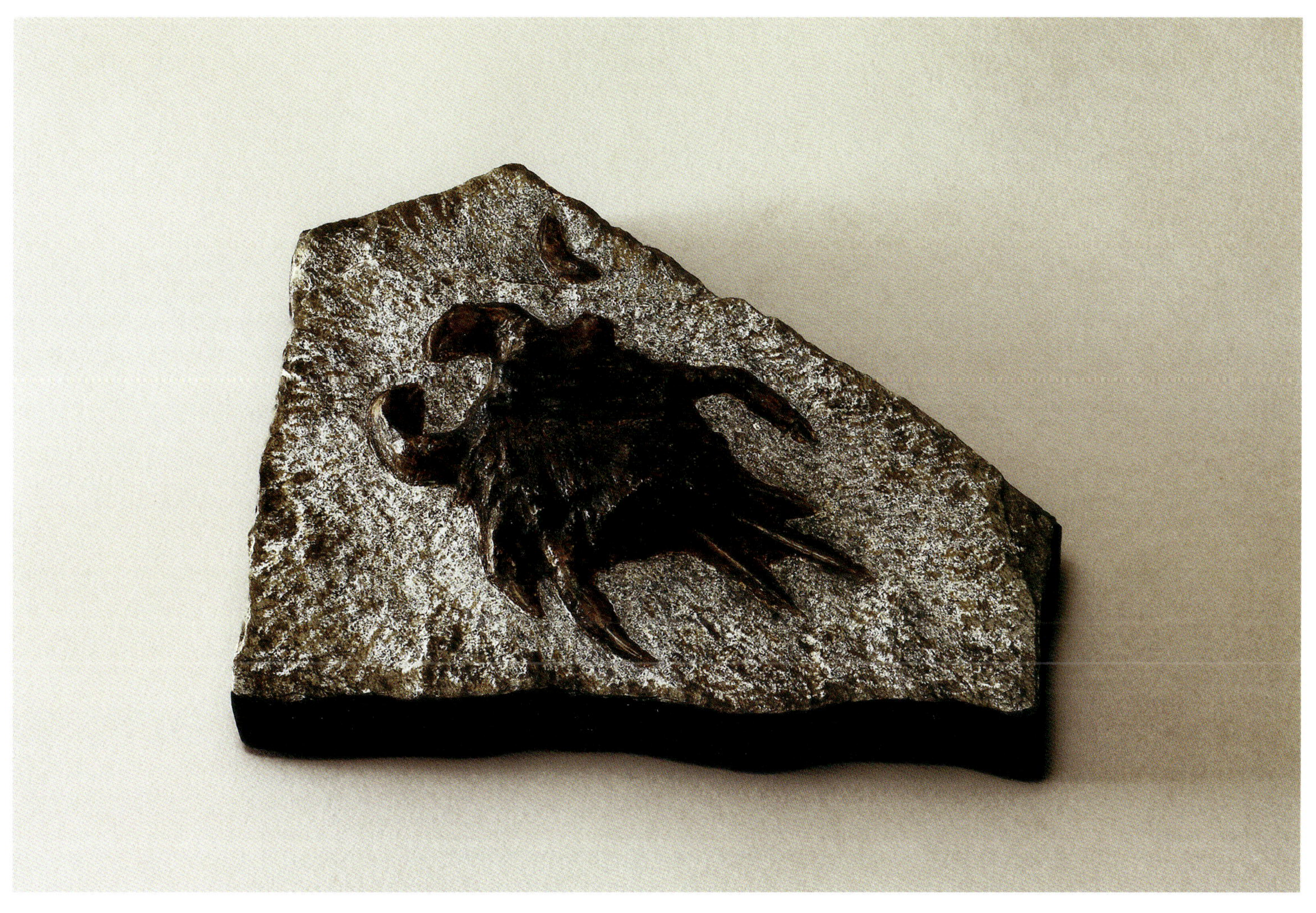

Ancient Creature III
2000
Slate, pinecones, and seashell fragments
1 × 8 × 5¾ in.
Collection of the artist

This unnamed creature had pincerlike front appendages—perhaps it was an early forerunner of a scorpion—a forked tail, and what appears to have been hard plating over its back. It might have been amphibious or aquatic, even a creature of the desert, equipped as it was for survival. This specimen is found preserved in a bed of slate.

Richter 8.5
2000
Fabricated stone and wood
H. 36¾ in.
Collection of Tim and Gail Bruce

The minimalist appearance of this divided diagonal stripe barely hints at the violence represented by the title. Fractures such as this one occur in bedrock when it cracks under great stress. That stress, which we experience as an earthquake, is measured by the Richter scale.[3] A magnitude 8.5 quake is stronger than the great 1906 earthquake in San Francisco, or the 1949 quake in the Queen Charlotte Islands. Such earthquakes can cause enormous destruction and loss of life up to fifty miles from their epicenters.

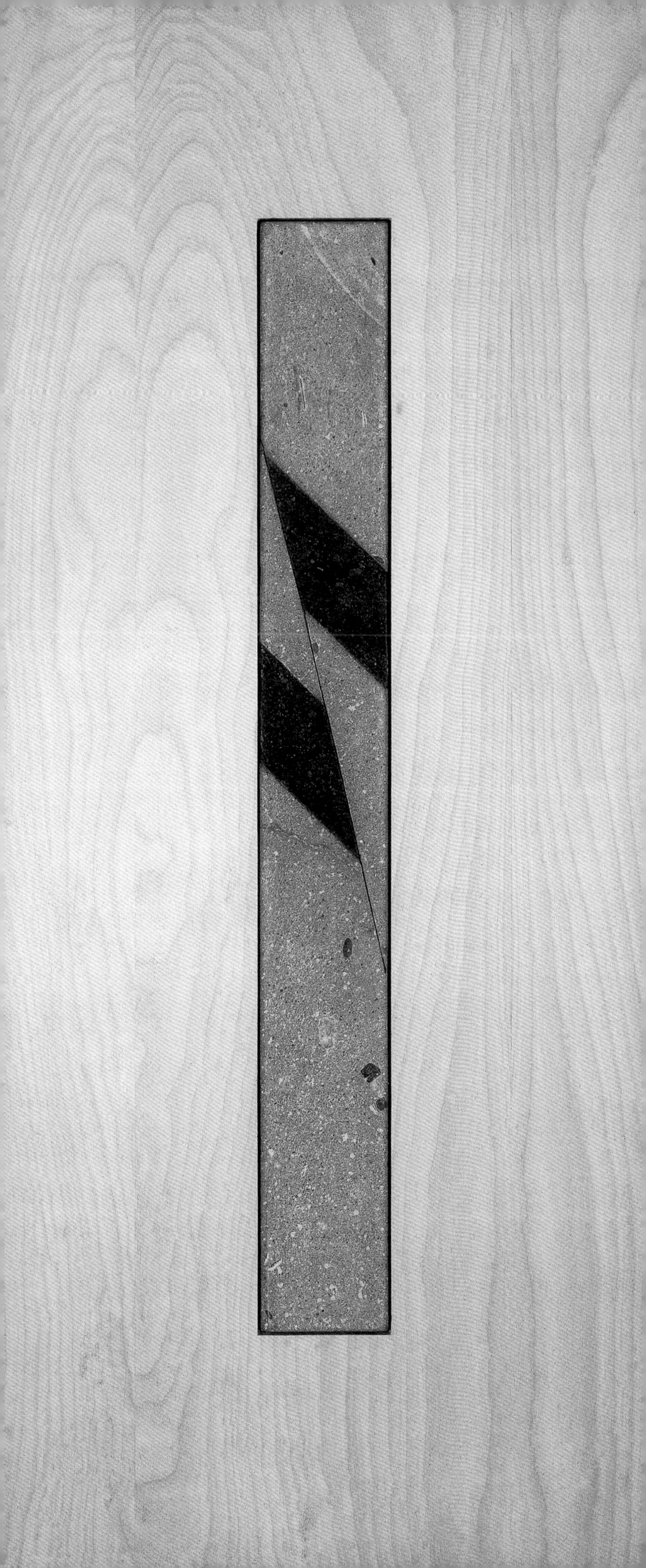

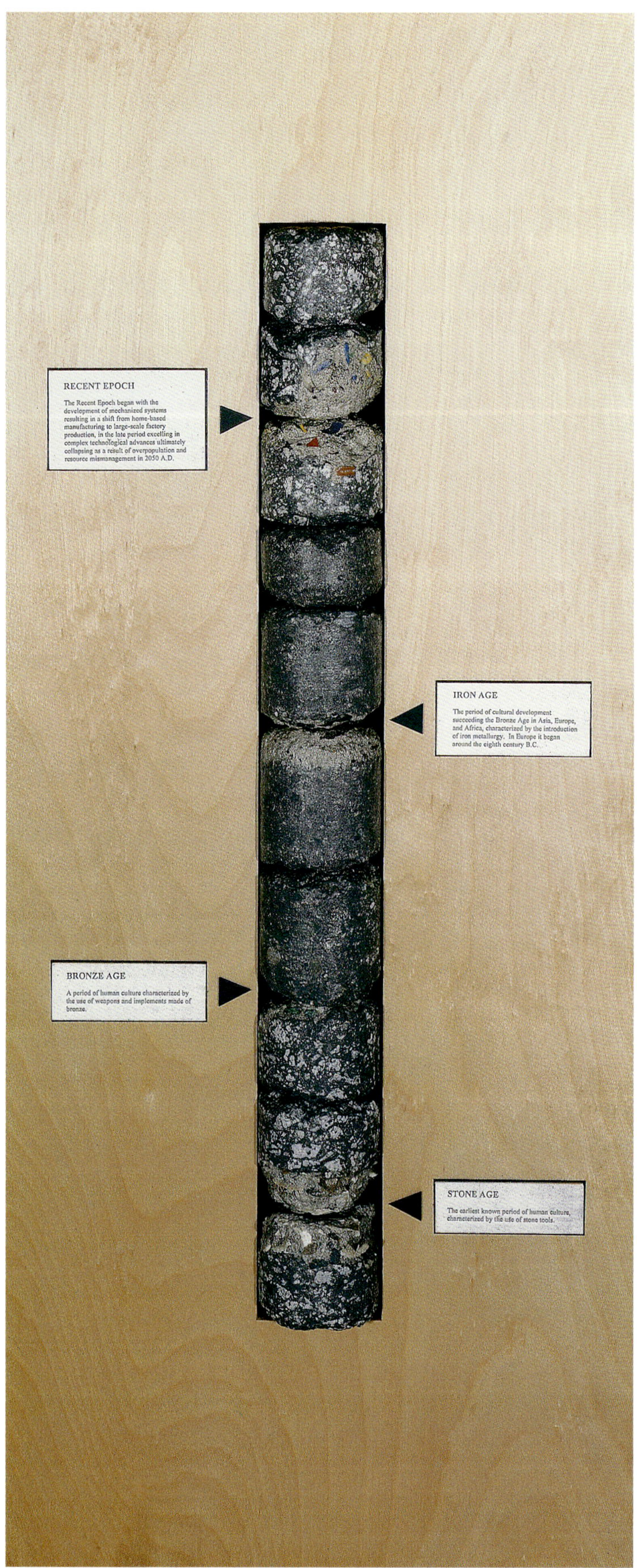

Ages of Man I
2001
Core-drilled fabricated stone,
bone fragments, metal, plastic, and wood
H. 35¼ in.
Collection of David and Heidi McCormack

In recent years an internationally sponsored oceangoing rig has been drilling and retrieving deep cores from the ocean bed. They have revealed remarkably detailed information about the earth's climates and plants from tens of thousands of years ago. McCracken became fascinated with geological cores after being given samples by a geologist friend. He filled a box with layers of earth and artificial rock, salted with materials typical of each age at the appropriate depth, then used a diamond core drill to cut a core sample for Ages of Man I *and a lapidary saw to cut* Ages of Man II.

Ages of Man I *presents a series of ten stacked layers, labeled in ascending order from Stone Age through the Bronze Age and Iron Age to a Recent Epoch. The oldest show coarse stones and flakes of flint from napped spear points. The texture gradually changes to layers that show bits of trapped bronze and brass, then to finer particle sizes packed almost as dense mud in the Iron Age. The particle sizes become coarser again in the Recent Epoch, with its bits of bright plastic and wire, already covered with a sifting of soil. The core sample is displayed in a column inset into a wood faceplate.*

Ages of Man II
2001
Fabricated stone, bone fragments,
metal, plastic, and wood
H. 14¼ in.
Collection of the artist

A slice with a diamond saw through a mélange that simulated a deep core of earth reveals eras of markedly different composition, suggesting the skeletal remains that settled on the ocean floor, up through leavings of the Stone Age, the Bronze Age, the Iron Age, and an epoch sufficiently recent to include bits of plastic. It stands as a handsome column of minimalist art that—to the knowing eye—reflects the state of the world and all in it as accurately as the most detailed landscape.

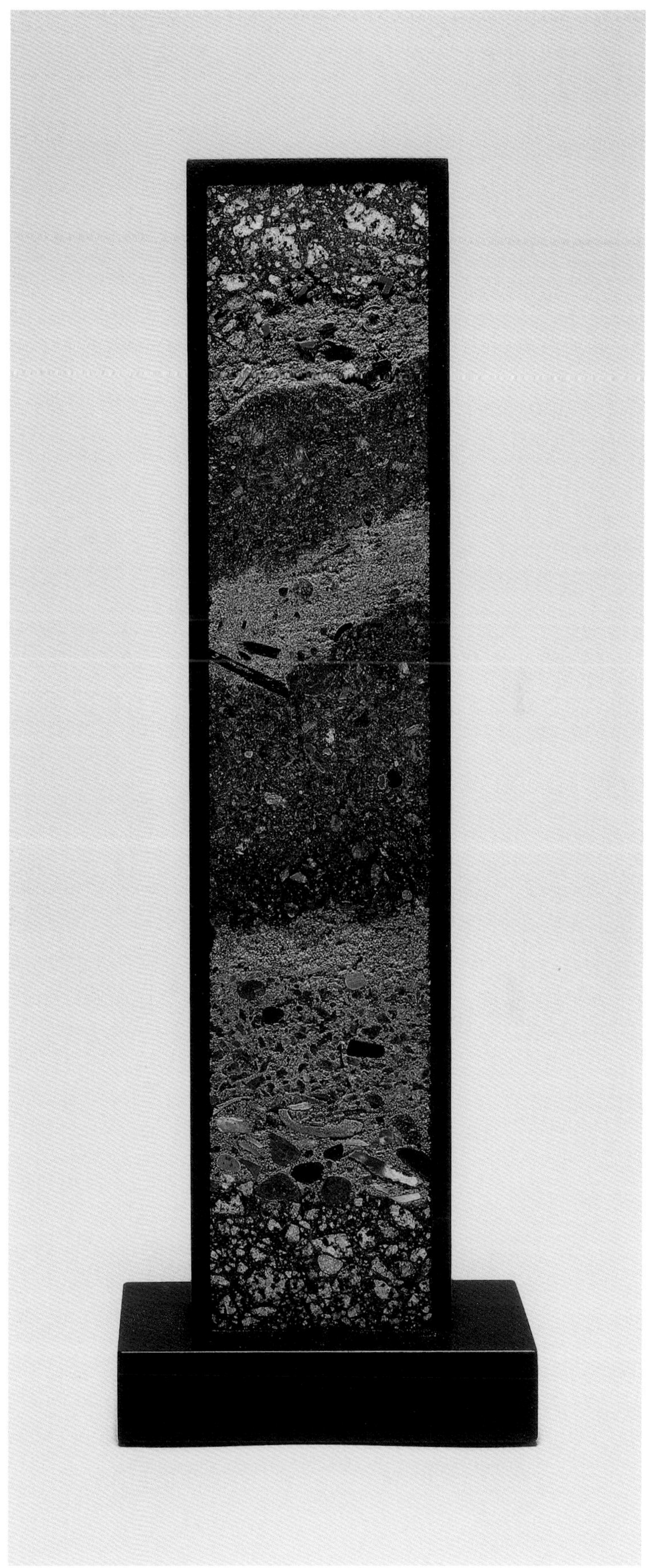

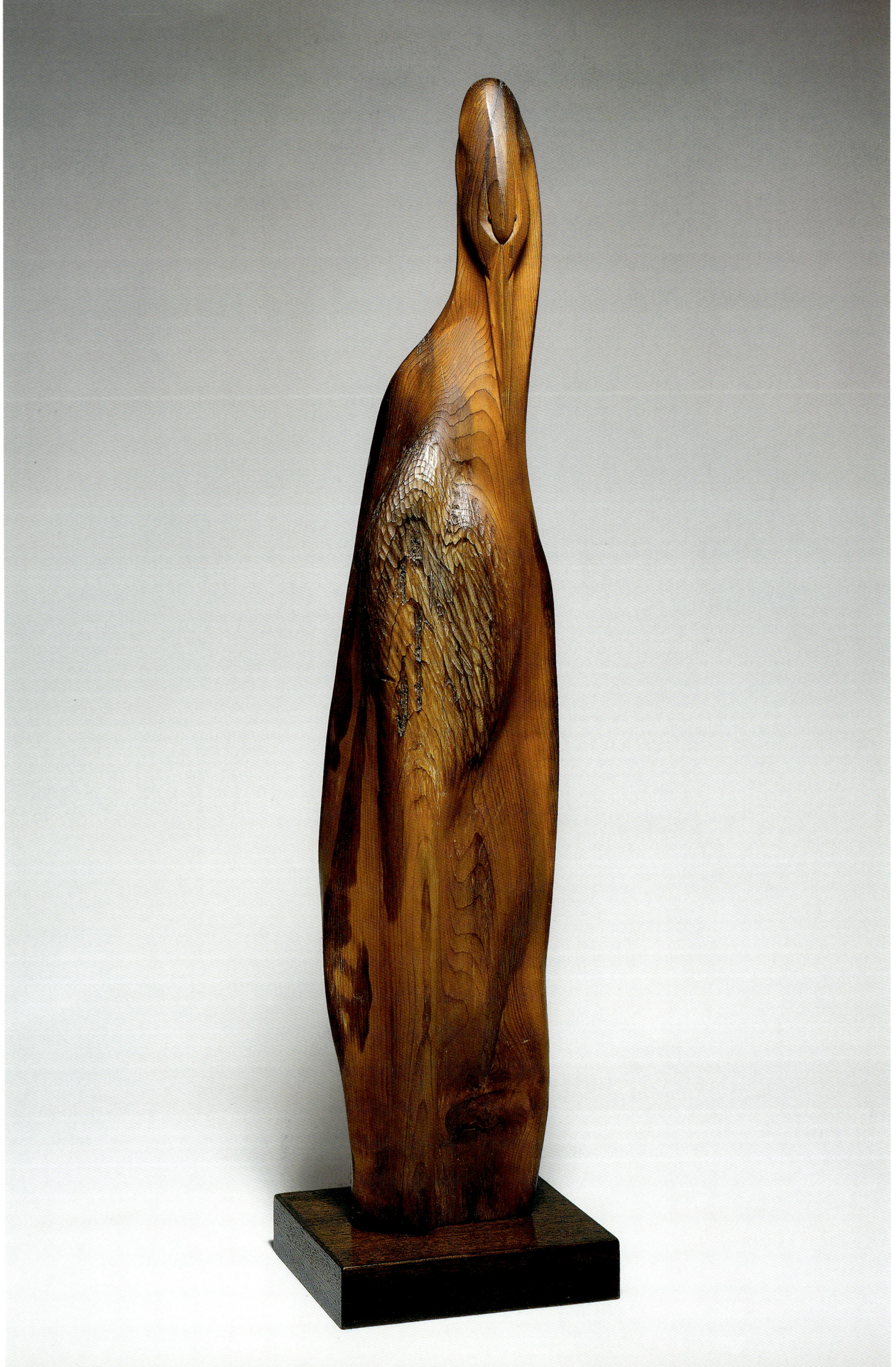

Birds

Since the earliest days of his work as a sculptor, McCracken has returned to abstracted images of birds, with a diversity as rich as Mozart playing with variations on a theme. It is no coincidence that he felt a particular kinship to painter Morris Graves, who won national acclaim with paintings of strange birds at New York's Museum of Modern Art in 1942. Like Graves, whose blind birds have otherworldly visions, McCracken's birds express unexpected resources. They burst free of bars, see through darkness into other dimensions, or act as fierce guardians, in addition to being consummate expressions of graceful form.

One of McCracken's earliest successful sculptures, a life-size heron carved from red cedar in 1952, was in Graves's collection until his death in May 2001, when it was returned to its maker. Shortly before Graves died, Philip and Anne McCracken visited him at The Lake, his home near Loleta, California. Graves was awestruck when, concurrent with their visit, the first heron ever seen to visit his lake cruised over the water and alighted. It may well have been the same heron that cried out from outside Graves's window at the moment of his death.

McCracken has sculpted other herons over the years, none better known than a 1977 bronze *Heron* perched hollow-eyed on a tall pedestal, with its wings hunched high around its head, creating its own shelter from the elements. It stands stoic and withdrawn into itself, its claws curled over the edge of the bronze block on which it perches, in the collection of the Whatcom Museum of History & Art in Bellingham.

A more recent heron is the 1999 bronze *Reflections*. The bird stands on a pyramidal hummock that wears the rippling surface of water. This time the bird's long neck, not visible in the 1977 sculpture, is the most prominent feature, stretched to an exaggerated length, in a sinuous curve that continues unbroken to the tip of its beak. In all of his bird sculptures, McCracken abstracts the overall form, rarely showing details other than eyes, beaks, and prehensile feet. From beak to talon, the heron is an undulant curve that divides at the shoulder, one line arching to follow the sleek back, the other tapering down the extended legs. Studying it, one is inclined to believe nature never

Heron
1952
Cedar
H. 33 in.
Collection of Anne McCracken

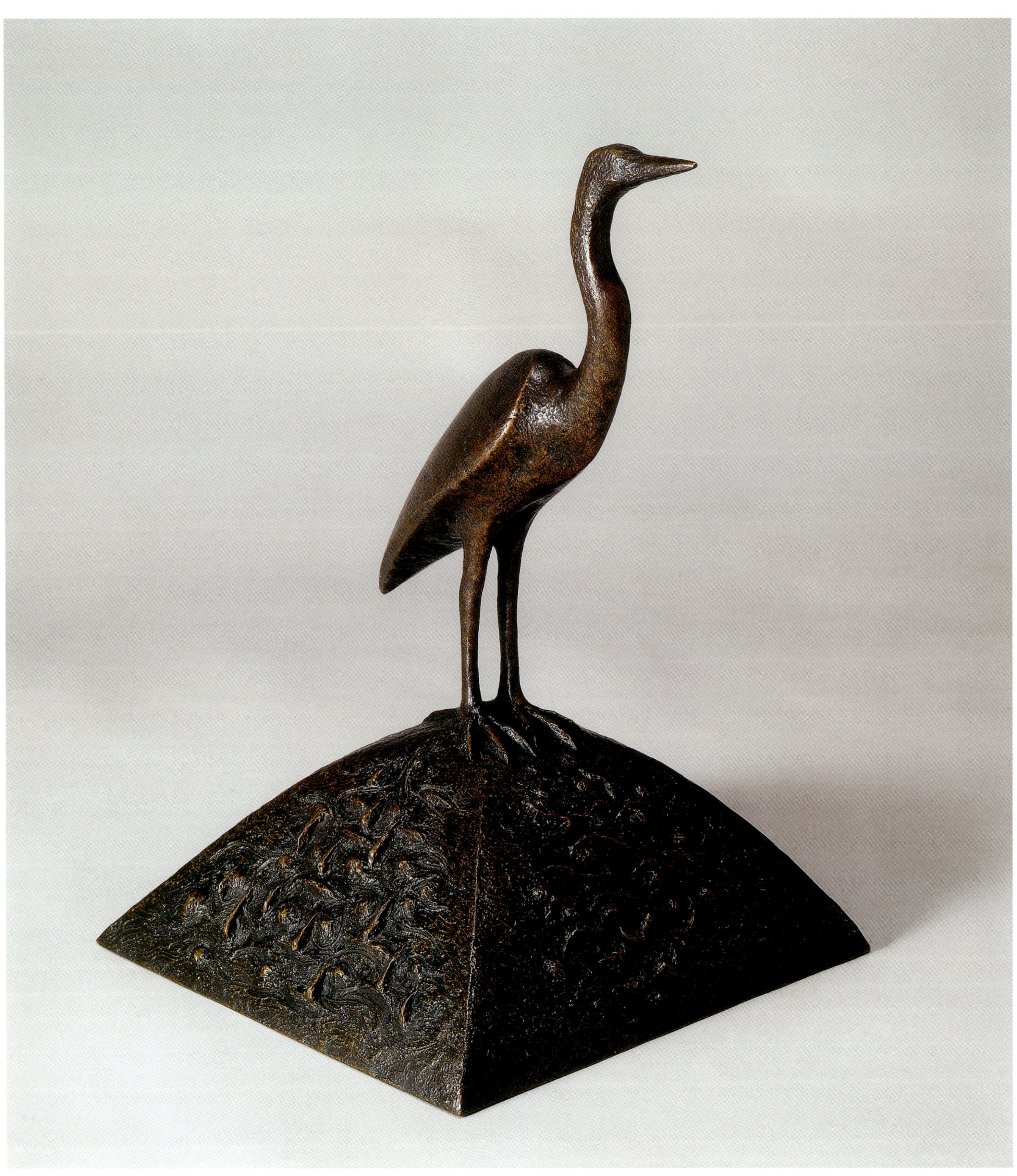

Reflections
1999
Bronze
H. 13⅝ in.
Private collection

made a more graceful shape than a heron. Living on Guemes Island, McCracken has had ample occasion to appreciate it, as he has the forms of owls.

While some symbolism may be read into his depictions of owls, they are, for the most part, done out of affection and admiration. His attachment to them was enriched by the experience of rearing a great horned owl as a member of the family. Back in 1957, a friend whose job was banding wild birds for later study of their migration patterns and territories, came upon a baby owl who appeared to have been pushed out of the nest. He brought it to the McCrackens to raise.

They gave the baby owl a sheltered nest on a bookcase shelf, and brought it a diet of mice and crushed chicken heads, understanding that bones and feathers are a necessary part of an owl's diet. Such indigestible elements enable it to regurgitate pellets. As soon as the owl could fly, they gave it free access to the outdoors, but found that it made itself at home with them, staking out the back of a large wicker chair as its favorite roost. The owl liked to watch TV with the family, shifting her head from side to side to try to gauge the distance of moving objects in the picture. She was especially fond of Western movies, and seemed to be a particular fan of John Wayne.

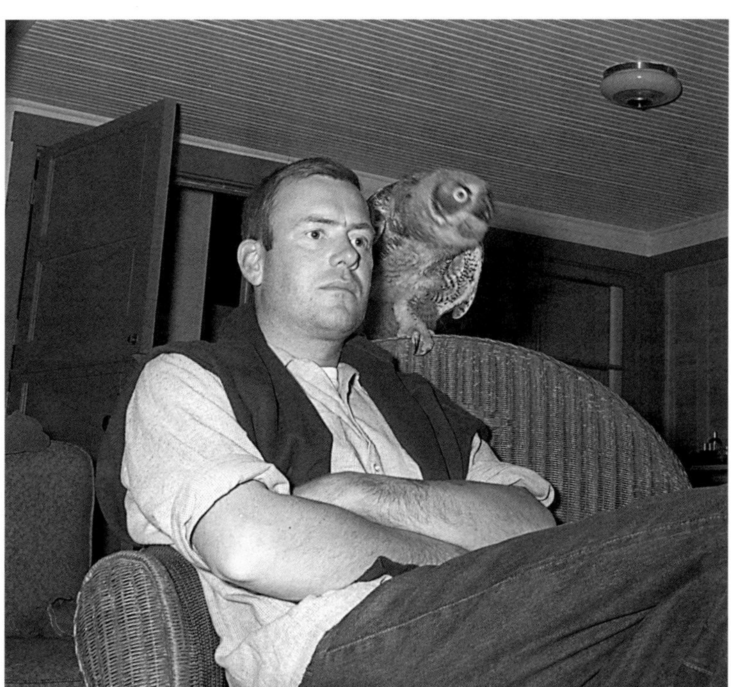

Philip and his owl watch TV, c. 1962
(photograph by Anne McCracken)

Realizing that the owl must be taught to hunt, McCracken took it out at night, and trained it with pigeons. "From then on, nothing was safe," he recalls. "From the time she was three weeks old, she was very aggressive. In the beginning, our cats would sometimes try to steal her food. But as she got bigger, the chase went the other way. The cats learned to respect her."

The owl paid regular visits to neighboring houses on Guemes. "I'd get a call from someone telling me my owl was there, and please come get it. So I'd hop in the car and drive to the house, then I'd get out and whistle, and the owl would fly up and perch on my shoulder, and we'd get back into the car and drive home."

On one occasion, the owl banked through the front door headed for its favorite chair, to discover an upsetting sight. A guest had thrown a coat with a fur collar over her favorite chair. Not knowing what to make of it, the owl flew instead to a kitchen sideboard, where she came to rest in a bowl of spaghetti sauce. When she rose to fly across the room, a hail of red spaghetti sauce spattered from her wings and dribbled from her feet as she flapped through the room, peppering the guest, along with everything else.

In the due course of things, a male owl captured her fancy. McCracken reports that she tried earnestly to get the object of her affections to fly into the house with her. "She'd fly in and perch on my shoulder and call out to him through the door. I could see him sitting out there with a disapproving look, as if she were embarrassing him by such behavior. He was having none of it. He wouldn't come near the house." At last, she flew out to join him, and together they flew off into the sunset—or wherever it is that courting owls fly—to build a nest of their own.

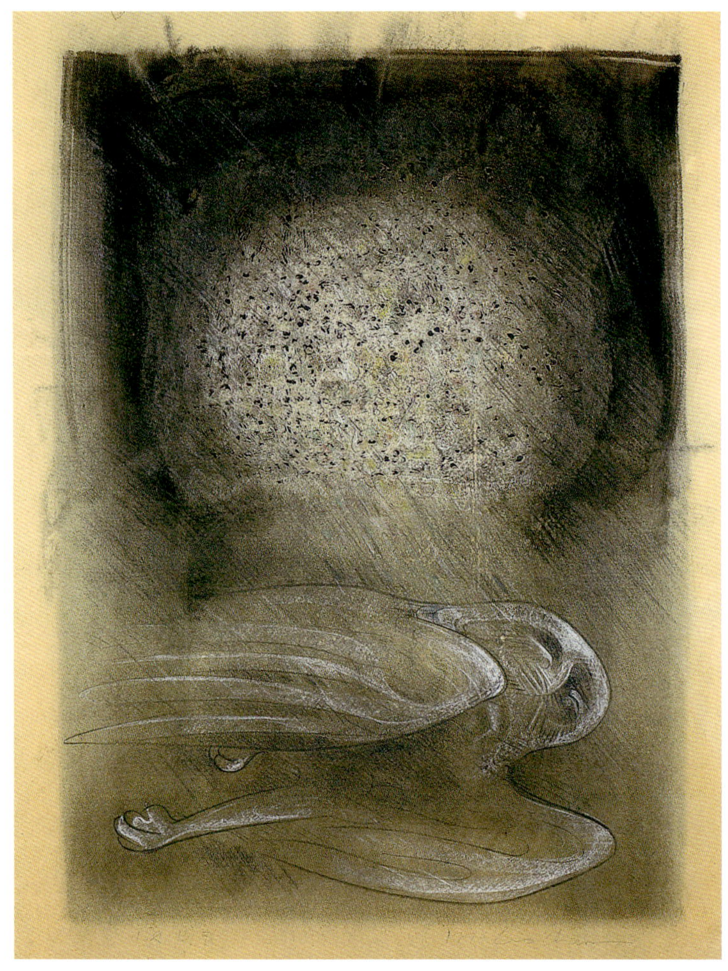

Dream of a Dying Owl
1963
Print, pencil, and ink wash on paper
24 × 17¾ in.
Collection of the artist

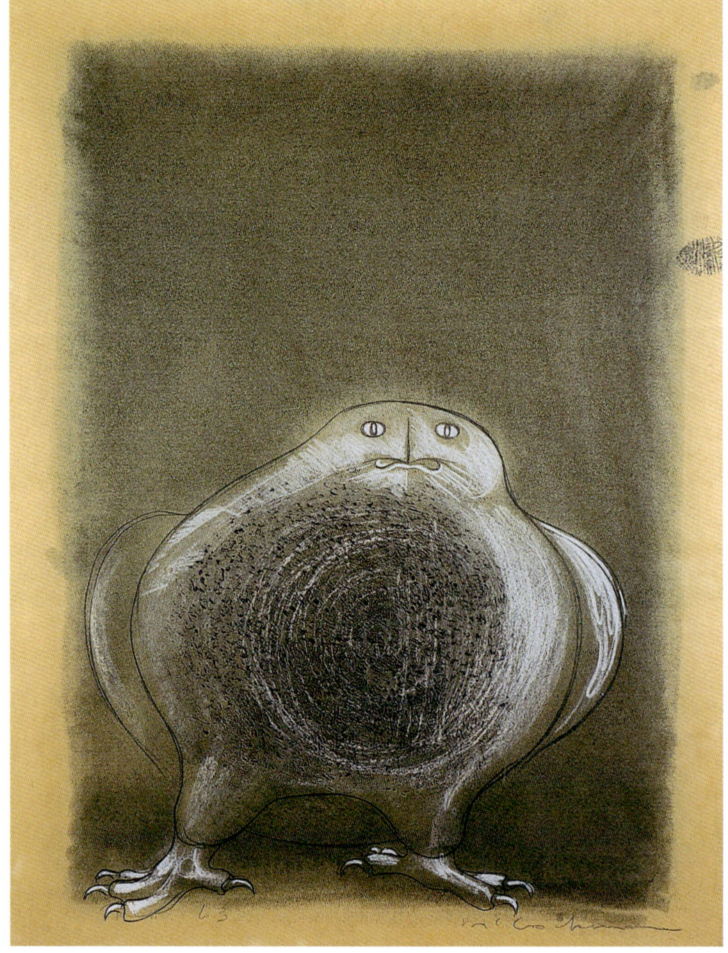

Angry Bird
1963
Print, pencil, and ink wash on paper
24 × 17¾ in.
Collection of the artist

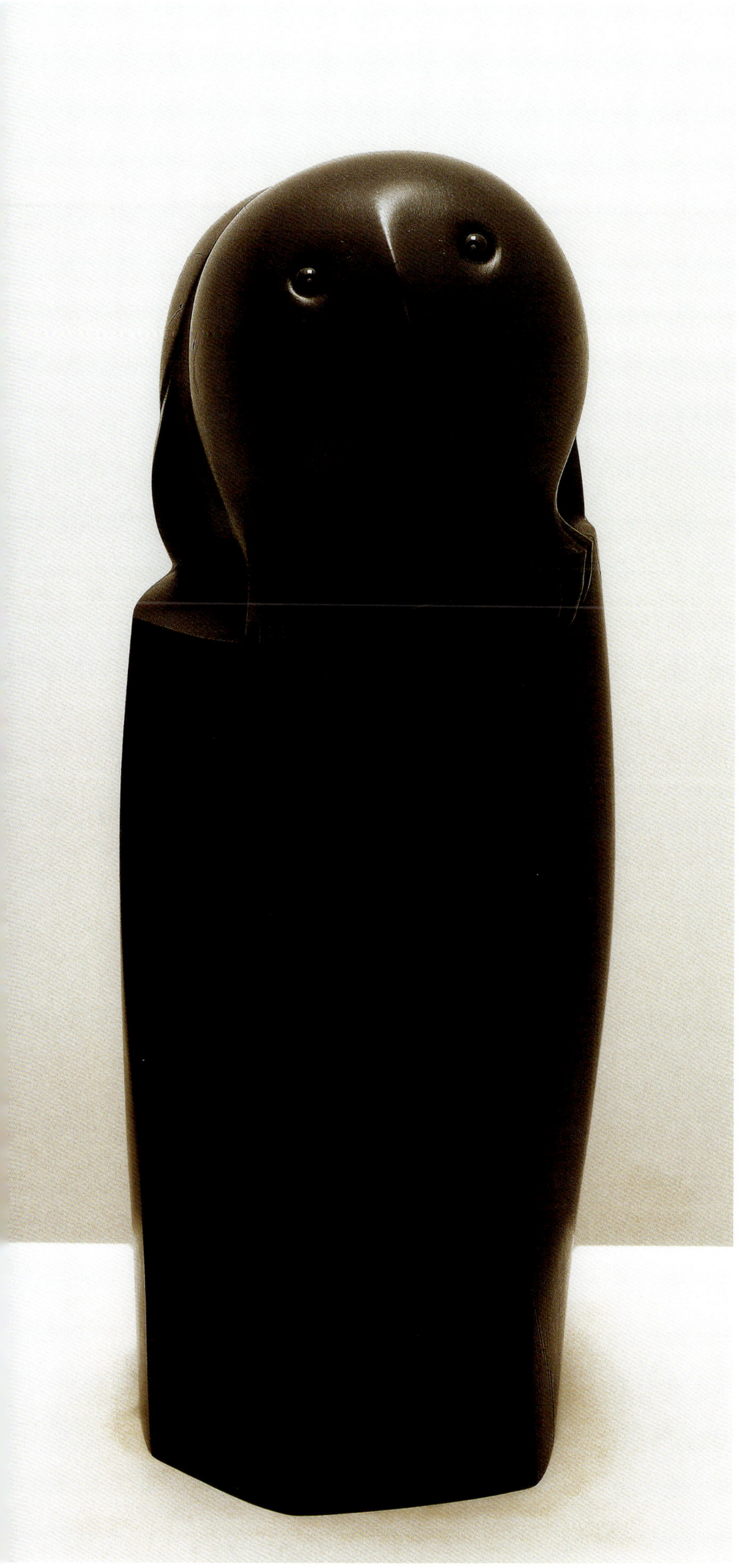

Bird Seeing Beyond
1984
Juniper and onyx
H. 16 in.
Private collection

The owl form has since made frequent appearances in McCracken's work. Its solid, compact shape, its keen night vision, and its haunting call have given the owl a special status. It has been called a cat with wings. Kwakiutl people see owls as possessing the souls of living people, and never harm them lest killing an owl might also kill the person to whom the soul belongs.

In his mixed-media image *Dream of a Dying Owl* (1963), McCracken rendered the bird with the chalky lines of a ghostly apparition, while above him a giant speckled egg, large enough to carry him to be hatched in another plane, appears to be in the process of dissolving even as he is drawn toward it.

McCracken's *Angry Bird* is a mixed-media drawing done about the same time, at the same size, with the same media. In it, McCracken captured the tendency of an angered bird to puff out its feathers to appear larger than life to face off a perceived threat. Defined by a crisp black outline softened by chalky white volume surrounding its expanded chest, this angry bird presents the image of a brawler, from the expression in the outraged eyes to the defiant stance of the taloned feet.

Owls' almost uncanny vision in the dark has given them the reputation of being able to pierce the veil that separates the physical from the spirit world. That quality is embodied in McCracken's 1984 sculpture, *Bird Seeing Beyond.* The bird is young. With its form indicated in a compact, minimalist curve of juniper, its most prominent feature is small, onyx-bright eyes that seem to be focused on nothing earthly, bulging in

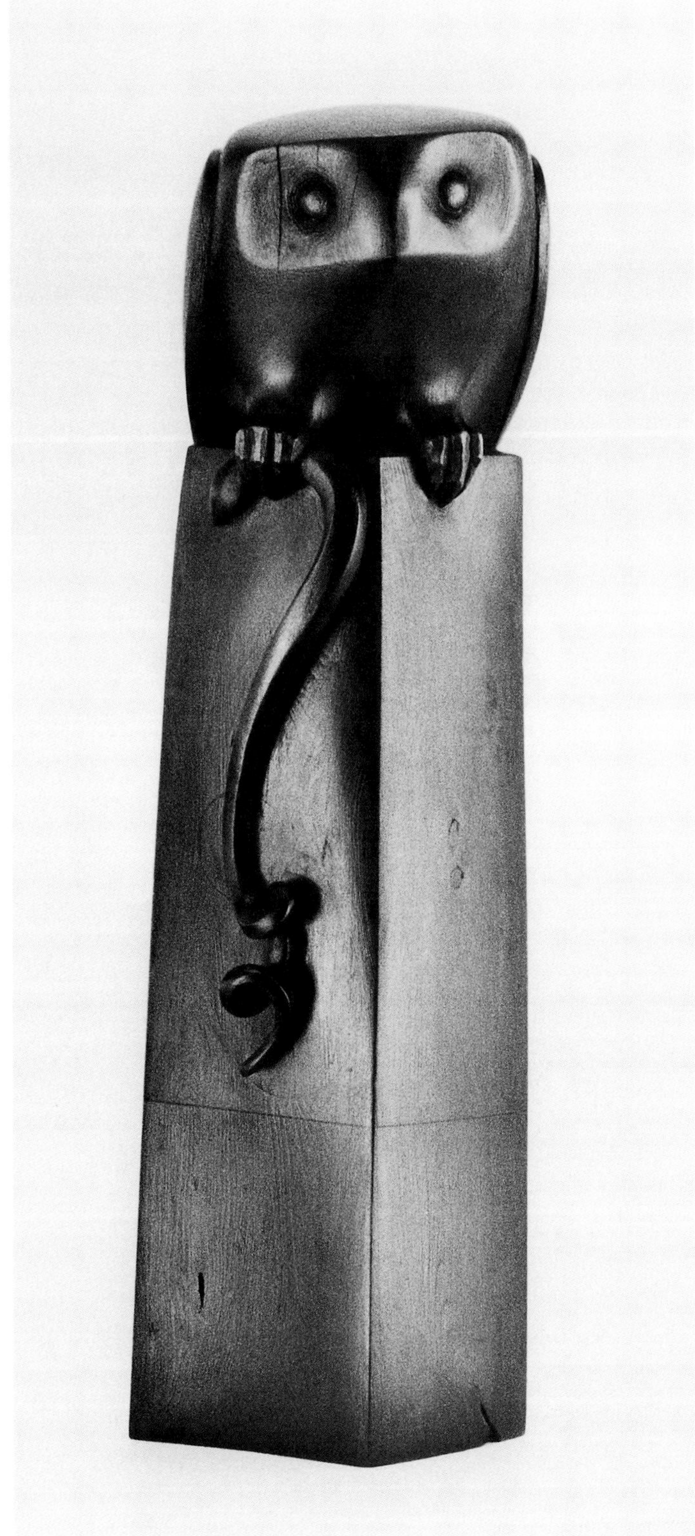

Owl and Snake
1983
Juniper
H. 12¼ in.
Collection of Jeannie and
Charles Gravenkemper

astonishment. Its claws are locked over its perch, holding steady through an awesome experience.

In maturity, an owl can appear almost as wide as it is tall. That mature shape is shown in *Owl and Snake* (1983). A writhing snake hangs from the claw of an owl that looks straight ahead, out of eyes whose surrounding aureoles of feathers cover most of its head, as they do in a barn owl. Talons clutching a defeated snake, a theme more often seen in depictions of a bald eagle, are a reminder that Native Americans honor the owl as the night eagle.

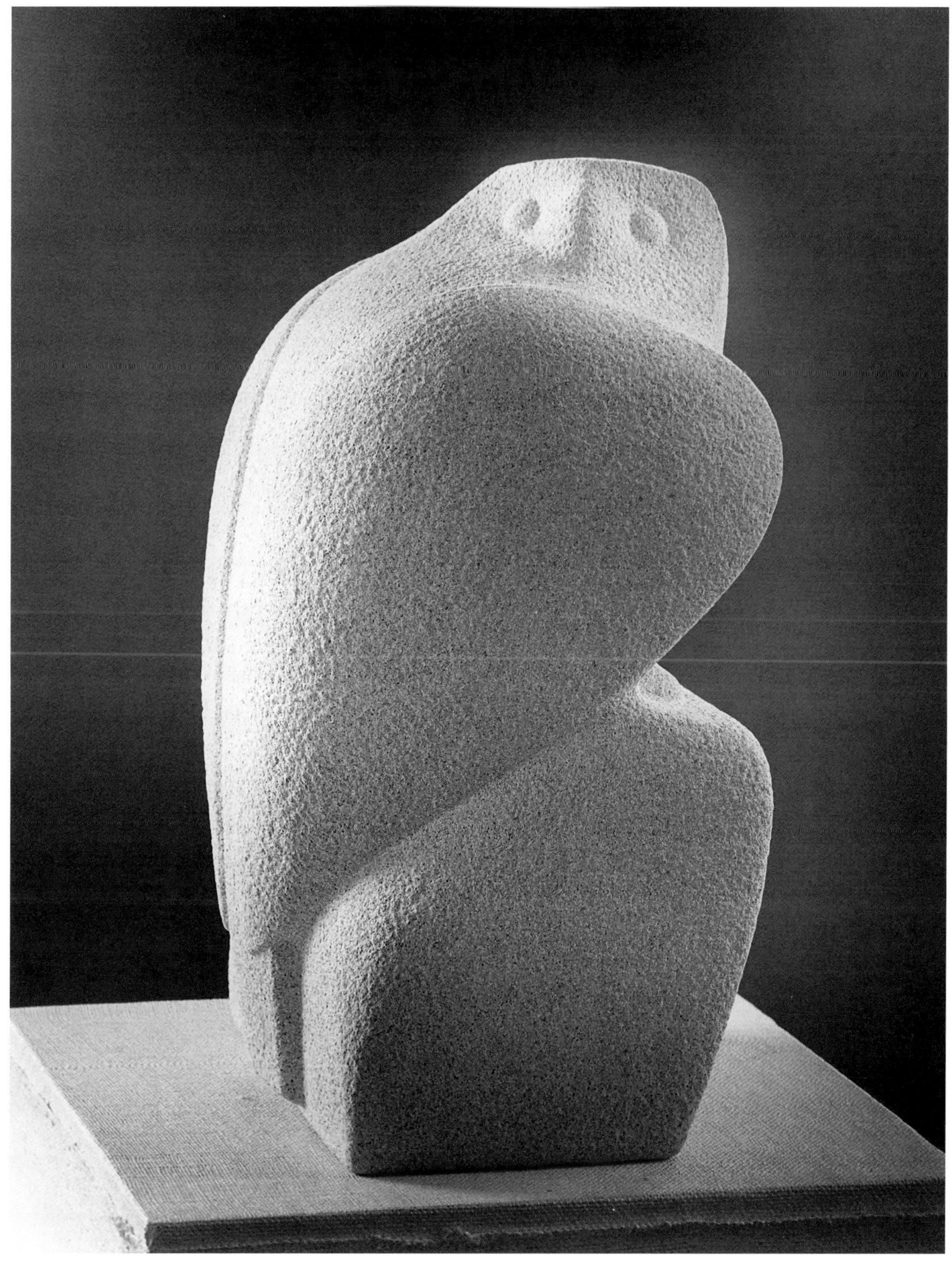

Night Bird
1982
Sandstone
H. 20 in.
Collection of Lance and J.P. Brigham

Night Bird *is a fat owl carved in sandstone, wings and back melding into the shape of a swelling bud, topped by a small, flat-topped head looking back with owlish eyes (not for nothing do we use this expression) over its shoulder, almost in surprise, as if the sculptor had caught a freeze-frame of a sudden sense of danger.*

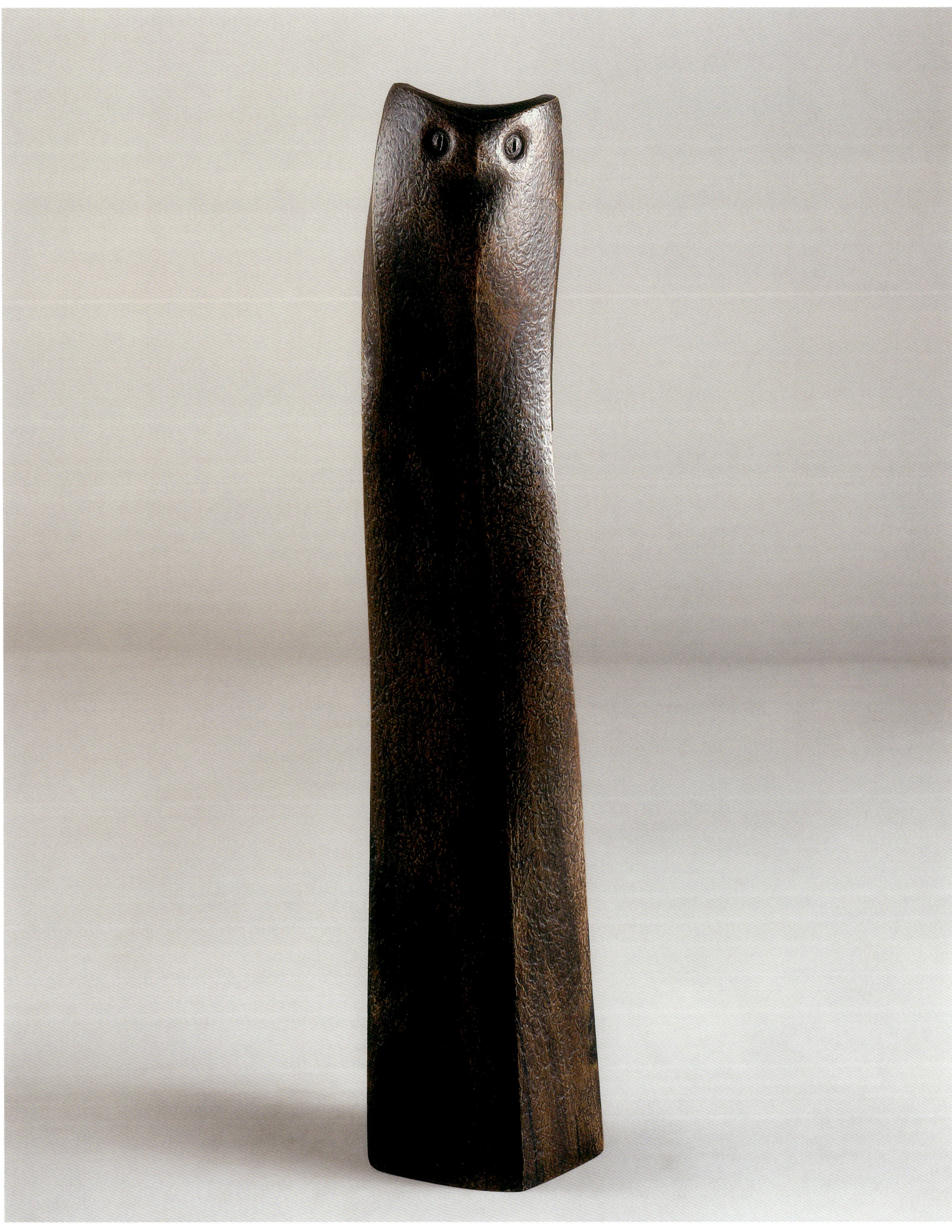

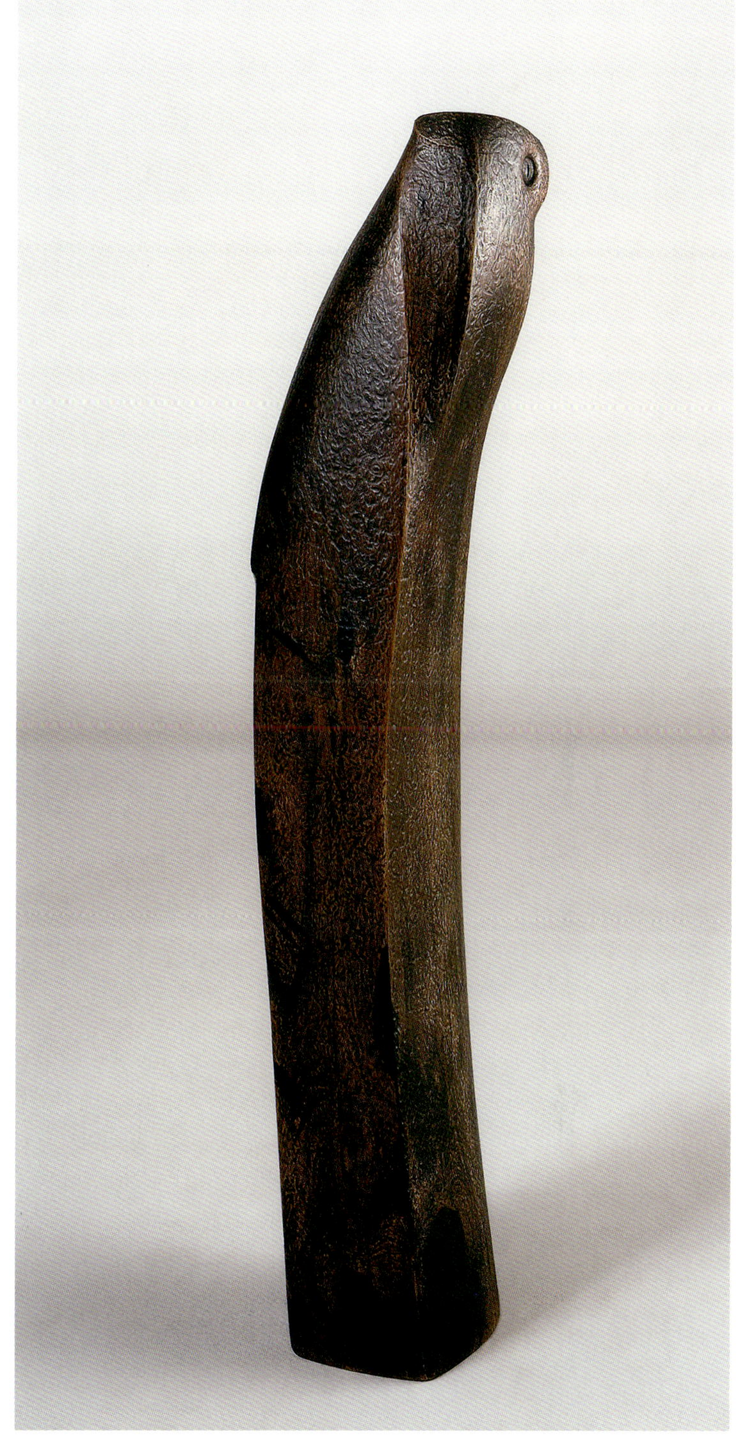

Owl Totem (two views)
1997
Juniper
H. 14¾ in.
Collection of Ruth McLuckie

In 1997, McCracken elongated the form of an owl into its own totem, carving it in a fifteen-inch length of juniper wood so that the body of the bird grows out of the thick pole—a visual way of saying that the owl is an integral part of the woods, and of nature. The piece is titled Owl Totem.

A word about the nature of totems is in order. At its simplest, a totem is a symbol of an individual, or—in the case of totem poles—of an entire family or clan. A totem animal indicates an aspect of one's personality that is closely tied to nature. In traditional belief, the totem animal is thought to choose the person, and not the other way around. In being chosen to rear a young owl, McCracken could be perceived as having been chosen to carry owl qualities. Certainly he and his owl communicated on some level.

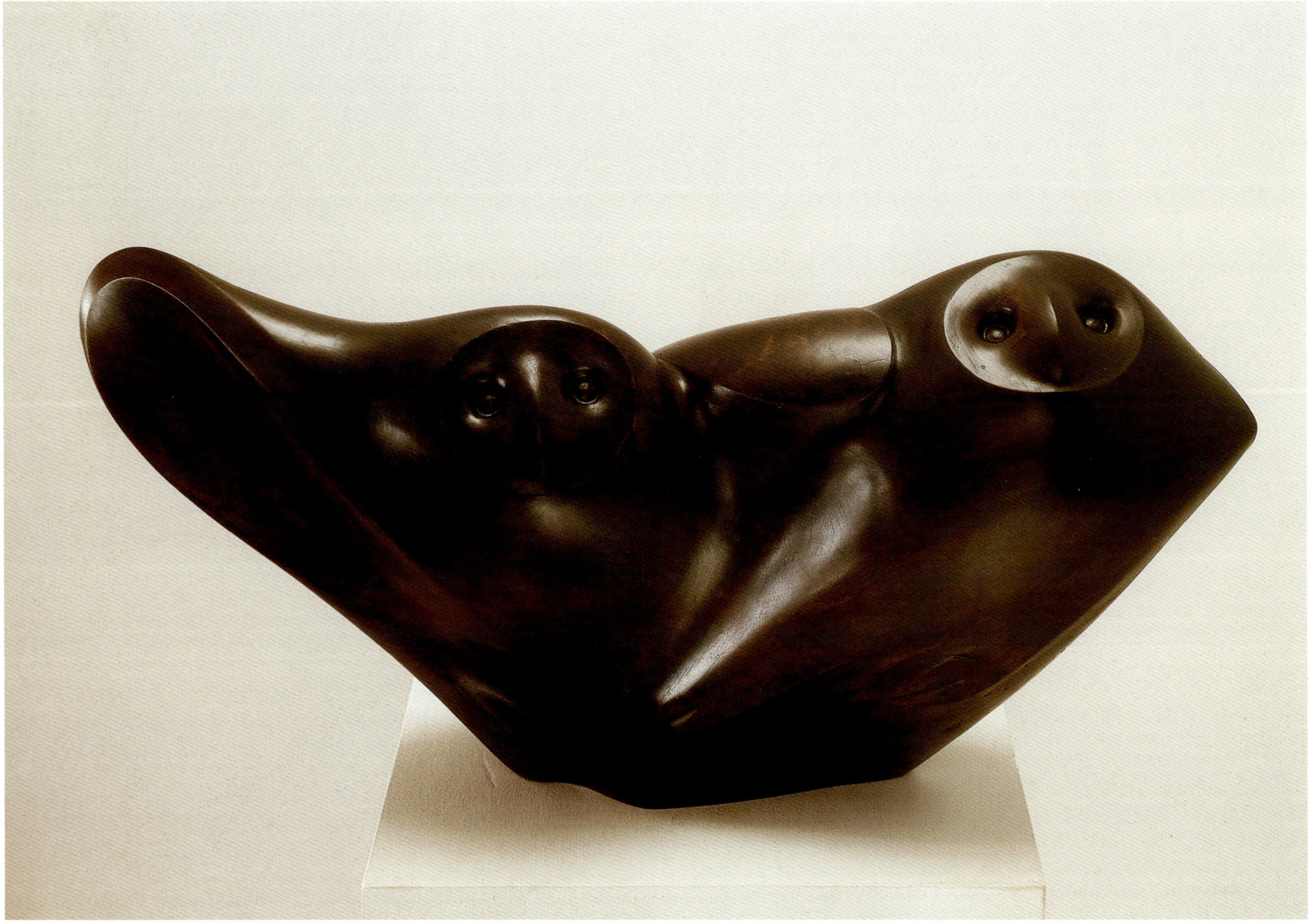

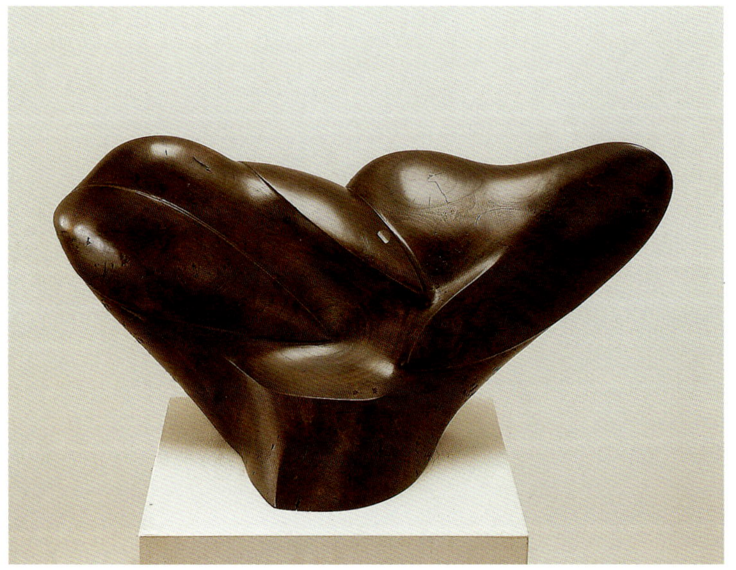

Night Journey (two views)
1982
Cherry wood
H. 11 in.
Collection of Lance and J.P. Brigham

Symbolism aside, the shapes of birds are among the sleekest and most compact expressions of energy imaginable. In Night Journey, *the abstracted shapes of a pair of young owls carved from dark cherry appear to share a common central wing as they thrust forward together into an unknown darkness.*

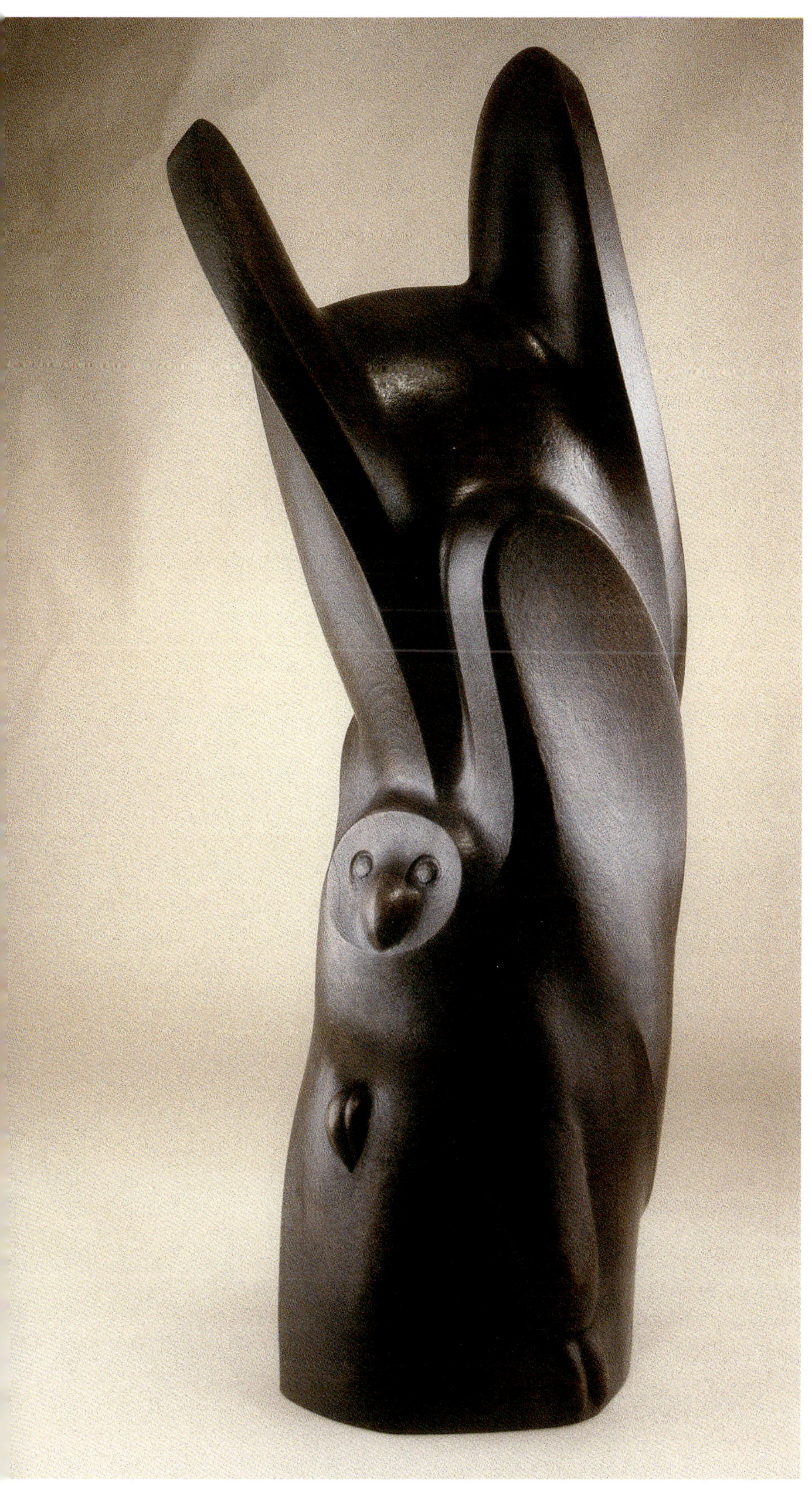

Owl Torrent
1990
Cherry wood
H. 31½ in.
Private collection

A sense of mystery surrounds Owl Torrent. *The abstraction of the owl shape takes the form of a fat cylinder with extensions on each side of the flat-topped head that can be read as the exaggerated ear feathers of a great horned owl. Two owls, alarmed and rising, face in different directions in this wraparound piece. The sleek lines of the sculpture carry unbroken curves from the scoop of the horns over the swell of the wings, to taper down the tail, through the base. As in* Owl Totem, *the birds and their base form an unbroken whole.*

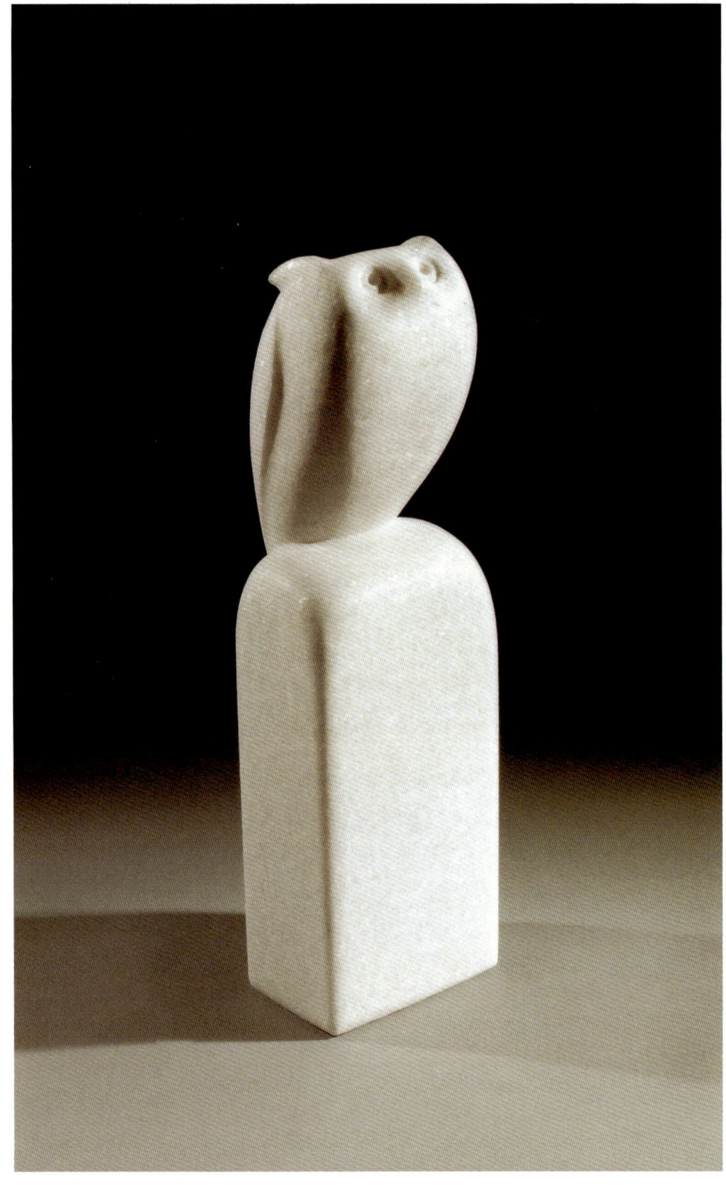

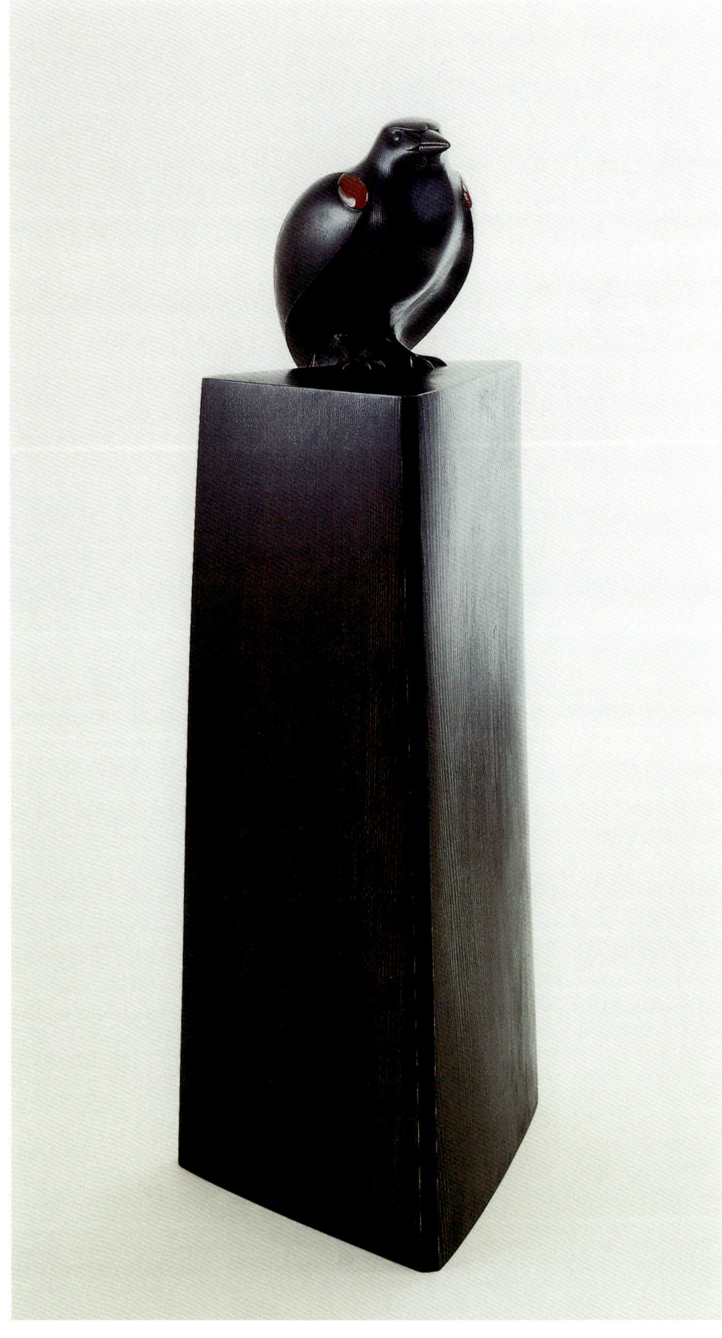

Edo Owl
1989
Marble
H. 12½ in.
Collection of Don Hebard

Inspired by a Japanese painting, Edo Owl *is carved in flecked white marble, its small eyes sunken into its face, staring up toward the viewer as if awestruck. McCracken has sleeked the form into the tapering shape of an amulet, at one with its lozenge-shaped base.*

Black Bird
1986
Cedar and carnelian
H. 26½ in.
Collection of Marshall and Helen Hatch

The white owl finds its polar opposite in McCracken's Black Bird, *the dark shape of a solitary Redwing Blackbird carved in cedar, perched on a tall wood pedestal.*

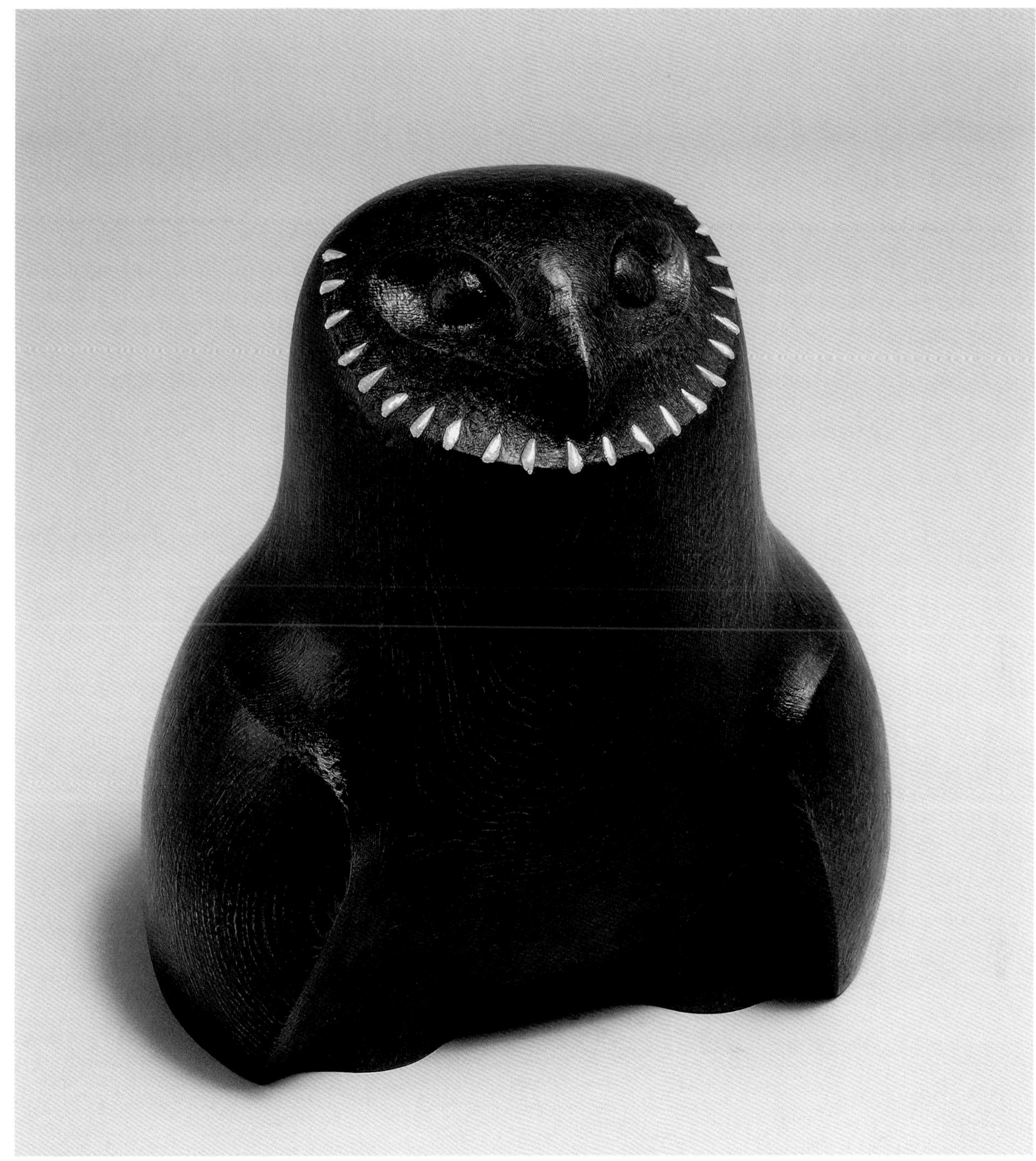

Northern Harrier
1998
Cedar and pearls
H. 9½ in.
Collection of Lisa Maki

Although they have owl-like faces, harriers are hawks, better known as the marsh hawk, for their breeding habitats in marshes and damp grasslands. They hunt on the wing, flying low, striking mice, voles, young rabbits and birds, and frogs. McCracken's Northern Harrier *is a husky specimen carved in cedar. Its short, strong down-curved beak protrudes from a flattened face with owlish eyes. The harrier's white ruff is indicated with inlaid "feathers" of baroque pearls.*

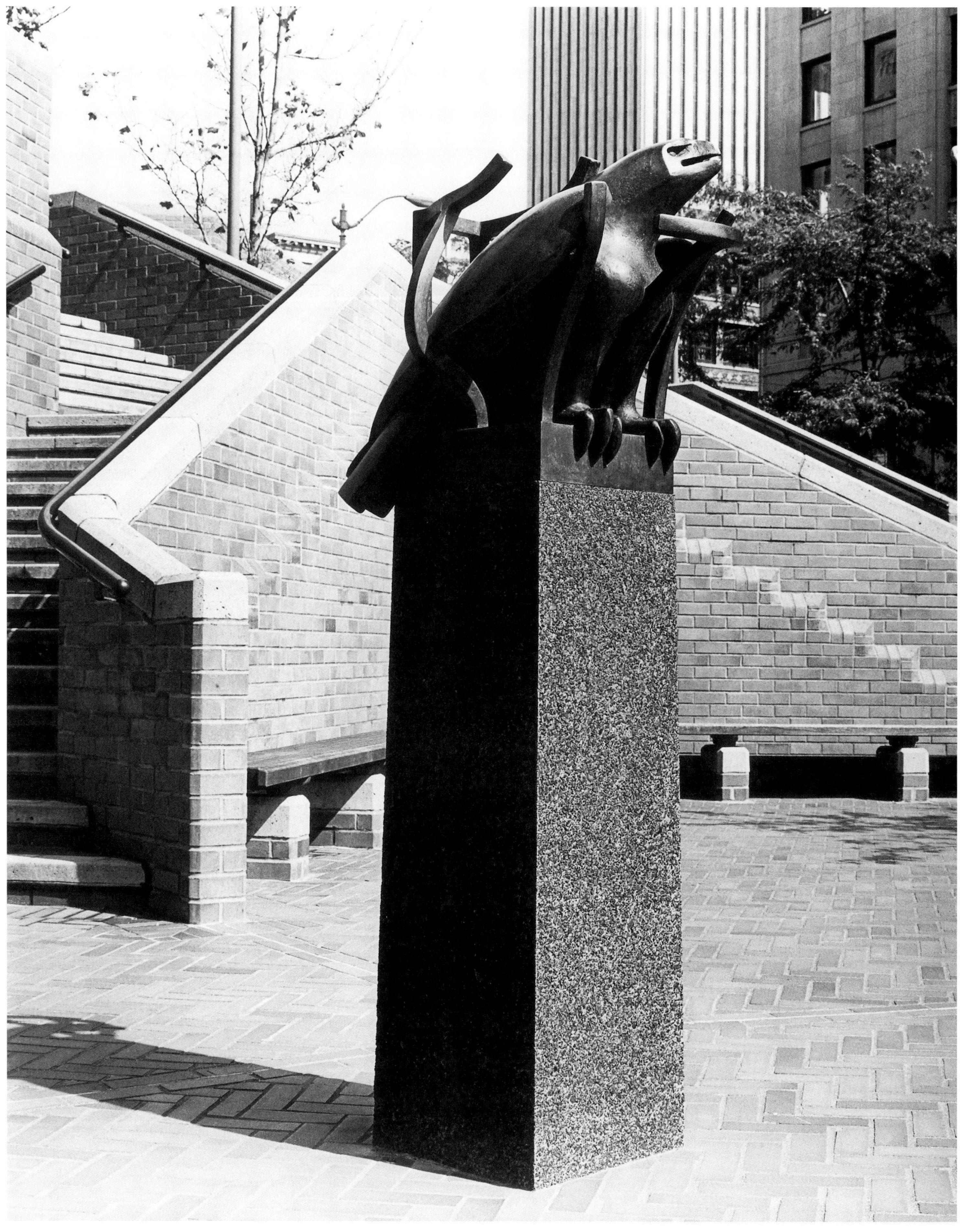

Freedom
1976
Bronze on cast-stone base
H. 23½ in.
Federal Building, Seattle,
General Service Administration, Region 10

McCracken's fondness for owls and herons extends to an admiration for raptors. Birds had been absent from McCracken's work for a full decade when in 1976 he received a commission marking the completion of the new Federal Building in Seattle. He created Freedom, *a bird that has burst from restraining bars to surge forward in an aggressive posture, his beak parted as in a cry of victory. The piece is a direct descendent of McCracken's 1958 sculpture* Caged Bird, *in which the bird is just beginning to push apart its restraining bars (p. 27).*

McCracken said, "Although I have done many bird-form sculptures, specific birds seldom appear in my work, and that is true of this piece. It is the birdness *as a vehicle for the expression of a vast range of life currents that interests me. Further, this sculpture is not intended to represent a specific religious or political condition, but is meant to be translated into the terms each viewer personally sees as representing his own freedom."*

Freedom *is sited on an exterior plaza directly over the Federal Building's lunchroom. Anxious that the bronze sculpture should be securely anchored and as impervious to vandalism as possible, McCracken attached it to bronze reinforcing rods that were to run down into a hollow concrete base which was filled with wet concrete before the rods were lowered into it and the piece was set into position. It had been finished for less than an hour when he yielded to the urging of friends who counseled that waiting for concrete to set up was even less interesting than watching paint dry. He left to join them for lunch.*

A few days later, he returned to show the piece to family members. Someone had swung on the freshly installed piece while the concrete was still wet, and pulled the bronze bird and its bars askew. The concrete had set with the piece off kilter. Fortunately, it had left small gaps in its wake, allowing the piece to be clamped back into position. To hold it there, McCracken's crew drilled up into the open space inside the bronze and pumped epoxy into the gaps behind the rebar, then waited and watched until it was firmly set.

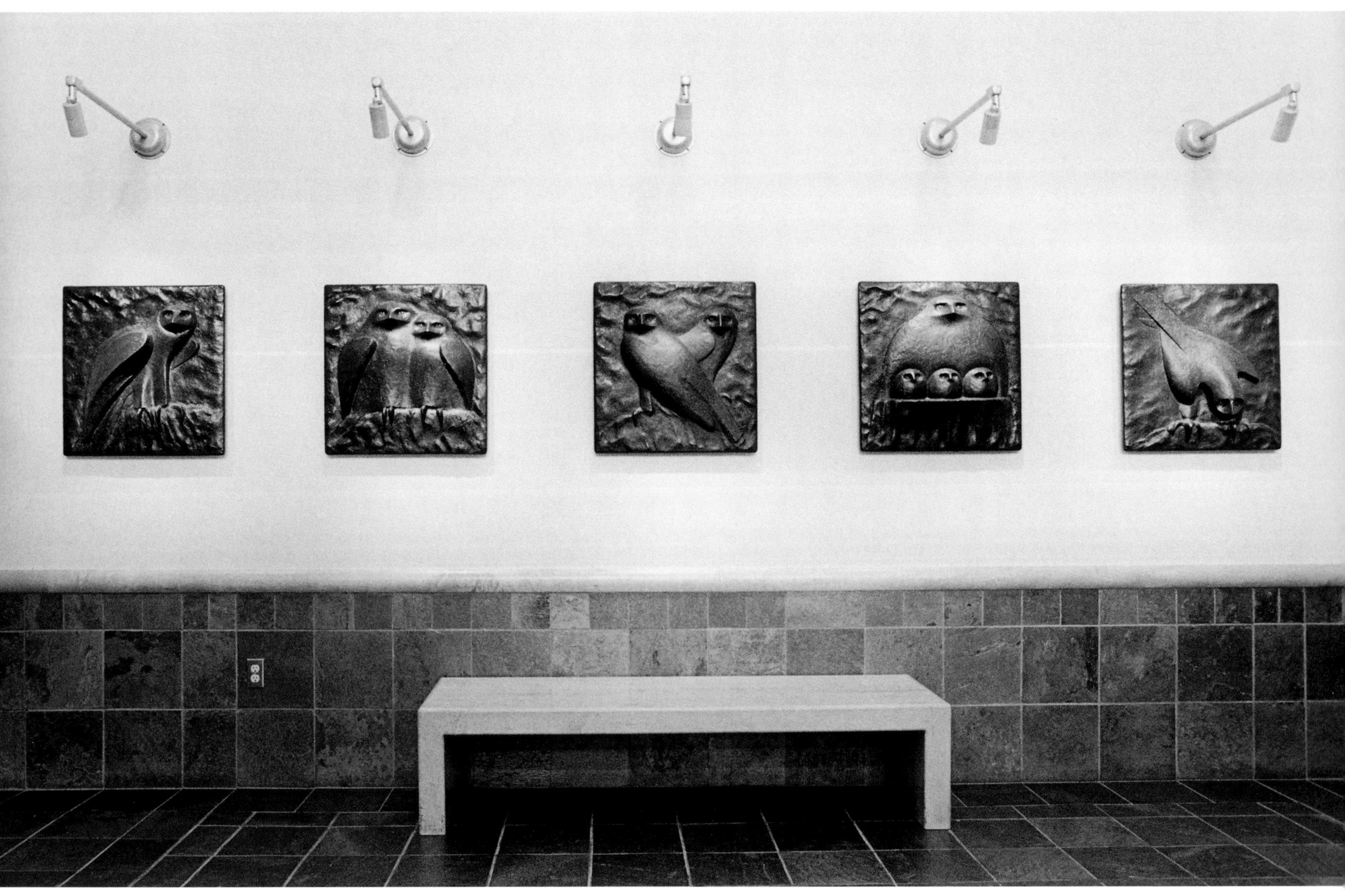

Raptors (Kingdome bronzes)
1978; reinstalled 1999
Bronze
Each, 26 × 25 × 3½ in.
King County District Courthouse, Issaquah, Wash.

Two years after Freedom, *another important public commission was installed. McCracken was one of four artists chosen to create works for the then-new Kingdome in Seattle. The Kingdome was built as a venue for sports events, and for commercial expositions such as boat and home shows. It was slated for hard use, with no obvious place for large sculptures.*

A trip back to England reminded McCracken of a group of ancient Greek stone wall reliefs depicting birds and animals that he had often admired in the British Museum during the time he worked with Henry Moore. They were his inspiration for a series of five dramatic bird shapes, rendered in bronze bas-relief. They were installed in April 1978. The Kingdome was imploded in March 2000 to make way for a new stadium. McCracken's bas-reliefs were moved to the new King County District Courthouse in Issaquah.

Ascending Lark II
1990
Bronze
H. 30¼ in.
Private collection

In 1990, recalling the skylarks in England that sing as they climb in flight from the ground to the sky, McCracken created the lyrical form of Ascending Lark II. *The tall bronze form is composed of a series of elongated shapes that turn against each other in a spiraling curve as smooth as phrases of music, culminating at the peak in the shape of a small bird, its head thrown back in song. It is a piece of pure visual poetry, expressing joy in every element.*

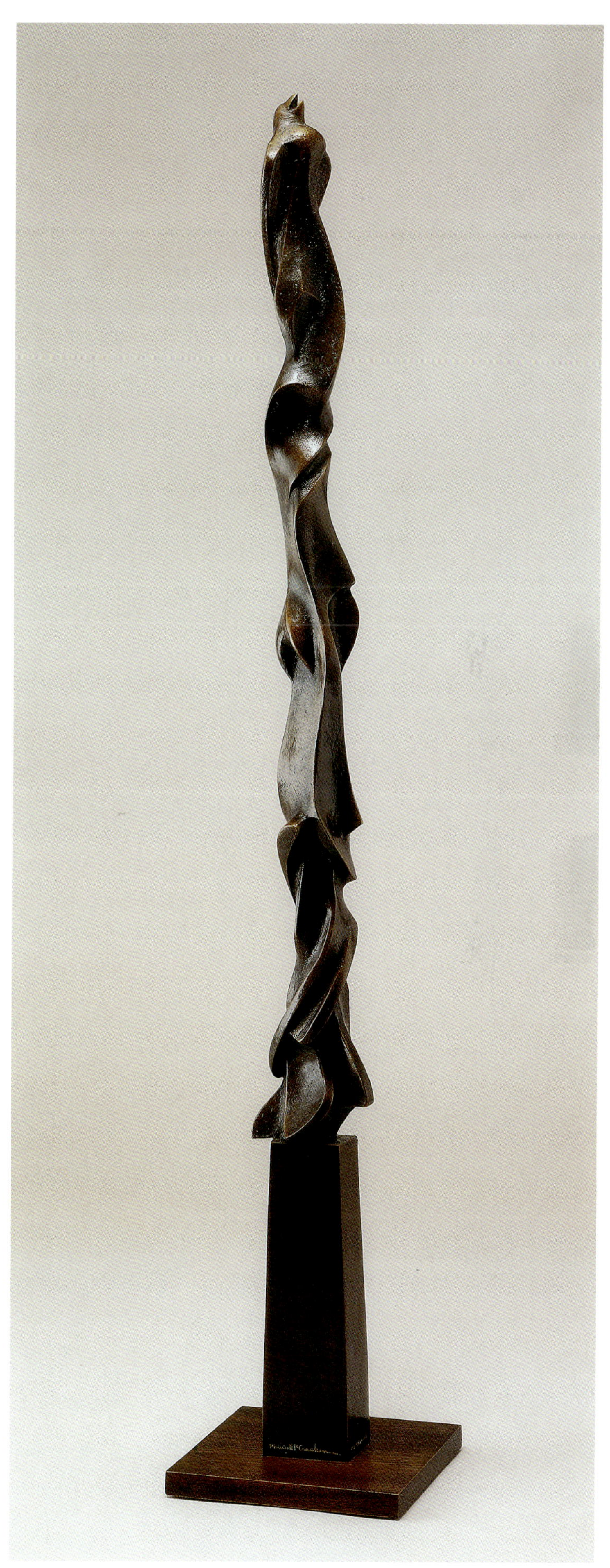

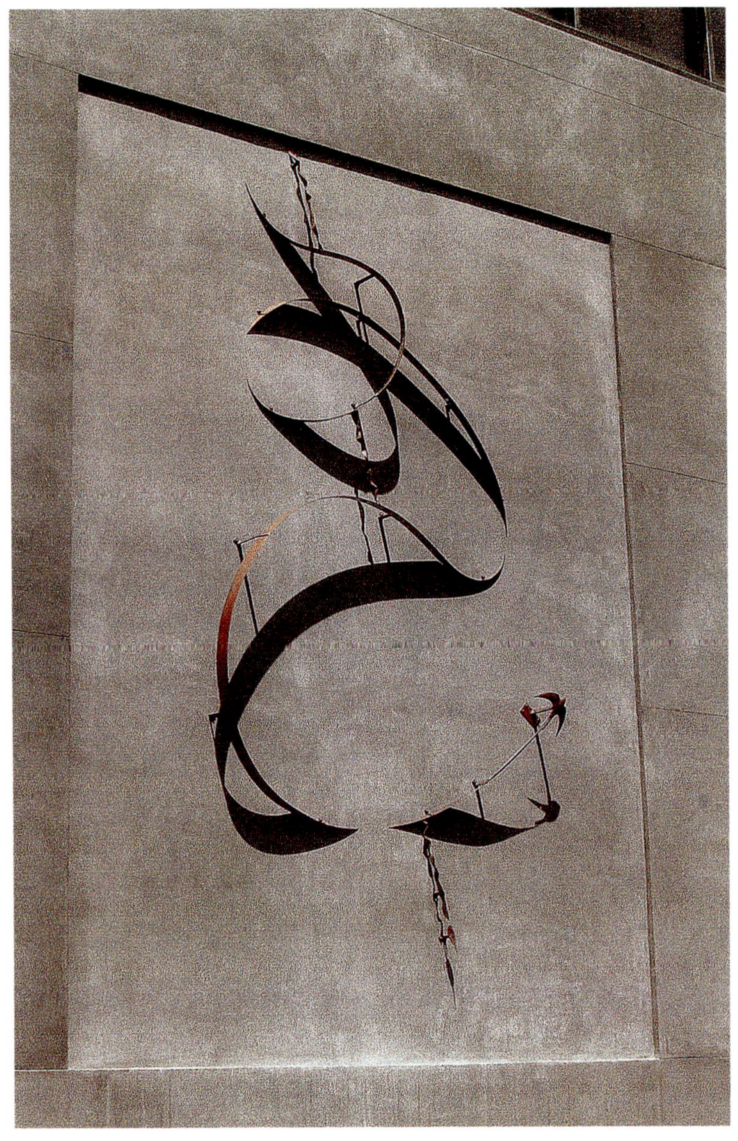

Aerial Play
2002
Cast and fabricated bronze
H. 168 in.
Private collection

McCracken's most original bird sculpture is a private commission titled Aerial Play. *A curving band of bronze traces the flight of a swallow that swoops and soars, playing with a dropped feather. The smooth, arcing metal band that terminates in the soaring swallow and the twisting band that traces the path of the feather are installed to stand forward from the concrete wall on which they are mounted, creating bands of shadow that move as the sun crosses the sky, giving the piece the appearance of Arabic calligraphy. Although McCracken is not the first to enlist the sun as an artistic collaborator, it is difficult to think of any piece in which it has been used to greater aesthetic advantage.*

Michael Gwost, McCracken's assistant, played a major part in the complex fabrication and installation of this piece. Gwost has been a valued assistant on a number of projects since coming to work in McCracken's studio as an apprentice in 1977.

Bird Family
1990
Bronze
H. 11½ in.
Private collection

Curious Birds
1995
Bronze
H. 8⅞ in.
Private collection

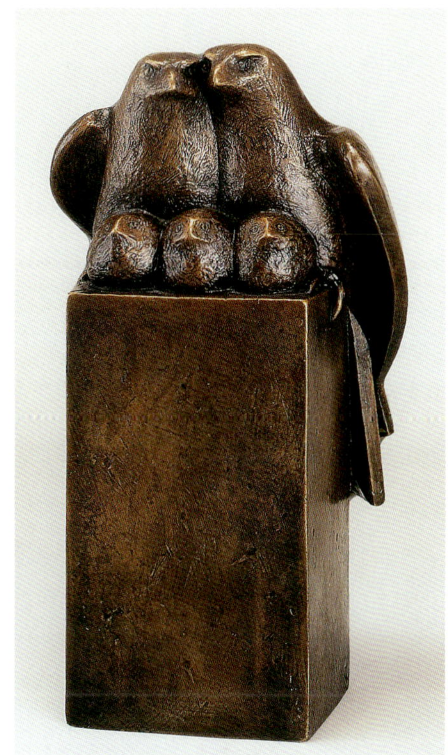

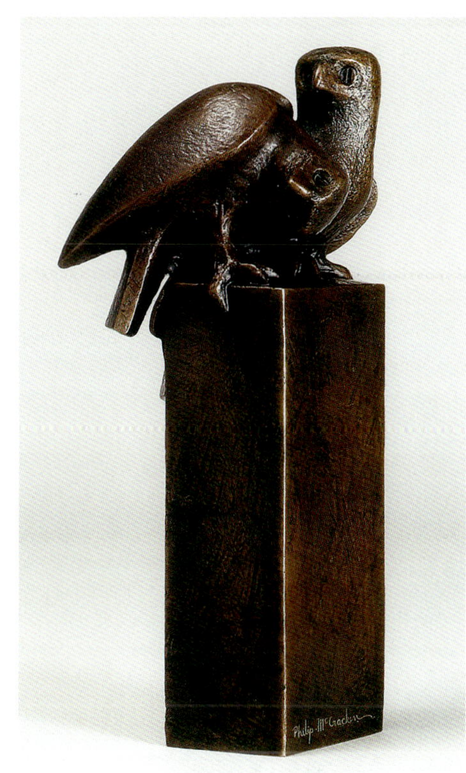

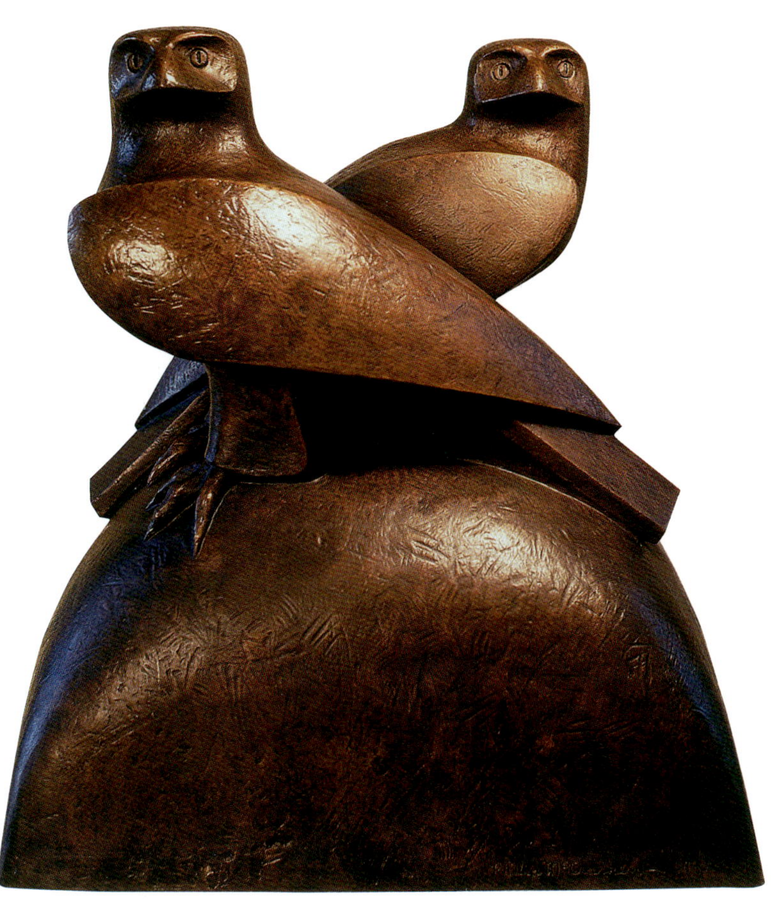

Raptors
1992
Bronze
H. 26½ in.
Private collection

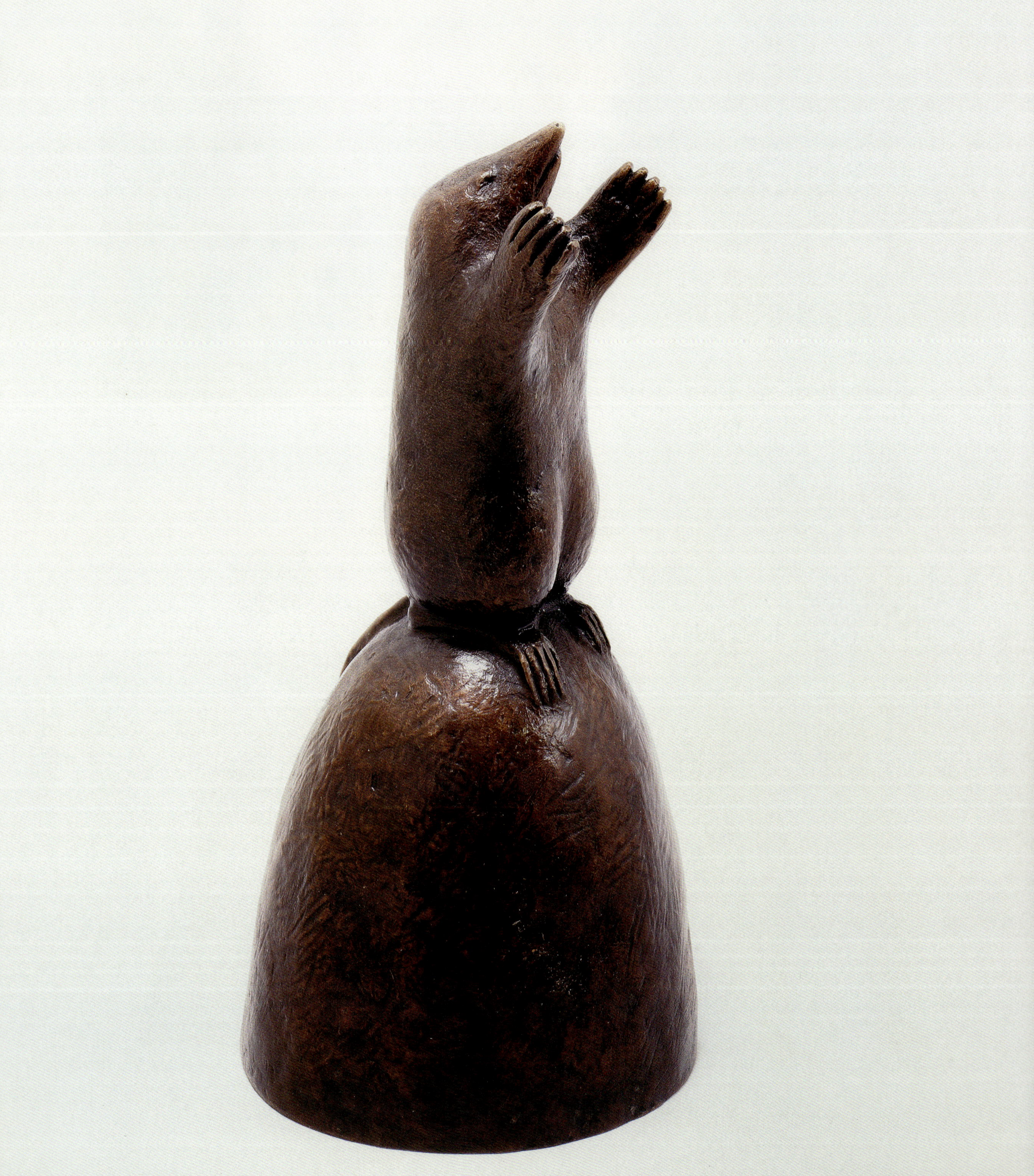

Later Lyricism

McCracken's most expressive works have consistently been those that isolated forms from nature in ways that cause us to look at them with fresh eyes. These pieces are never academic; rather, they are evocative impressions in which lines are sleeked and simplified—honed to the essence of the subject. The style is less minimalist than extractive; it employs an economy of form akin to haiku.

His particular genius has been the ability to translate Northwest flora and fauna into a visual language appropriate to the vision of an enchanted world in which animals stand on equal footing with humans. The tone of such pieces is one of affection leavened by humor. Increasingly, McCracken has chosen the humble and the improbable as subjects for his sculptures: plants such as skunk cabbage and creatures such as jumping spiders. His sensuous forms often carry the dimension of being a hieroglyph on a pedestal. In each case, they illustrate his ability to "see a world in a grain of sand."[1]

It is substance as well as form that makes his sculpture lyrical. Bird skins, and rose burls, and opalescent seashell, and gold leaf—these sensuous materials are evocative in themselves. We are presented with subjects including a mandala, and a meditating frog, and a creature in the midst of metamorphosis. He also takes on that ultimate beauty, a dividing cell, the genesis and the mechanism of life itself.

Mole Greeting the Sun
2003 (see p. 146)

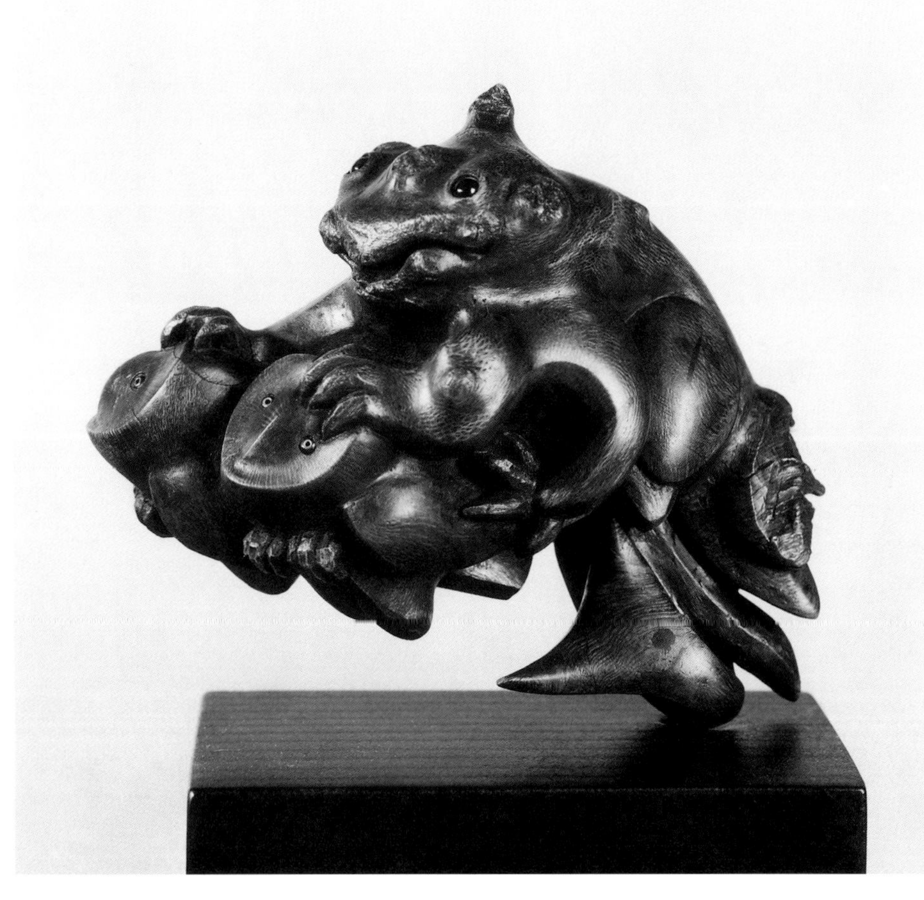

Out of the Garden
1982
Rose burl
H. 10¼ in.
Private collection

The garden of the title is Eden; paradise itself. A creature who resembles a four-armed toad appears to be giving the boot to a pair of flat-faced owl forms. This being, carved of a rose burl that did, indeed, come out of the artist's garden, is without precedent or successor in McCracken's body of work. It is purely a beast of the imagination, which would do credit to a Hieronymus Bosch nightmare. Its form suggested by the burl, the creature balances on a point of his split fish tail. The knot at the top of his head harks back to a fairy tale by Hans Christian Anderson that speaks of a jewel in the head of a toad.

Metamorphosis
1983
Juniper
H. 24 in.
Private collection

This is possibly the most ambiguous form ever to issue from McCracken's studio. Carved in juniper wood, seemingly a creature morphing from an alert bird to a fish—possibly an orca—it is impossible to say in which direction the transformation is proceeding. The form flows with a hydrodynamic shape that appears to be in the process of dividing to twin itself. The body extends from a blunt head aimed slightly downward, a form that has resonance in the hunting posture of Restless Bird *(p. 29). In* Metamorphosis, *the shape is transmuted to become curved and flowing, with rising fins and a ruddered tail, so that it is easy to imagine this creature flying through the water.*

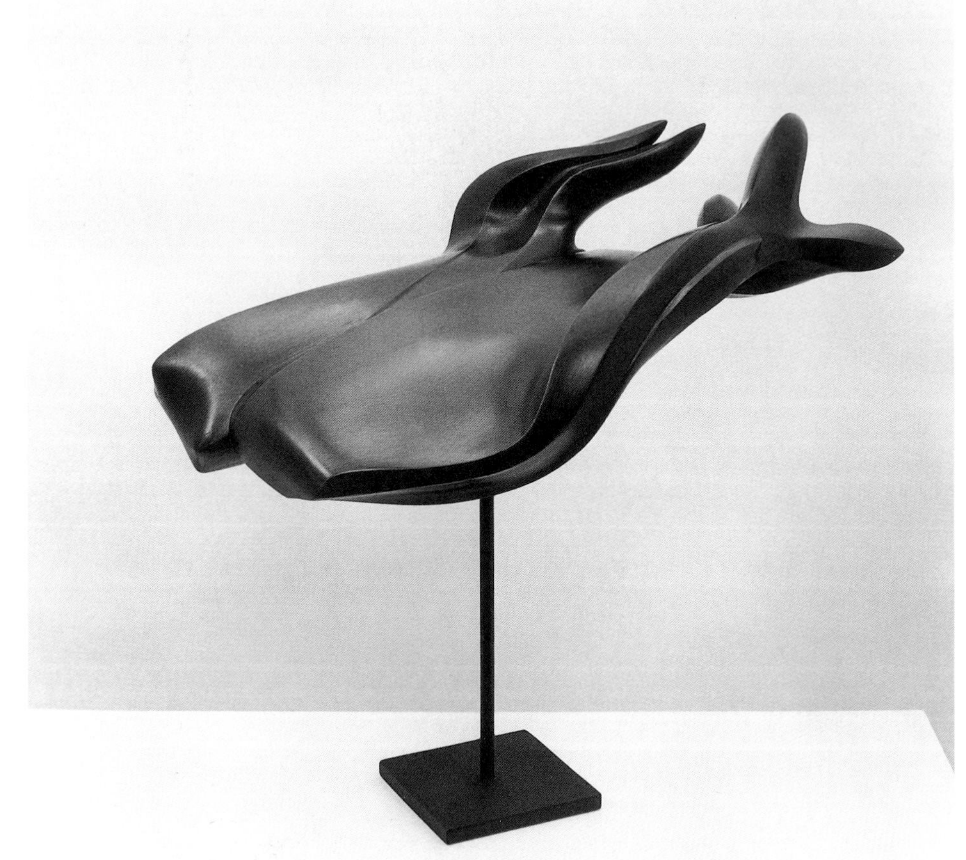

Dark Presence
1983
Juniper
H. 21½ in.
Courtesy of the Kennedy Galleries, New York

A headless creature hurtles upward with the wide-sprung legs of a frog in mid-strike. The impression it gives of nonspecific threat is visceral, as if this nameless creature were startled from some hidden place. Since McCracken brings to pedestal-top scale subjects that, in normal experience, are stellar or cellular, this could as well be a malignant cell isolated as it launches an invasion. Notwithstanding its sinister aspect, the smoothly honed lines of juniper carry a sensuous beauty, with its descending offshoots that terminate in what might be germinal buds.

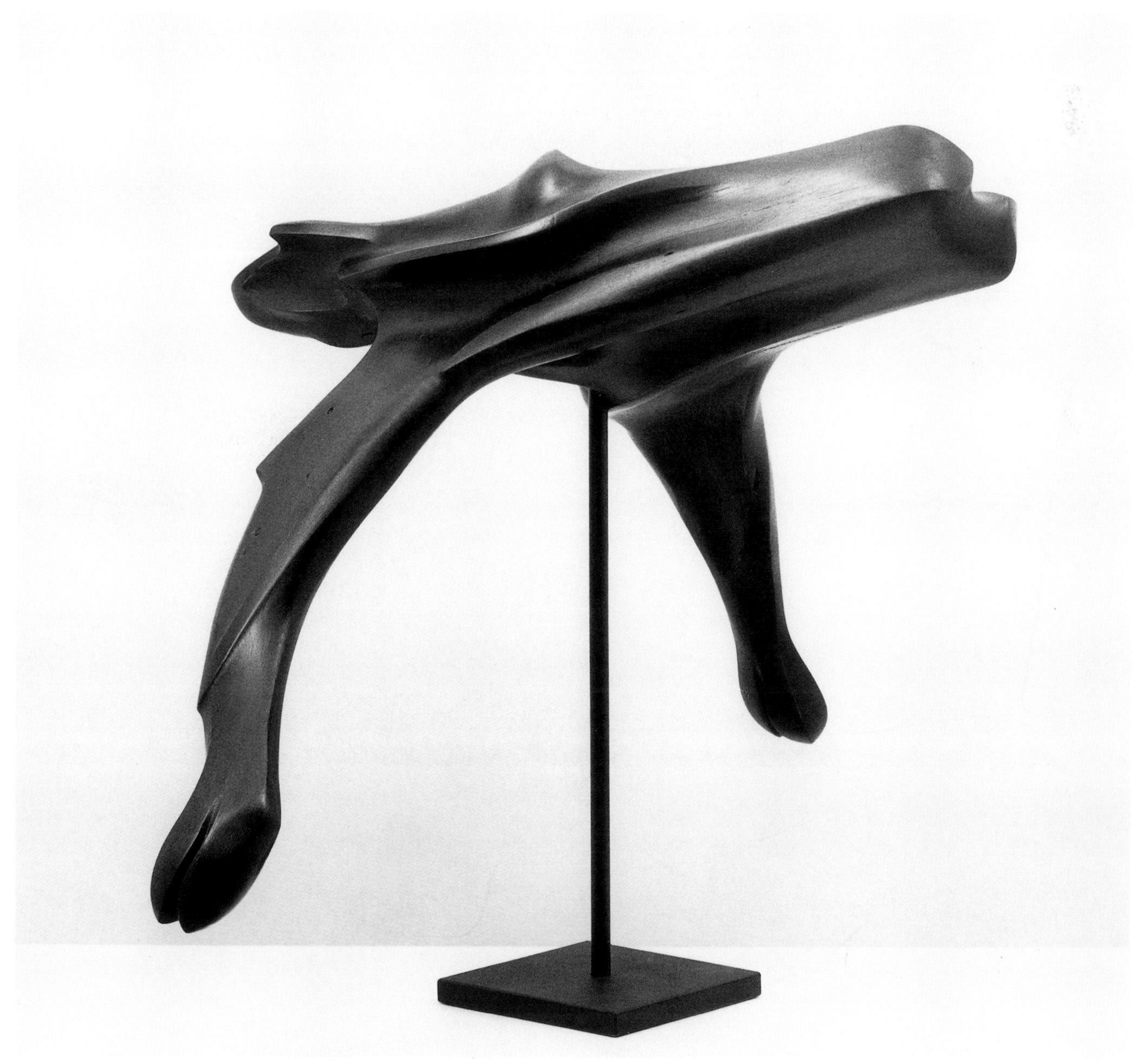

Dark Feathered River
1983
Cedar and feathered bird skins
20 × 52 × 20½ in.
Tacoma Art Museum,
Gift in memory of Marian Willard
by Philip and Anne McCracken

The concept of feathers as a stand-in for water is another of McCracken's unprecedented visions. Once he had the design in mind, he put an ad in the paper and tacked a note to the wall of a local feed store seeking game birds with colorful feathers. From the many that were offered, he chose game birds with hackles—the colorful feathers that rise around the neck of an aroused fighting bird—and starlings, whose green-black feathers are speckled like the bubbles in a stream. He mounted the feathers on a carved matrix suspended over a mirrored base. In 1983, the year Dark Feathered River *was completed, Marian Willard died. She was the McCrackens' beloved friend, as well as having been Philip's gallery representative in New York.* Dark Feathered River *was a gift to the Tacoma Art Museum in her memory.*

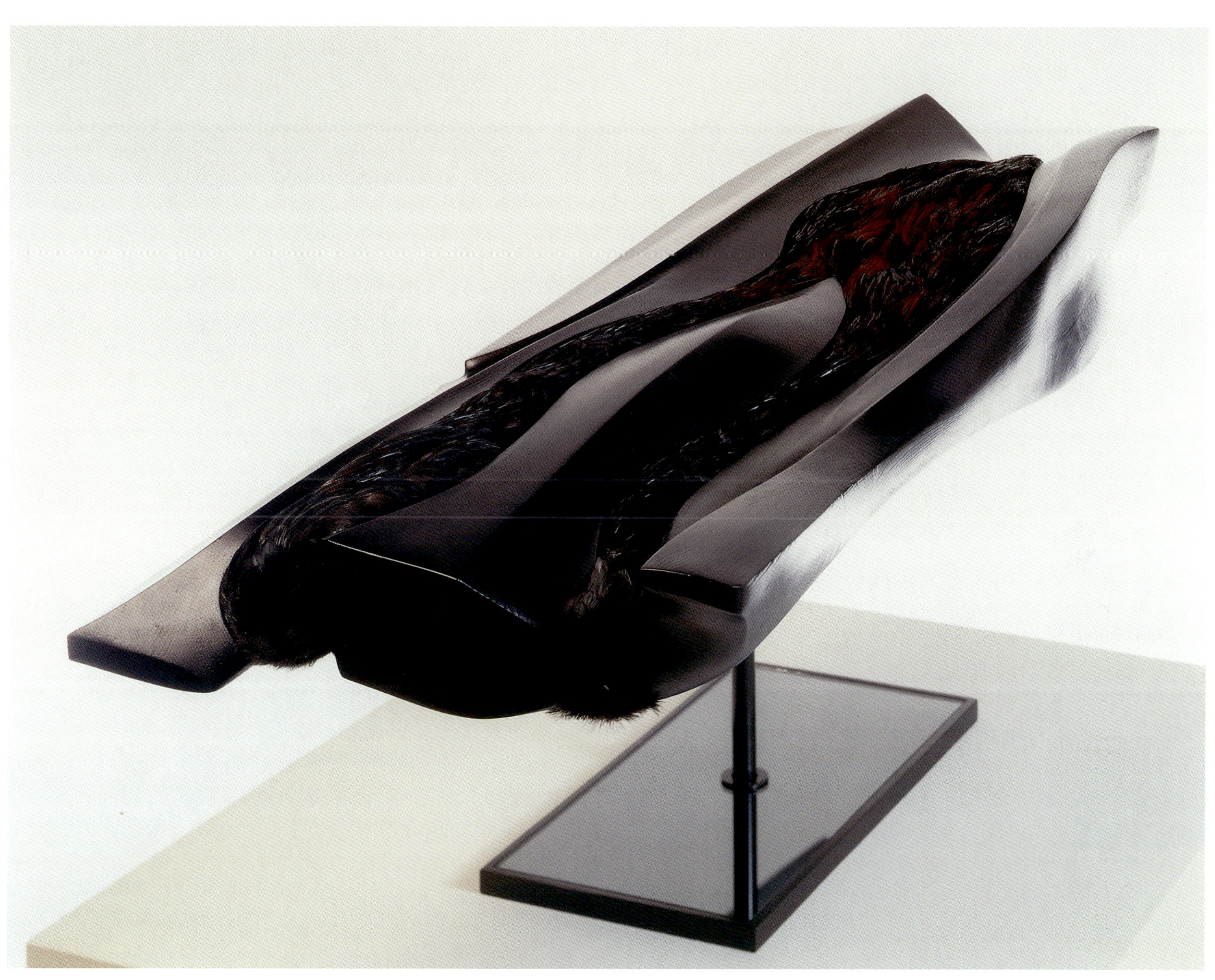

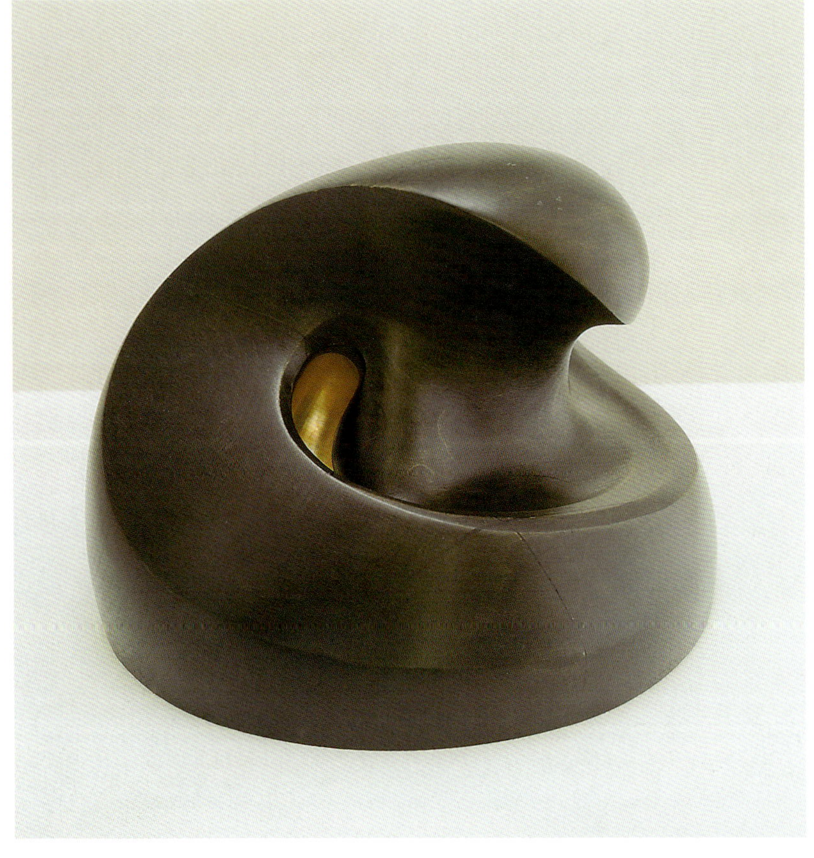

Within Each Wave
1985
Juniper and shell
H. 5½ in.
Collection of Joyce Lovett

The curling peak of a breaking wave is caught in this juniper carving, pierced with opalescent shell. The shape echoes the chiefly headdresses of Hawai'ian royalty, and the ceremonial headgear of certain Tibetan priests. The hovering crest also bears an unmistakable kinship with the nagaraja, *the hooded serpent (cobra) of Hindu lore. The wave's form, in which inside and outside are one continuous surface, carries an almost magnetic fascination. The shining inner surface suggests that transformative energies are in play.*

Genesis
1985
Granite
H. 7 in.
Collection of Colin and Sylvia Graham

Genesis *portrays the true ultimate beauty: the dividing zygote, the cell from which all else proceeds. A single fertilized egg cell will divide into groups of cells, some of which go on to form bones, others brain, and still others all of the organs as well as the eyes, ears, nose, mouth, fingers, hair, and brains of a living person. This is the cell possessed of magic. It is small wonder that McCracken initially thought of this form as "Venus Enclosed." One is struck afresh by the artist's radical originality in creating a sculpture representing one single cell.*

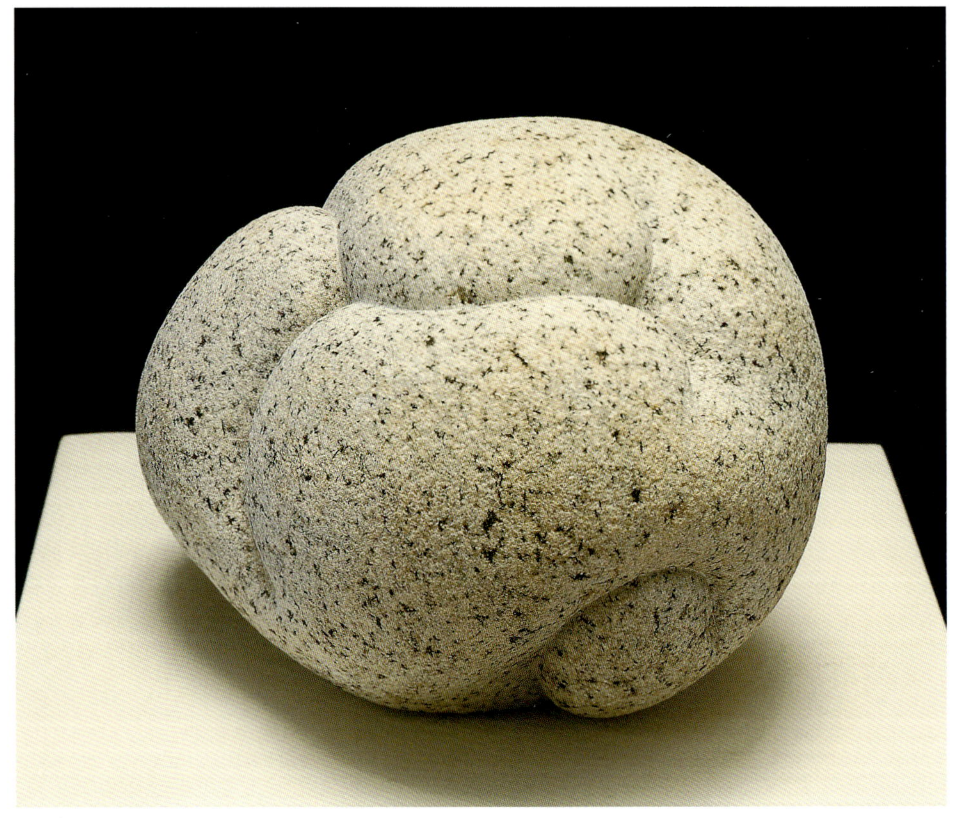

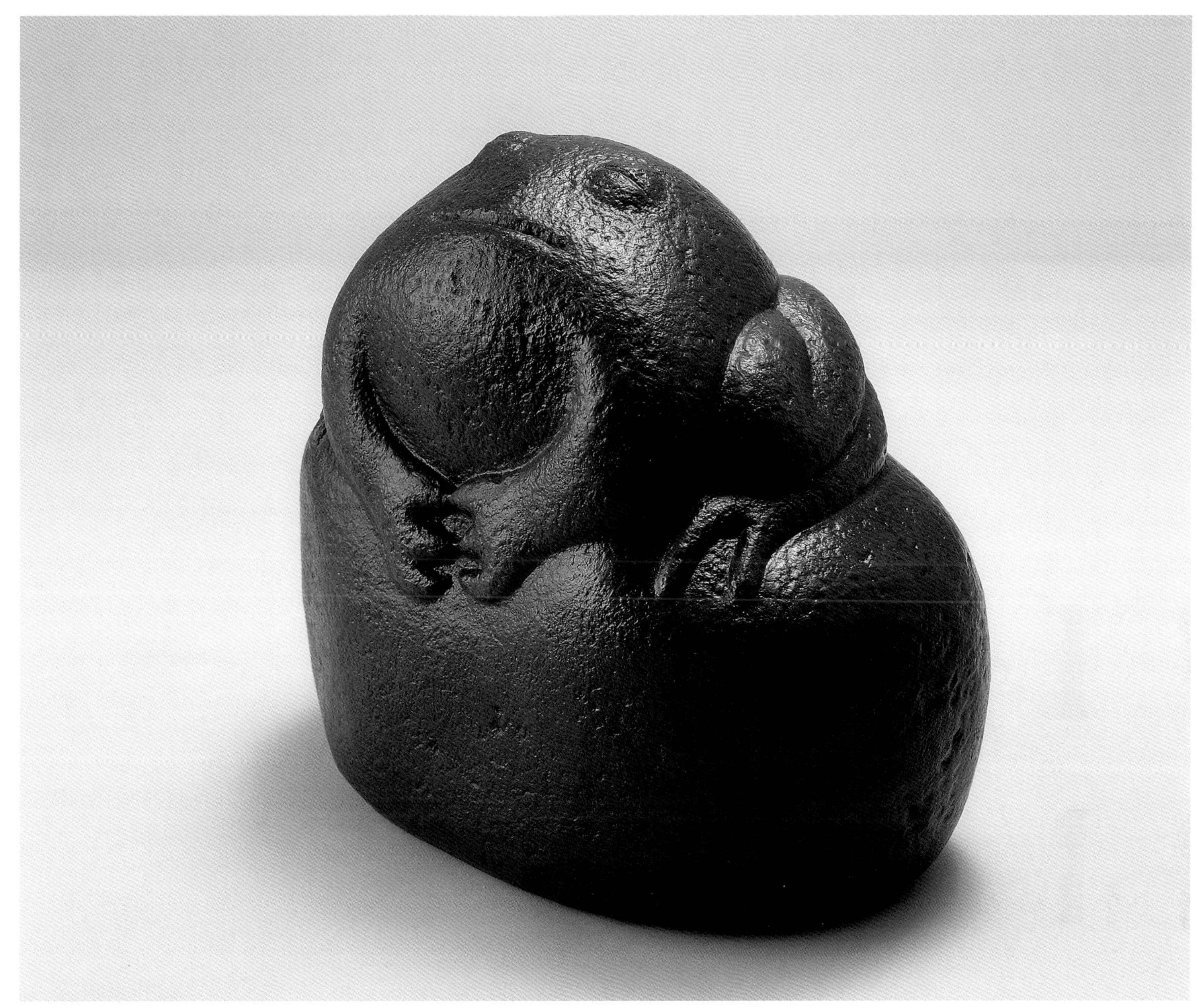

Meditating Frog
1995
Bronze
H. 10¾ in.
Collection of Rod Arnzen and Kathi Gardner

The latent shape of this meditating frog might have existed within a rounded river rock, so compact and minimally altered is its form. Two green ponds in front of McCracken's house nurture tadpoles. A half-concealed frog can often be seen at the water's edge, waiting patiently for a passing insect. The state of motionless alertness is not unlike that of meditation. McCracken's rendering of this frog suggests a precedent in nature for the practice of mindful alertness. First carved from fieldstone, Meditating Frog *was later cast in bronze, which reflects light from its pebbled surface in much the same way as does moist frog skin.*

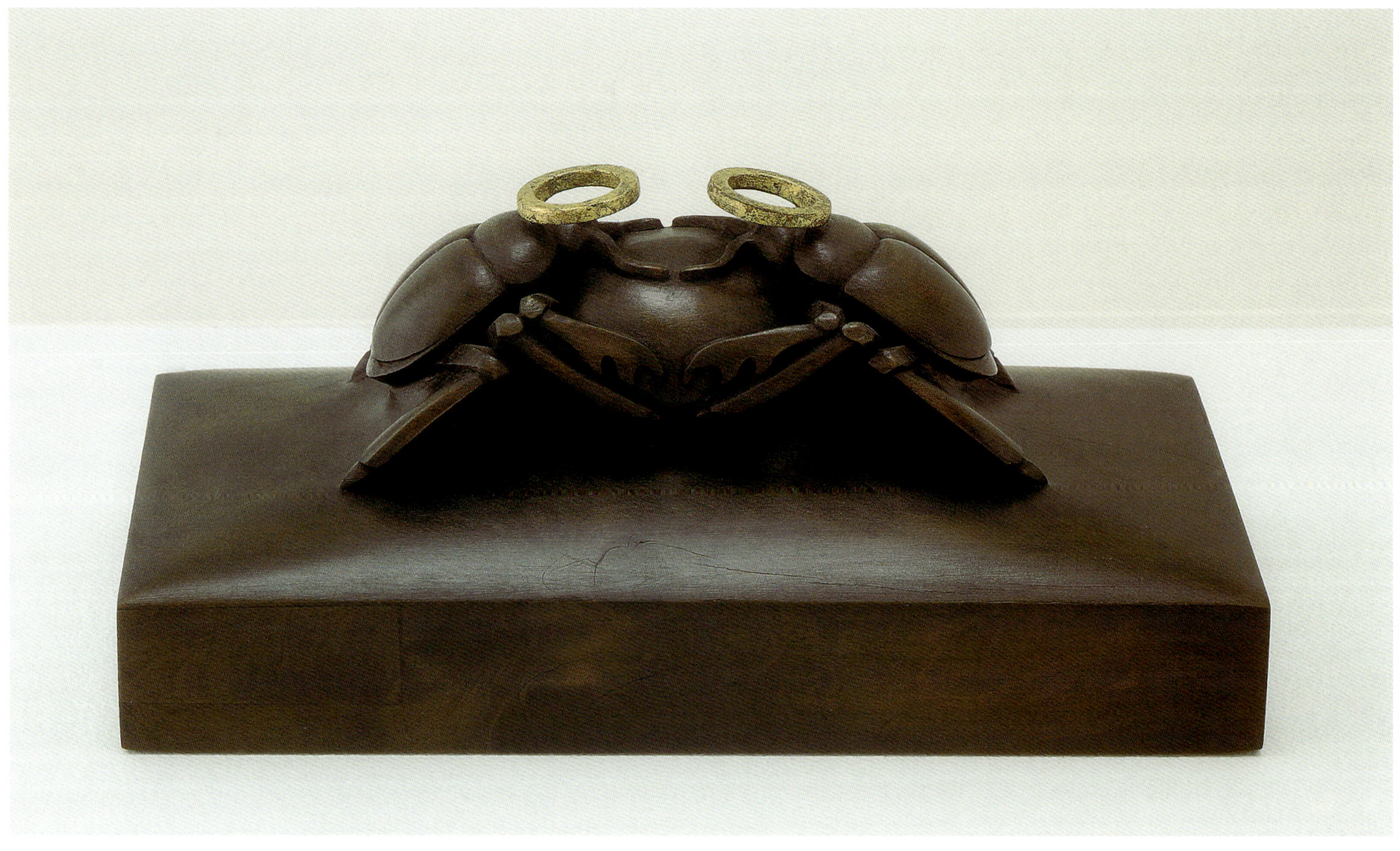

Scarabs
1985
Juniper and gold leaf
3¾ × 8½ × 4¼ in.
Collection of Marshall and Helen Hatch

A pair of dung beetles with haloes recall a famous quip attributed to the British biologist and geneticist J.B.S. Haldane. Purportedly asked by a group of bishops what might be learned about the Creator from his scientific examination of the world, Haldane replied that the Creator had "an inordinate fondness for beetles." This notion doubtless was inspired by the fact that beetles are among the oldest known species—the earliest fossil dates from 265 million years ago—and the most numerous. There are 350,000 described species of beetles. The scarab, a common dung beetle, was revered by ancient Egyptians as a symbol of the eternal renewal and reemergence of life. The birth of scarabs from a dung ball signified to Egyptians a rebirth to life after being buried. The scarab therefore symbolized the eternal cycle of life after death. McCracken's haloed scarabs resonate with that ancient conviction about their sacred nature. "It is a matter of recognizing that all forms of life are sacred," McCracken said. "In the order of things, all creatures have an equal place. An eagle is not superior to a dung beetle."

Birth of a Charmed Quark
1995
Apple wood and gold leaf
8½ × 18 × 6¼ in.
Collection of Margaret Wesselhoeft

A charmed quark is one of the more elusive components of subatomic particles. It is perceived in the decay of the neutral K-meson, in a way that defies the rules of common sense. To those of us who are not nuclear physicists, McCracken's rendering, in apple wood and gold leaf, appears to show the instantaneous confluence of two entities, rising in collision like battling animals locking horns.

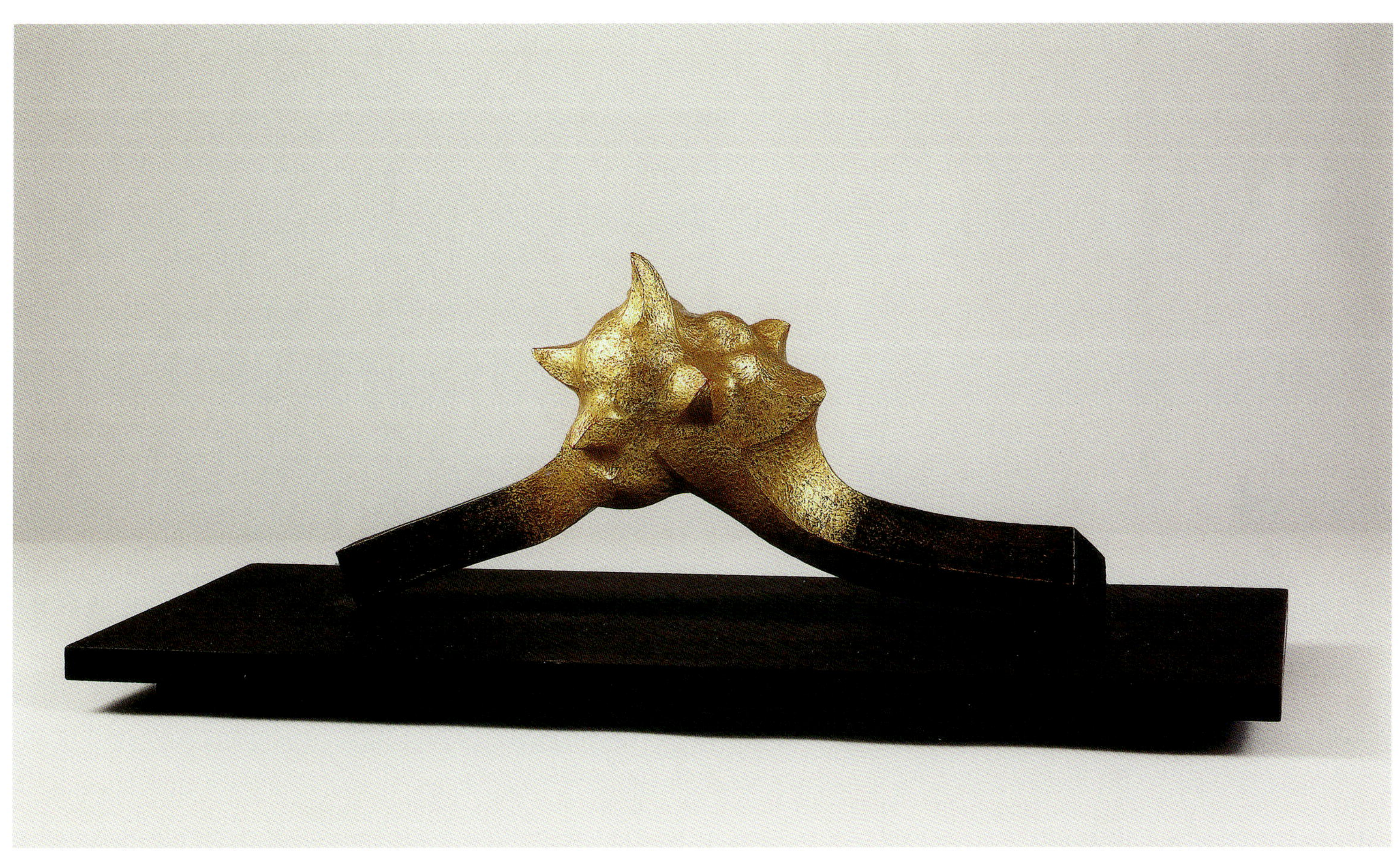

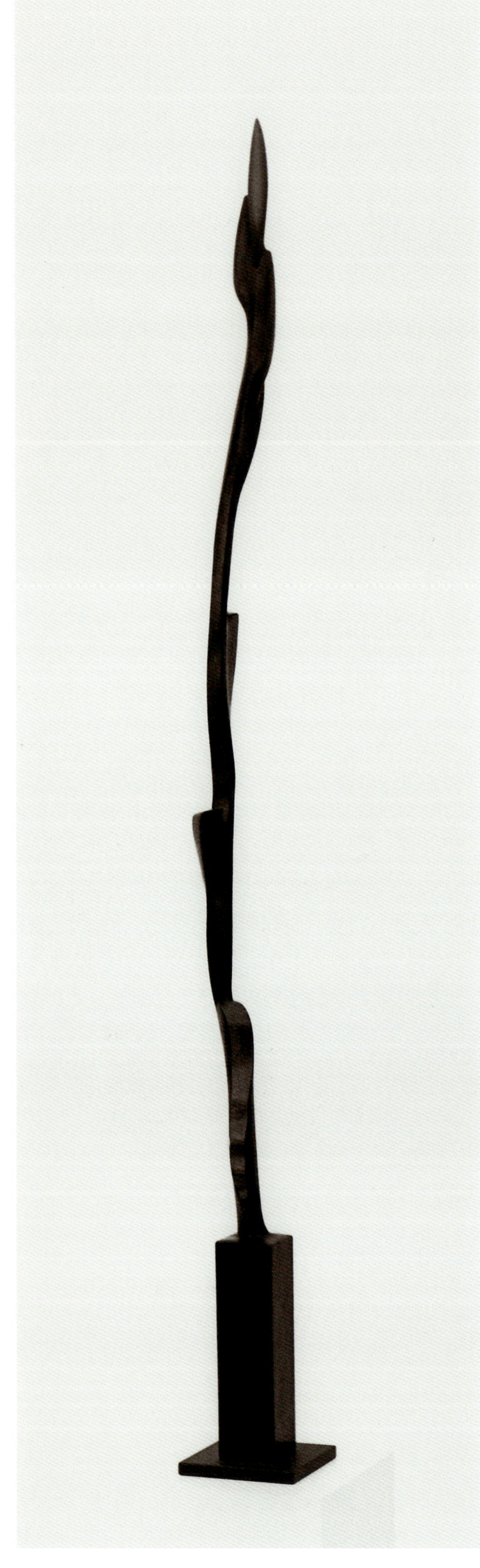

Wild Grass
1998
Juniper
H. 65½ in.
Collection of Marshall and Helen Hatch

The vigor of a weed is visible in this slender, thrusting form that has but one urgency: Grow. Grow. Each upward stab of stem pauses only to emit another burst of the shoot until we reach the freeze-frame instant of a ripe bud. The form gives us the understanding that a thousand shoots of wild grass are not a thousand times more beautiful than one. Rather, they may be one-thousandth as beautiful.

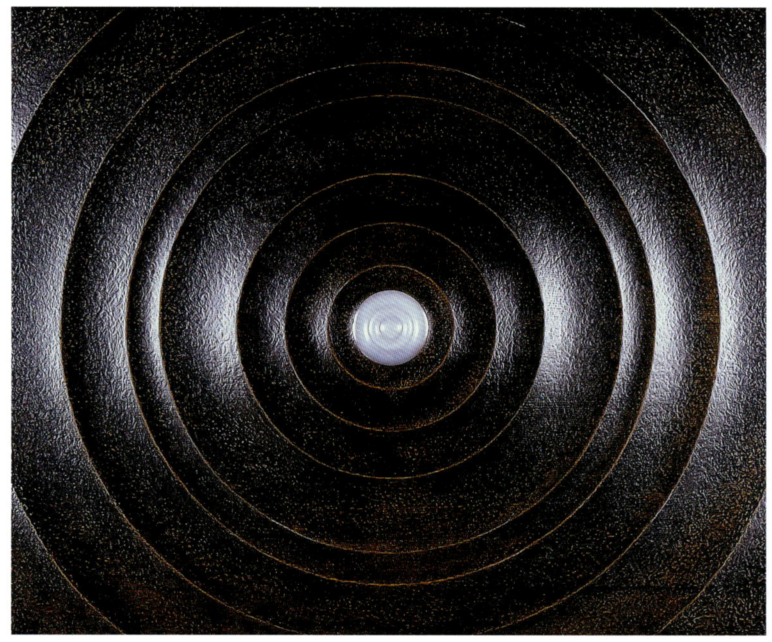

Mandala III
1995
Cedar and quartz
H. 18½ in.
Collection of the artist

Like the ripples of a still pond into which a pebble is dropped, concentric rings of cedar expand out from the nugget of quartz at their center. The form is symbolic of the manner in which a seed thought planted in the meditating mind influences ideas and behavior. The still, bright center inspired McCracken's subtitle for the piece: The Chamber Where Brightness Is Born.

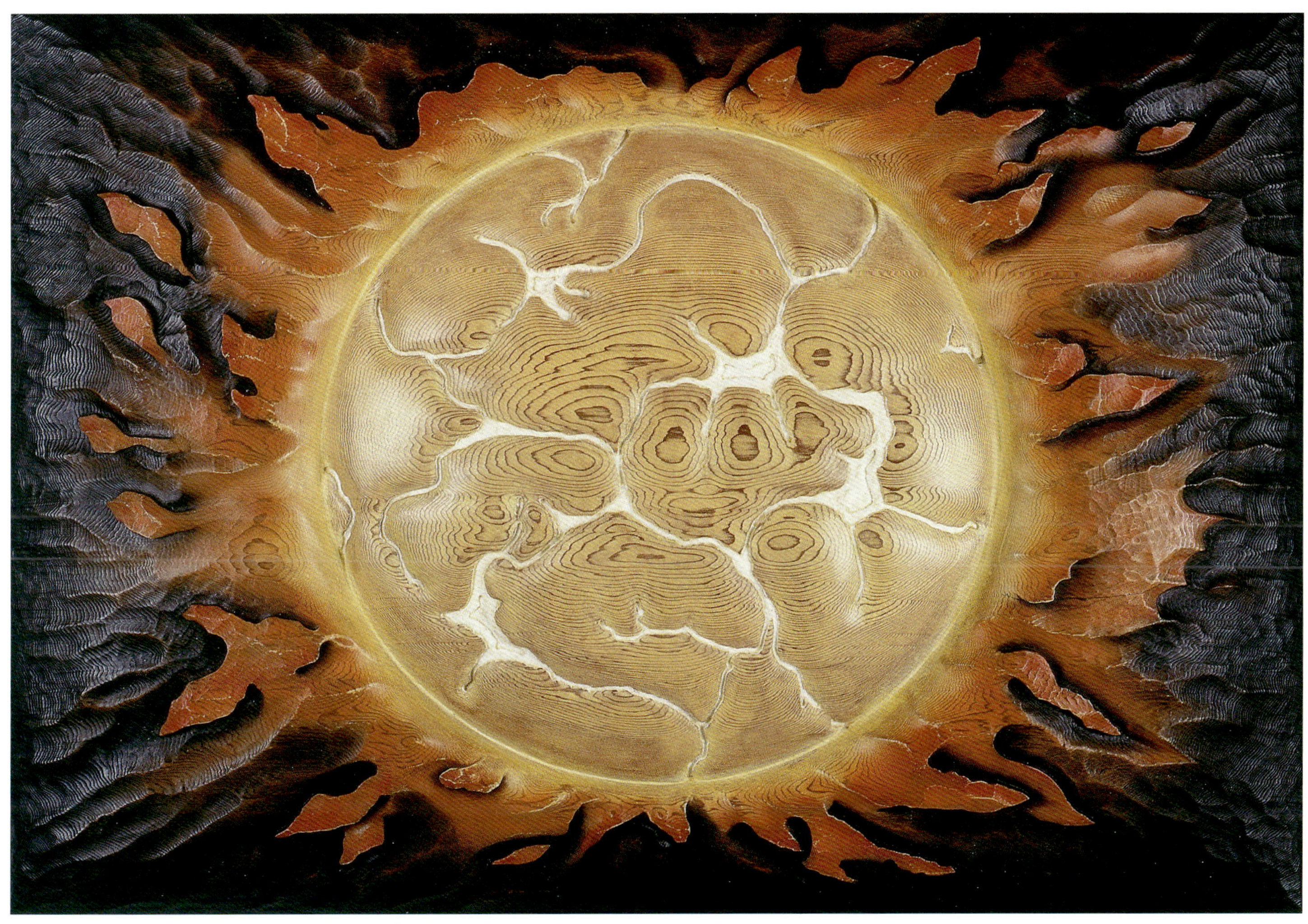

Yang/Sun
1982
Polychromed cedar
H. 25½ in.
Museum of Northwest Art,
Gift of Marshall and Helen Hatch

A surface that resembles a bulging, cracked mud flat burns with inner heat that radiates an aurora of flame. It is the essence of Yang, the bright power that symbolizes the male principle in Han Chinese philosophy.

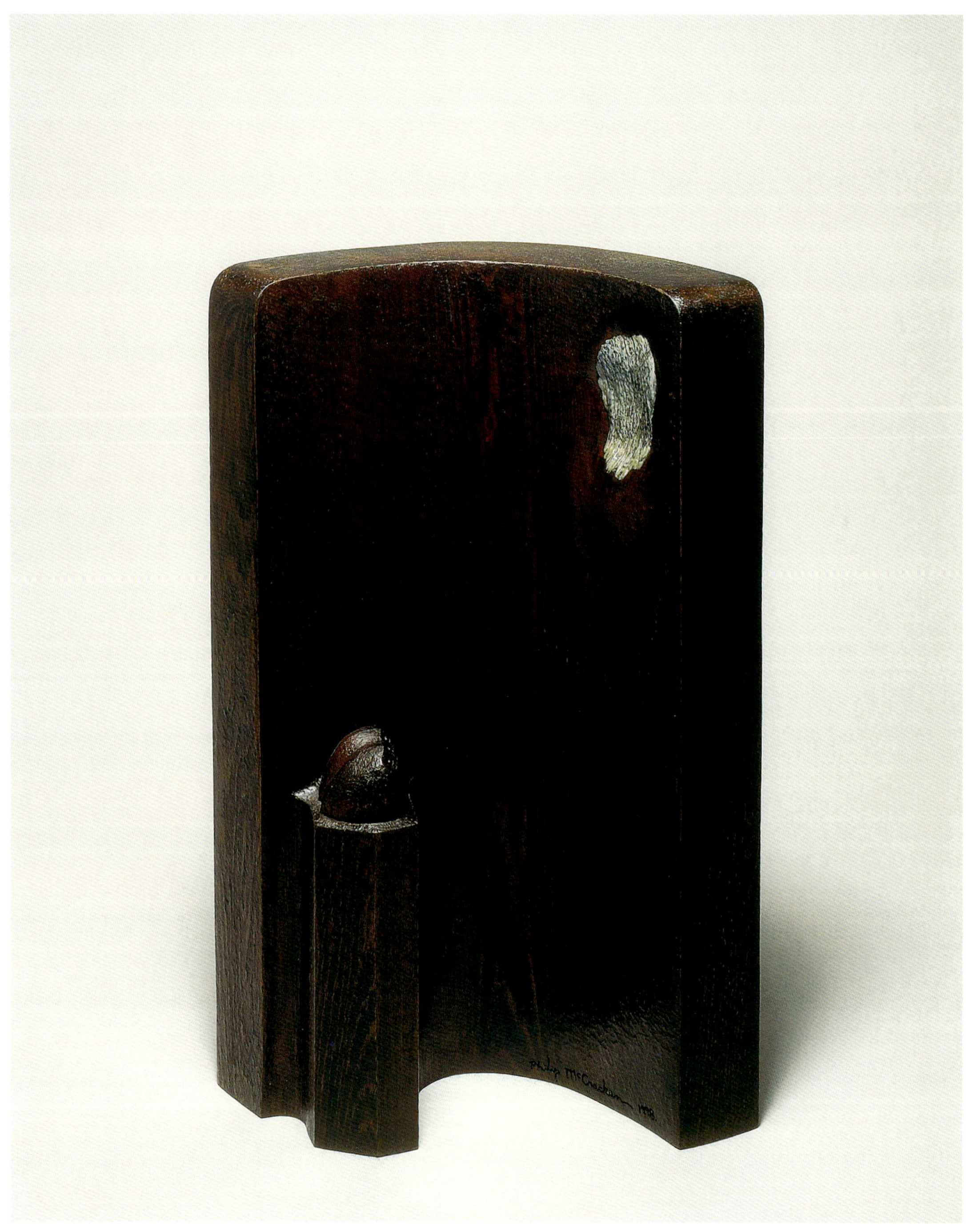

Night Sky
1998
Cedar and shell
H. 16 in.
Private collection

A pair of young birds, small against the night sky, huddle together, held in thrall by a blaze of moonlight, in the form of iridescent abalone shell, in the dark curve of the enveloping night sky. The birds and their perch are cut from a piece of wood continuous with the arc of the sky, which was given its curve to create the form of an enclosed theater. In making this shape, McCracken said he had in mind the closing words of Shakespeare's play The Tempest: *"We are such stuff as dreams are made on, and our little life is rounded with a sleep."*

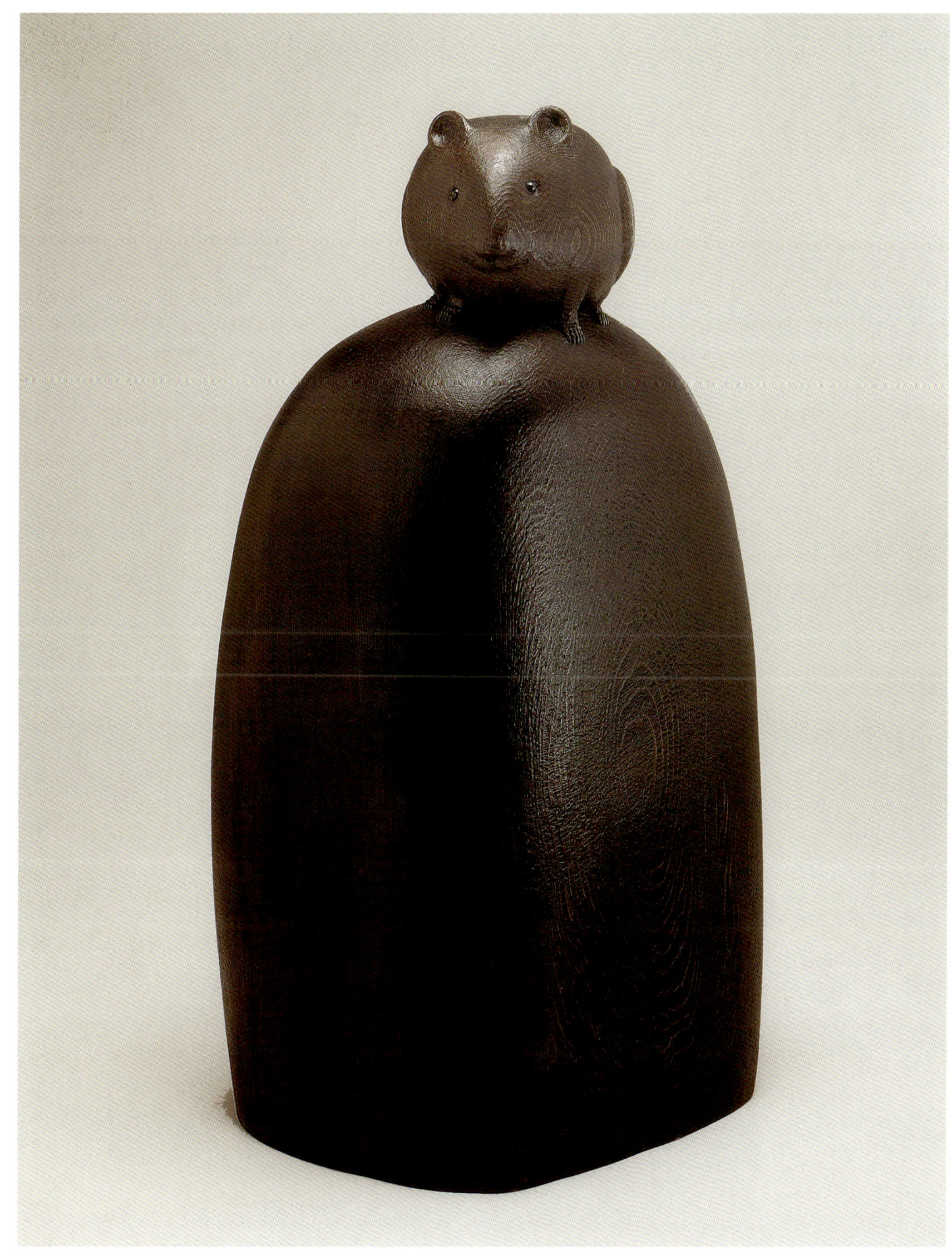

Pika/Mountain Sentinel
2001
Cedar and onyx
H. 21½ in.
Collection of Tim and Gail Bruce

This is one of McCracken's rare life portraits of a wild creature. The cedar carving captures the direct stare of a curious pika. Pikas, with their shrill whistle, are common sights on high trails of Western mountains. They are not rodents, as they might appear, but short-eared, short-legged, tailless lagomorphs—members of the same order as rabbits.

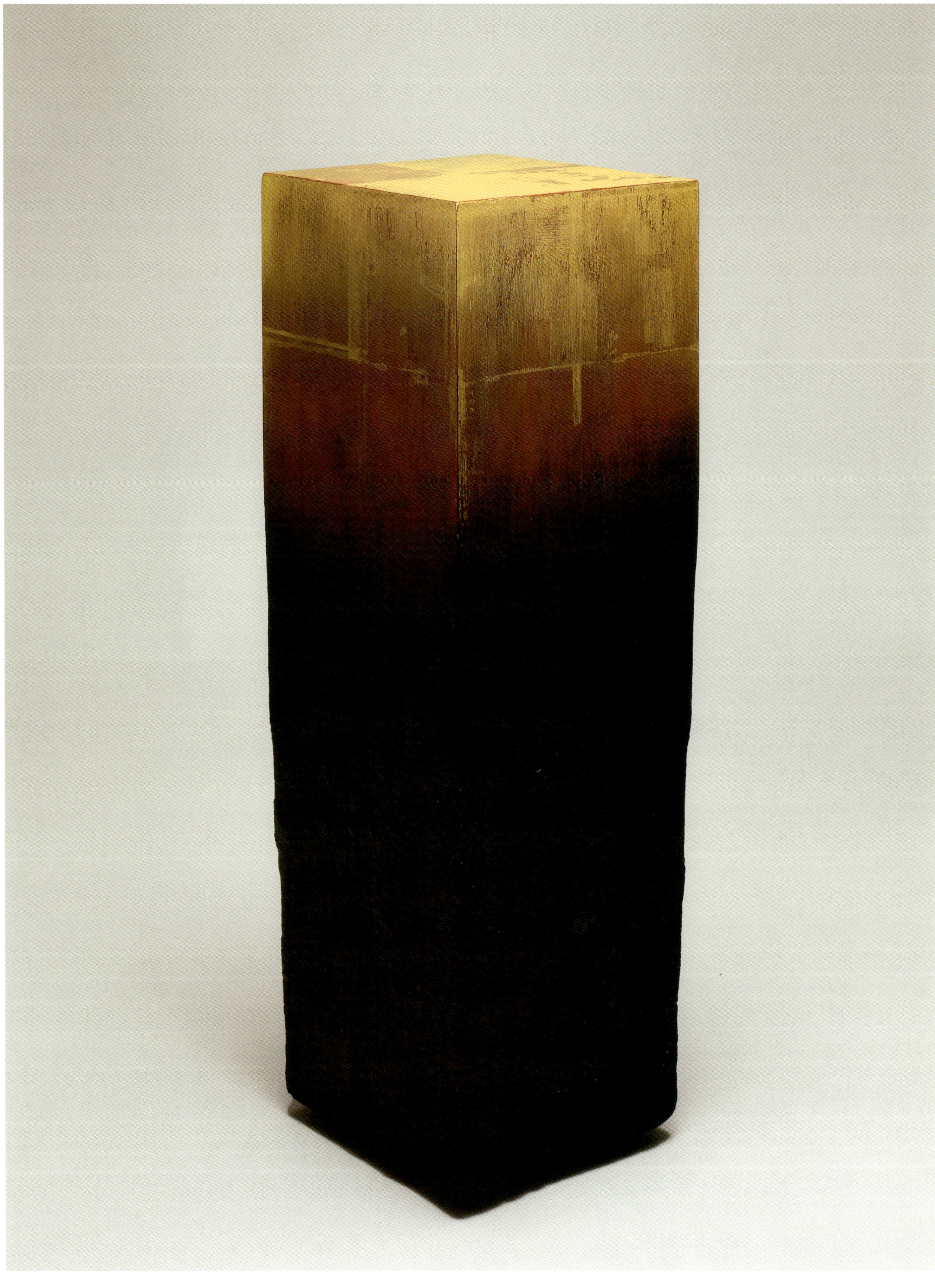

Plan A, Plan B
2001
Scorched cedar and gold leaf
H. 20⅛ in.
Collection of the artist

On a cool artistic level, the sculptor could see two equally interesting possibilities for a pillar of cedar—Plan A: its surface burnished with gold (symbolic of birth), or Plan B: charred and fissured (symbolic of death). The plans are yin and yang, burnished on top, charred on the bottom, symbolic of the course of a life from birth to death. Because it speaks of movement and the essential flow of life, showing them together, as "Plan A, Plan B," is more beautiful and more meaningful than either of them alone.

Cryptic works such as Plan A, Plan B *invite more than a single interpretation. Although the piece was created before the World Trade Center tragedy of September 11, 2001, some have seen in it a premonition of what was to come.*

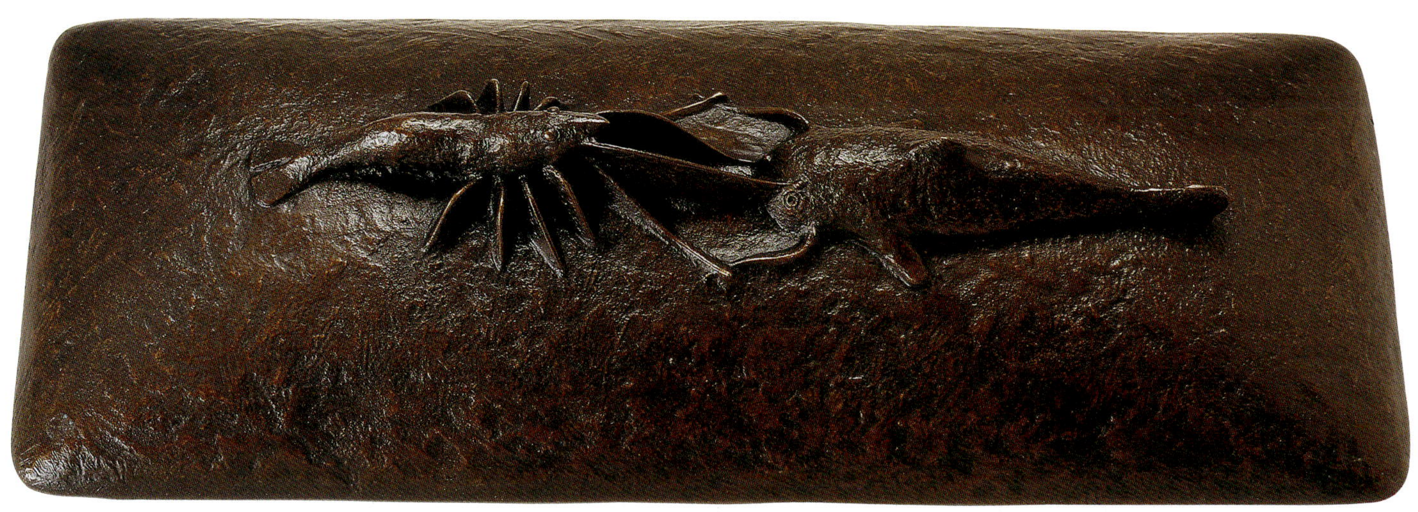

Encounter
2001
Bronze
3 × 13¾ × 2¼ in.
Collection of the artist

A shrimp and a catfish face off, touching antennae in mutual exploration. They are vastly different from each other, yet they employ only the lightest touch to sense the strangeness each has encountered.

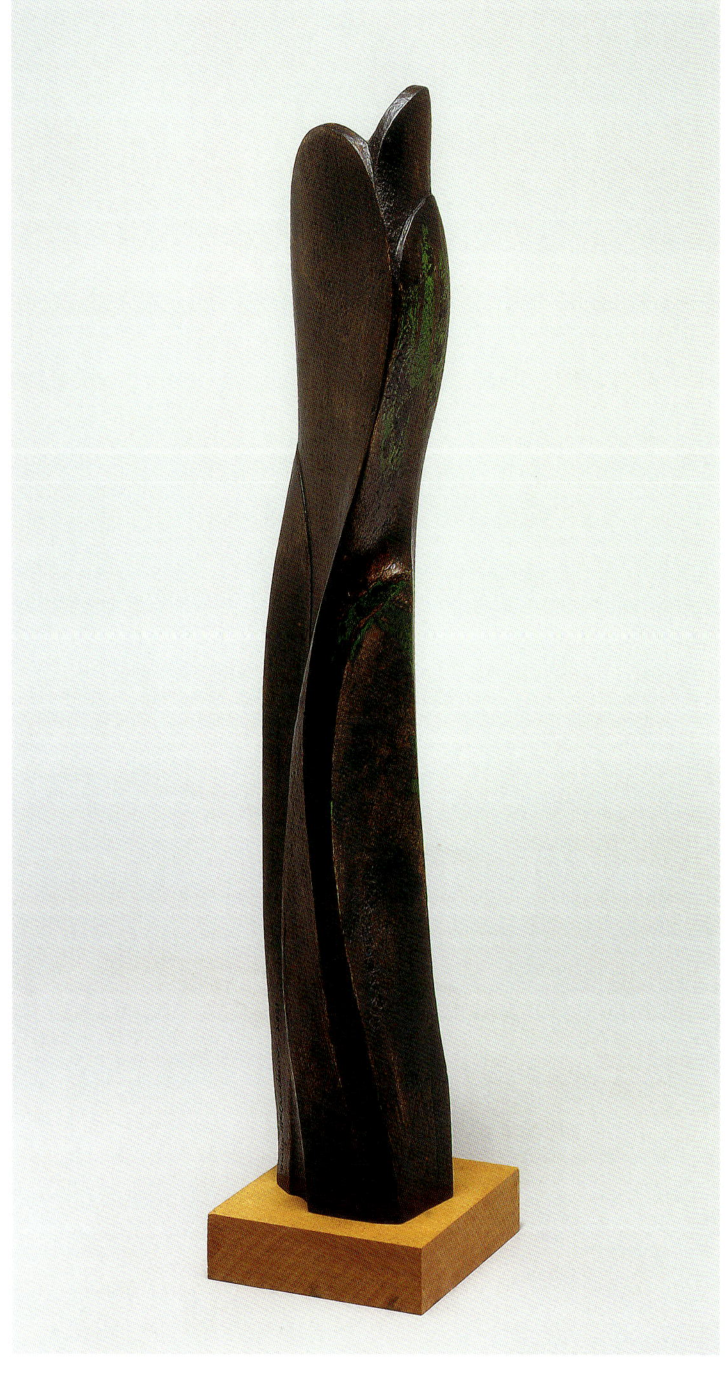

Spring Arum
2001
Alder
H. 18 in.
Private collection

The thrusting bud of Spring Arum *is stylistically related to McCracken's 1972 sculpture,* Spring. *Rendered in softly polished alder, this arum—a family that includes the calla lily, skunk cabbage, jack-in-the-pulpit, and the anthurium—may be generic. Or it might well have been inspired by the Titan arum, the world's largest flower, which blooms in early May, carries more a stink than a scent, and can reach more than six feet in height.*[2] Spring Arum *is a budding shoot seeking the sun. Like McCracken's* Scarabs, *it honors a little-appreciated life form.*

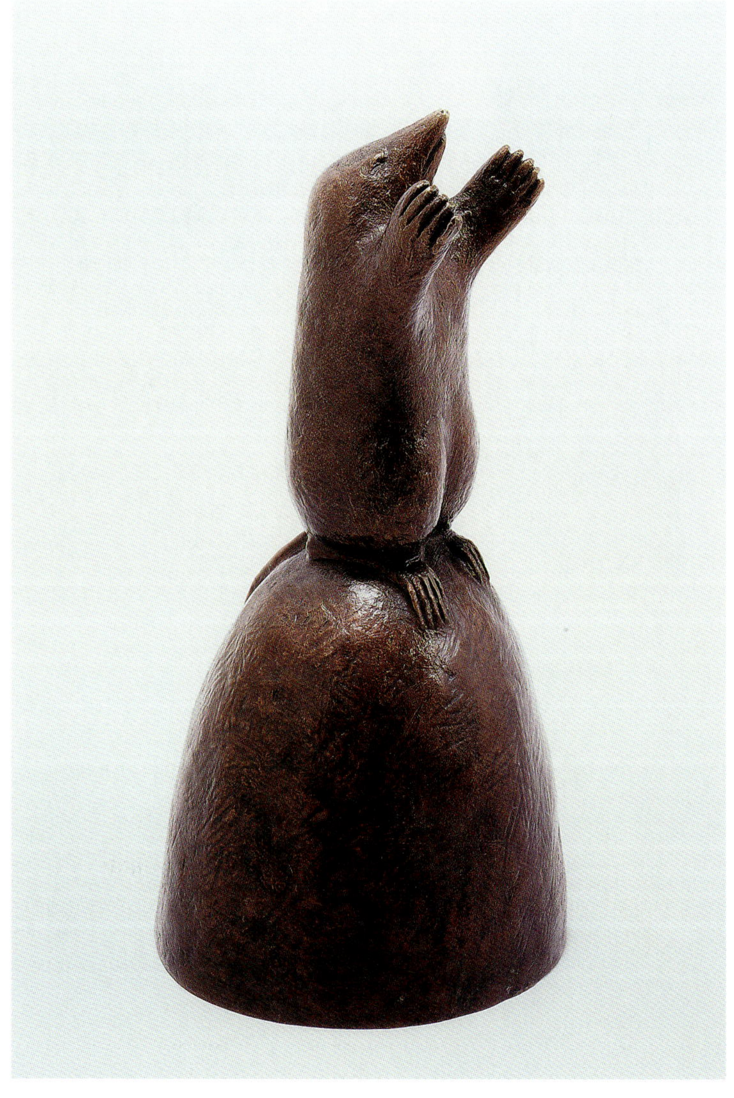

Mole Greeting the Sun
2003
Bronze
H. 6½ in.
Private collection

This small bronze signifies a process of transformation. A mole, a creature who lives its life in darkness, has crawled out of its burrow, and is seeing the light perhaps for the first time. McCracken understood it as a depiction of enlightenment; a process of being transformed into a spiritual being by "seeing the light."

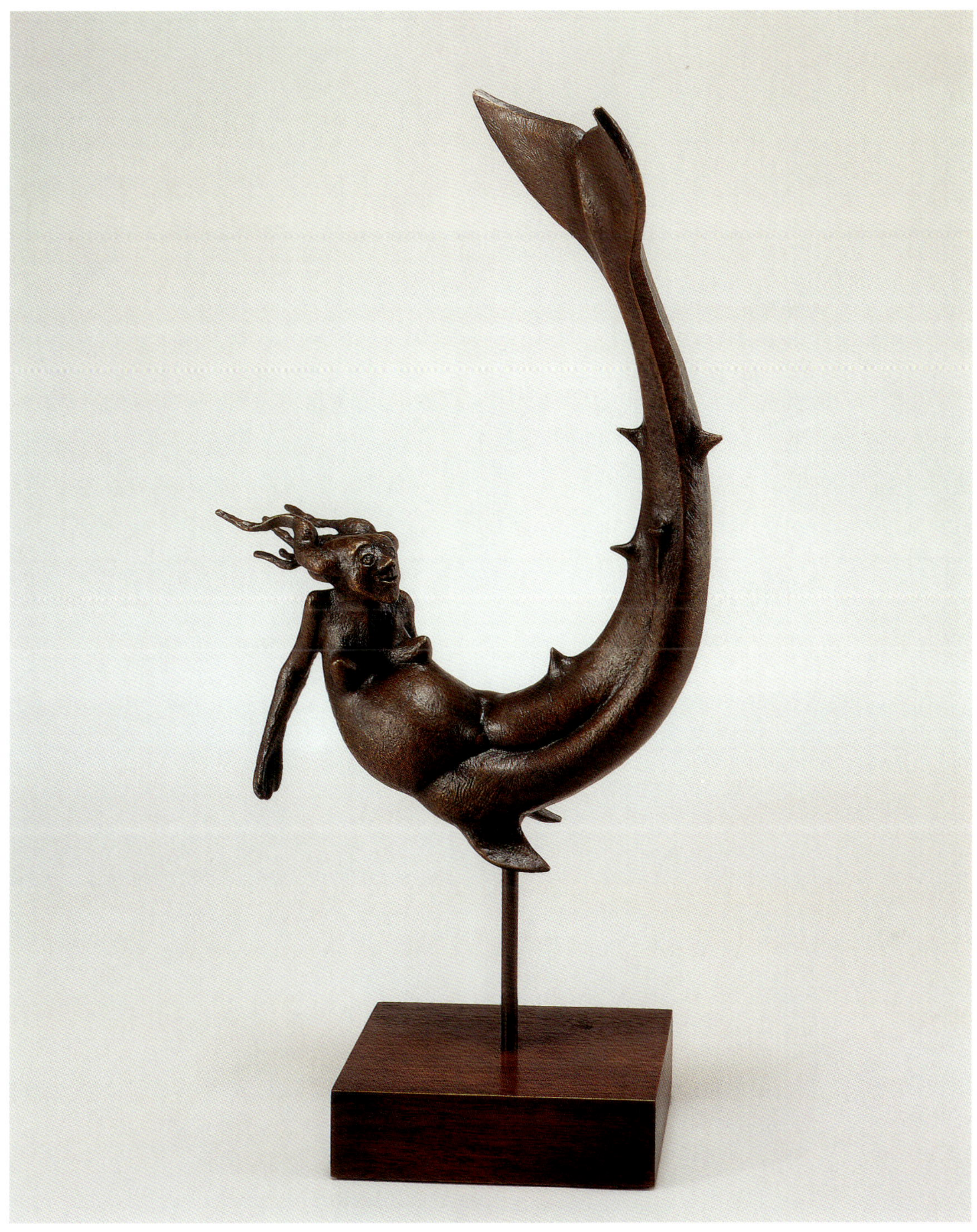

Pregnant Mermaid
2001
Bronze
H. 22 in.
Collection of the artist

Some ideas are so natural and inevitable that it seems nearly impossible they should not have been presented before. So it is with the pregnant mermaid. The image is particularly arresting because one cannot avoid speculating on the paternity of the merchild-to-be. Cast in bronze, the mermaid appears to have been discovered and stopped in action as she swims, her hair flowing in the current. Her face is that of a wild, non-human creature, neither benign nor evil, from another realm of being.

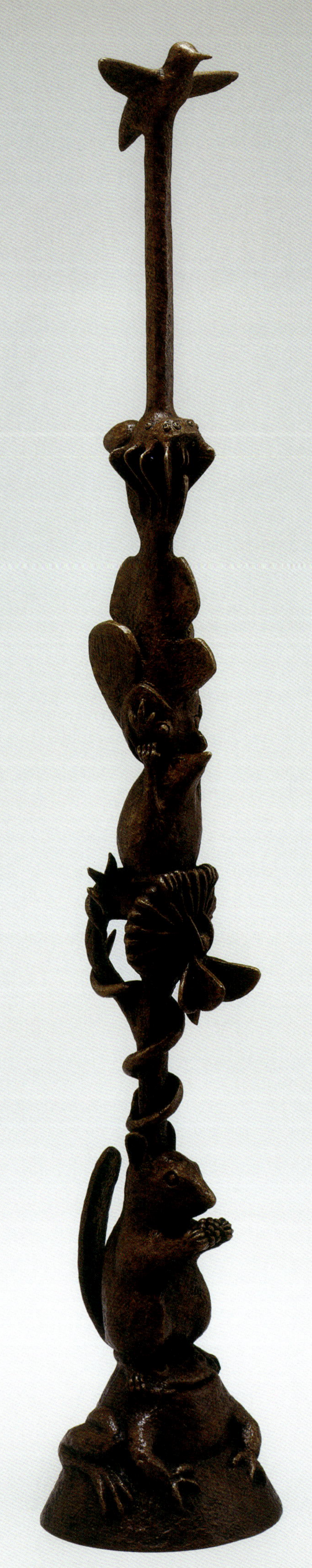

Guemes Island Totem
2001
Bronze
H. 23¼ in.
Private collection

In 2001, McCracken created a Guemes Island Totem, *which he said gave him great pleasure. The totem pole is a time-honored Northwest tribal art form,*[3] *but the animals used here are unusual. In place of the wolf, raven, whale, and other powerful animals seen on traditional totem poles, McCracken again honors creatures thought of as less important. A frog, a squirrel, and a snake support a group topped by a hummingbird.*

"This piece," he wrote, "is not about the big bear, the killer whale, and the eagle. Instead, it honors the small creatures not often found in traditional totemic forms. They are some of the small beings found here that I am very familiar with and have a particular fondness for. Some of them have very high metabolisms and intense lives: the chipmunk, the shrew, and the hummingbird. Others have very different and singular lives: the skipper, the staghorn sculpin, and the jumping spider. I am at peace with the thought that we are all a part of this great continuum." The space on McCracken's pole between the hummingbird and the jumping spider beneath it is similar to spaces left vacant in memorial and funerary poles.

Steve Mesler, who cast this piece at the River Dog Fine Arts Foundry in Port Townsend, cites it as "one of the most remarkable pieces we've ever cast. I hope it ends up in a museum one day, because it is extraordinary. The shapes are so complex that we had to cast it in four pieces, then join them."

Mesler, who has been doing McCracken's casting since 1998, says, "His work is the yardstick by which every artist in the Northwest should measure themselves. His requirements are simple: he wants it perfect. One piece, titled Four Seasons, *he sent back to us twenty times before we got it right. Nothing that is less than spectacular from a craft standpoint goes out his door.*

"The first time I went up to his place with a casting, I was terrified. I had heard he was tyrannical. I didn't sleep the night before. I got to the ferry an hour and a half early. He has turned out to be the exact opposite of what I feared. He is compassionate and patient—one of the great human beings of all time.

"He is attuned to things the rest of us don't have access to. I was talking to him on the phone once, and there was a robin somewhere in my vicinity. I wasn't even particularly aware of it. But Philip caught the sound in the background, and heard it as an alarm; something or someone was present in the woods that the robin didn't care for.

"Through him I have gotten one of the most thorough educations possible in what a great sculpture is. He has an eye for detail like no one else I know. He can spot bad form in an instant. As soon as he points it out, it's irrefutable. As a result of working with him, our quality level has gone way up. My eye has been trained to his standards. I'm going to work for him for the rest of his life."

Notes

Introduction

1. In this and subsequent places in which I quote Philip McCracken, I refer to his written reflections on his work. They are unpublished, although some of them have been reproduced by galleries to accompany a pertinent exhibition.

2. Published for the Tacoma Art Museum by the University of Washington Press. Colin Graham, the author, is director emeritus of the Art Gallery of Greater Victoria, where he served as director from 1951 to 1974, and a former lecturer at the California College of Arts and Crafts.

The Artist's Life

1. Keats's 1818 sonnet reads: "When I have fears that I may cease to be / Before my pen has glean'd my teeming brain / Before high-piléd books in charact'ry / Hold like rich garners the full-ripen'd grain; / When I behold, upon the night's starred face, / Huge cloudy symbols of a high romance, / And think that I may never live to trace / Their shadows, with the magic hand of chance; / And when I feel, fair creature of an hour! / That I shall never look upon thee more, / Never have relish in the faery power / Of unreflecting love!—then on the shore / Of the wide world I stand alone, and think / Till Love and Fame to nothingness do sink."

2. Those interests are reflected in McCracken's sculpture series, including the Future Past series and the Fragments of Night Sky series, and *Birth of a Charmed Quark*.

3. The insect specimens were, in later years, chewed up by one of the family's monkeys.

4. Stuart Preston, untitled clipping, *New York Times,* January 10, 1965, artist's archive.

5. Jeanne Paris, untitled clipping, *Long Island Press,* January 10, 1965, artist's archive.

6. "People Are Talking About," *Vogue,* March 1, 1965, artist's archive.

Early Sculpture

1. *Philip McCracken* (Tacoma and Seattle: Tacoma Art Museum and University of Washington Press, 1980), p. 23.

2. Pewter, a mixture of tin, lead, and a small admixture of antimony or other metals, has a melting point of 450 to 500 degrees F.—a manageable temperature for a studio casting. Bronze, which melts at 1,800 to 2,250 degrees, must be cast in a professional foundry.

Early Lyricism

1. Forty-six similar circles are known north of Wyoming, in the province of Alberta, Canada.

From the Potato Patch

1. Theodore F. Wolff, untitled clipping, *The Christian Science Monitor,* September 29, 1983, p. 20, artist's archive.

2. Anthony Trewavas, "Plant Intelligence: Mindless Mastery," *Nature* 415 (21 February 2002): 841.

3. Michael Pollan, *The Botany of Desire* (New York: Random House, 2001), pp. xix–xx.

4. B.M. Shapiro, "The Control of Oxidant Stress at Fertilization," *Science* 252 (2001): 533–36.

5. An amusing version of this superstition is seen in a class at Hogwarts School for Wizards in the film *Harry Potter and the Chamber of Secrets.*

6. Morris Graves to Philip McCracken, February 17, 1985.

7. Pollan, *Botany of Desire,* p. 199.

8. Ibid., pp. 195, ix–xv; quotes on pp. 195, xiv, xv.

Fragments of Night Sky

1. "Mathematics, rightly viewed, possesses not only truth, but supreme beauty—a beauty cold and austere like that of sculpture, without appeal to any part of our weaker nature, without the gorgeous trappings of painting or music, yet sublimely pure, and capable of a stern perfection such as only the greatest art can show" (Bertrand Russell, "The Study of Mathematics," 1902).

2. John Russell, *The Meanings of Modern Art* (New York: Harper & Row, 1974), p. 271.

3. Edna St. Vincent Millay, sonnet "Euclid Alone Has Looked on Beauty Bare," in *The Harp-Weaver and Other Poems* (New York: Harper Brothers, 1923).

4. Chryssa Kouveliotou et al., "Discovery of an X-ray pulsar with a superstrong magnetic field in the Soft Gamma Repeater called SGR 1806-20," *Nature* 393 (21 May 1998): 235–37.

The Future Past

1. Abraham Lincoln, address to the Wisconsin State Agricultural Society, Milwaukee, Wisconsin, September 30, 1859.

2. The reader is referred to a science fiction treatment of this theme in *A Canticle for Liebowitz* by Walter Miller (Philadelphia: Lippincott, 1960).

3. The Richter scale is logarithmic; an increase of one magnitude unit represents a factor of ten times in amplitude. The seismic waves of a magnitude 6.0 earthquake are 10 times greater in amplitude than those of a magnitude 5.0 earthquake. However, in terms of energy release, a 6.0 earthquake is 31 times greater than a 5.0.

Later Lyricism

1. William Blake, "Auguries of Innocence."

2. The huge phallic flower rarely blooms in cultivation, and is not much sought after, possibly because it has an aroma described as a cross between rotting flesh and excrement.

3. Traditional Native American totem poles are carved and raised to represent a family-clan and its kinship system, as well as its accomplishments, stories, rights, and prerogatives. They are tokens of ancestry.

Chronology

Philip Trafton McCracken

1928 Born November 14, Bellingham, Washington
Grows up in Anacortes, Washington

1954 B.A., University of Washington, Seattle
Spends summer as assistant to sculptor Henry Moore, Hertfordshire, England
Marries Anne McFetridge, August 14

1955 Moves to Guemes Island, Washington

One-Person Exhibitions

1960 Willard Gallery, New York

1961 Seattle Art Museum

1964 Washington State Capital Museum, Olympia
Art Gallery of Greater Victoria, British Columbia, Canada

1965 Willard Gallery, New York

1968 Willard Gallery, New York

1970 La Jolla Museum of Art, La Jolla, California
Anchorage Museum of History and Art, Anchorage, Alaska
Willard Gallery, New York

1977 Kiku Gallery, Seattle

1980 *Philip McCracken Retrospective Exhibition,* Tacoma Art Museum, Tacoma, Washington

1985 *Philip McCracken: New Sculpture and Drawings,* Kennedy Galleries, New York

1986 *From the Potato Patch,* Lynn McAllister Gallery, Seattle

1990 Willard Gallery, New York

1993 Valley Museum of Northwest Art, La Conner, Washington

1994 Whatcom Museum of History and Art, Bellingham, Washington
Gordon Woodside/John Braseth Gallery, Seattle

1997 Southern Oregon State College, Ashland

1999 Monterey Museum of Art, Monterey, California

2001 *Uncovered,* Port Angeles Fine Arts Center, Port Angeles, Washington

2002 *Philip McCracken: Bronze Sculpture,* Kurt Lidtke Gallery, Seattle

2004 *600 Moons: Fifty Years of Philip McCracken's Art,* Museum of Northwest Art, La Conner

Selected Group Exhibitions

1957 Ogunquit Museum of American Art, Ogunquit, Maine

1958 Art Institute of Chicago
Pennsylvania Academy of the Fine Arts, Philadelphia
Detroit Institute of Arts
Contemporary Arts Museum, Houston

1959 Santa Barbara Museum of Art, Santa Barbara, California

1960 Dallas Center for Contemporary Art
M.H. de Young Memorial Museum, San Francisco
Los Angeles Municipal Art Gallery
Galerie Claude Bernard, Paris

1961 Walker Art Center, Minneapolis
University of Illinois, Urbana-Champaign
1963 Ball State Teachers College Art Gallery, Muncie, Indiana
1966 The Phillips Collection, Washington, D.C.
Governor's Invitational, Olympia, Washington, and Osaka, Japan
Corcoran Gallery of Art, Washington, D.C.
1967 Akron Art Museum
1968 Finch College Museum of Art, New York
Rutgers University, New Brunswick, New Jersey
1969 Grand Rapids Art Museum, Grand Rapids, Michigan
1970 La Jolla Museum of Art
1975 Washington State Capital Museum, Olympia
1976 Portland Art Museum, Portland, Oregon
1978 Whitney Museum of American Art, New York
1979 Montana State University, Bozeman
1980 Brigham Young University, Provo, Utah
1986 American Academy and Institute of Arts and Letters, New York
Bellevue Art Museum, Bellevue, Washington
1991–92 National Gallery of Canada, Ottawa, Ontario
1991–93 Smithsonian Institution, Washington, D.C.
1993 Gallery Three-Zero, New York
1994 Downtown Park, Bellevue, Washington
Seattle Art Museum
1996 CSA Gallery, Christchurch, New Zealand
1998 Spanierman Gallery, New York
2001 Seattle Art Museum
2002 Art and Culture Center, Fallbrook, California
2003 Spanierman Gallery, New York

Selected Public Commissions

Norton Building, Seattle, 1959
Kankakee State Hospital, Kankakee, Illinois, 1961
Gus Hensler Memorial, City of Anacortes, 1966
United Nations Association, New York, 1968
Seattle First National Bank, Mount Vernon, 1974
Swinomish Indian Tribal Center, La Conner, 1974
Federal Building, Seattle, 1976
Pacific Northwest Bell, Seattle, 1979
Everett City Hall, 1980
La Conner School District, 1998 and 2000
King County District Courthouse, Issaquah, 1999
City of Seattle, 2001

Selected Public Collections

Anchorage Museum of History and Art, Anchorage, Alaska
Art Gallery of Greater Victoria, British Columbia, Canada
Henry Art Gallery, University of Washington, Seattle
International Minerals and Chemical Corporation, Skokie, Illinois

Museum of Contemporary Art San Diego, La Jolla, California
Museum of Northwest Art, La Conner
Saint Louis Art Museum
Seattle Art Museum
Tacoma Art Museum
Whatcom Museum of History and Art, Bellingham
Whitney Museum of American Art, New York
University of Oregon Museum, Eugene
Schneider Museum of Art, Southern Oregon University, Ashland

Honors and Awards

Ruth Nettleton Award, 1954
University of Washington School of Art Prize, 1954
Norman Davis Purchase Award for a Sculptor Under 40, 1957
Certificate for Superior Design and Execution, American Institute of Architects, 1960
Governor's Award, Washington State Artist of the Year, 1964
Irene D. Wright Memorial Award, 1965
Governor's Arts Award, Washington State Arts Commission, 1994
Cornish College of the Arts Lifetime Achievement Award, 1999

Selected Bibliography

Philip McCracken. Text by Colin Graham. Tacoma and Seattle: Tacoma Art Museum and University of Washington Press, 1980.

Essays and Reproductions

Dore Ashton. *Modern American Sculpture.* New York: Abrams, 1967.
Faith Medlin. *Centuries of Owls in Art and the Written Word.* Norwalk, Conn.: Silverline, 1967.
James J. Kelly. *The Sculptural Idea.* Minneapolis: Burgess Press, 1970.
Donald W. Thalacker. *The Place of Art in the World of Architecture.* New York: Bowker, 1980.
Theodore F. Wolff. "Artists at Work," *Christian Science Monitor,* July 17, 1986.
James M. Rupp and Mary Randlett. *Art in Seattle's Public Places.* Seattle: University of Washington Press, 1992.
Deloris Tarzan Ament. *Iridescent Light: The Emergence of Northwest Art.* Seattle: University of Washington Press, 2002.

Reviews and Articles

Christian Science Monitor, Long Island Press, New York Herald Tribune, Seattle Post-Intelligencer, Seattle Times, Art in America, ARTnews, Northwest Arts, Saturday Review of Literature, Time, and *Vogue.*

Acknowledgments

Special thanks are due to Colin Graham, who began this book, but because of illness was unable to continue. His research and biographical information were invaluable.

No book was ever a greater pleasure to write than this one. Being a longtime fan of Philip McCracken's art would, in itself, have made it gratifying to write about at length. But research involved another bonus: a series of visits to the McCracken home and studio on Guemes Island, during which I had not only the opportunity to see the art more closely but the pleasure of Philip and Anne's company. I particularly want to acknowledge the suggestions and ideas of Anne McCracken, whose sweet nature and loving support enrich the lives of all who know her.

Mary Randlett and Dick Garvey, photographers who are also friends of the McCrackens, have been documenting Philip's work and his studio for many years. Their photographs add immeasurably to an understanding of the art.

DTA

Checklist of the Exhibition

Heron, 1952
Cedar
H. 33 in.
Collection of the artist

Black Mask, 1953
Cedar
H. 28¼ in.
Collection of Lang and Anne Simons

Photograph of *Birds of Passage,* 1958
Bronze
H. 84 in.
La Conner Middle School, La Conner, Washington
Photograph: Mary Randlett

Photograph of *Caged Bird,* 1958
Cedar and steel
H. 16¼ in.
Mayor's Office of Arts & Cultural Affairs, City of Seattle 1% for Art Program
Photograph: Geoffrey Clements

Photograph of *Restless Bird,* 1959
Cast stone
H. 108 in.
Norton Building, Seattle
Photograph: Mary Randlett

Angry Bird, 1963
Print, pencil, and ink wash on paper
24 × 17¾ in.
Collection of the artist

Dream of a Dying Owl, 1963
Print, pencil, and ink wash on paper
24 × 17¾ in.
Collection of the artist

Photograph of *Mountain Bird,* 1966
Bronze on cast-stone base
H. 48 in., on 96 in. base
City of Anacortes, Gus Hensler Memorial
Photograph: Art Hupy

Poems, 1966
Cedar and mixed media
H. 5½ in.
Collection of Leeds and Wendy Gulick

Healed Up Sky, 1967
Canvas, oil, and acrylic sheets
46¼ × 96 in.
University of Oregon Museum of Art, gift from the Haseltine Collection of Northwest Art, 1975

I Love You Tree, 1967
Steel and wood
H. 14 in.
Private collection

Lights Out, 1967
Acrylic sheets, light fixtures, and wood
H. 17¼ in.
Art Gallery of Greater Victoria

Hornet's Nest, 1969
Wood, hornet paper, and wild rose bushes
H. 26 in.
Museum of Northwest Art, Gift of Anne Gould Hauberg

Wild Honey, 1970
Cedar, gold wire, and gold leaf
H. 21¼ in.
Collection of Marshall and Helen Hatch

Moon, 1971
Cedar
H. 26¼ in.
Collection of Anne McCracken

Photograph of *Spring,* 1972
Polychromed cedar
H. 192 in.
Private collection
Photograph: Mary Randlett

Barnacles, 1973
Juniper
H. 5⅜ in.
Collection of Dr. Harold and Martha Clure

Medicine Wheel, 1974
Polychromed cedar
H. 26½ in.
Private collection

Photograph of *Freedom,* 1976
Bronze on cast-stone base
H. 23½ in.
Federal Building, Seattle, General Service Administration, Region 10
Photograph: Mary Randlett

Red Dwarf Mandala, 1976
Mixed media
30½ × 30½ in.
Collection of Mary Randlett

Photograph of *Raptors (Kingdome bronzes),* 1978, reinstalled 1999
Bronze
Each, H. 26 in.
King County District Courthouse, Issaquah, Washington
Photograph: Mary Randlett

Photograph of *Autumn Leaves,* 1979
Fiberglass, concrete, and steel
H. 58 in.
Skagit County Park, Guemes Island, Anacortes, Washington
Photograph: Kevin Kelley

Red Inside, 1981
Cedar and steel
H. 13 in.
Collection of Marshall and Helen Hatch

Night Journey, 1982
Cherry wood
H. 11½ in.
Collection of Lance and J.P. Brigham

Out of the Garden, 1982
Rose burl
H. 10¼ in.
Private collection

Yang/Sun, 1982
Polychromed cedar
H. 25½ in.
Museum of Northwest Art, Gift of Marshall and Helen Hatch

Bad Potato, 1983
Epoxy, pencil, and oil on paper
13½ × 8½ in.
Collection of the artist

Carrot with Attendants, 1983
Print, pencil, and ink wash on paper
26¼ × 20¼ in.
Collection of the artist

Mandrake Root, 1983
Print, collage, pencil, and ink wash on wood panel
46½ × 23¾ in.
Private collection

New Potatoes, 1983
Print, pencil, and ink wash on paper
H. 19 in.
Collection of Tim and Gail Bruce

Genesis, 1985
Granite
H. 7 in.
Collection of Colin and Sylvia Graham

Scarabs, 1985
Juniper and gold leaf
H. 3¾ in.
Collection of Marshall and Helen Hatch

Within Each Wave, 1985
Juniper and shell
H. 5½ in.
Collection of Joyce Lovett

Black Bird, 1986
Cedar and carnelian
H. 26½ in.
Collection of Marshall and Helen Hatch

Alpha, 1990
Polychromed cedar and gold
H. 26 in.
Collection of Dorothea and Murray Adaskin

Ascending Lark II, 1990
Bronze
H. 30¼ in.
Private collection

Bird Family, 1990
Bronze
H. 11½ in.
Collection of Rita Hupy and sons, Hal, Guy, and Todd

Hexahedron, 1991
Redwood, acrylic, and gold leaf
H. 21 in.
Private collection

Comet, 1992
Polychromed cedar
H. 31 in.
Collection of Mrs. William H. Bryant

Decahedron, 1992
Cherry wood and epoxy
H. 17 in.
Collection of Anne McCracken

Raptors, 1992
Bronze
H. 26½ in.
Collection of Lance and J.P. Brigham

Euclid's World, 1993
Apple wood and epoxy
H. 15 in.
Collection of Marshall and Helen Hatch

Beyond the Sun, 1994
Maple and epoxy
H. 19 in.
Collection of the artist

Southern Cross, 1994
Apple wood, gold, and epoxy
H. 23 in.
Collection of Marshall and Helen Hatch

Birth of a Charmed Quark, 1995
Apple wood and gold leaf
H. 8½ in.
Collection of Margaret Wesselhoeft

Mandala III, 1995
Cedar and quartz
H. 18½ in.
Collection of the artist

Meditating Frog, 1995
Fieldstone and bronze
H. 10¾ in.
Collection of Rod Arnzen and Kathi Gardner

Comet Birds, 1996
Cedar
H. 30 in.
Collection of Ron and Mila Hart

Cigarette Butt, 1997
Polyester resin, petrified wood, and cigarette butt
H. 4½ in.
Collection of the artist

Ancient Creature, 2000
Bone fragments and plaster
H. 11½ in.
Collection of the artist

Ancient Creatures, 2000
Sandstone, pinecones, and fish spines
H. 1¾ in.
Collection of the artist

Dot.com, 2000
Polyester resin, computer chips, and petrified wood
H. 12½ in.
Private collection

Pan, 2000
Bone fragments and plaster
H. 6¾ in.
Collection of the artist

Ages of Man II, 2001
Fabricated stone, bone fragments, metal, plastic, and wood
H. 14¼ in.
Collection of the artist

Pika/Mountain Sentinel, 2001
Cedar and onyx
H. 21½ in.
Collection of Tim and Gail Bruce

Photograph of *Aerial Play,* 2002
Cast and fabricated bronze
H. 168 in.
Private collection
Photograph: AESTUS

Between Infinities, 2003
Cedar and gold leaf
13½ × 32½ × 12 in.
Collection of the artist

A Cedar's Summer Memory, 2003
Cedar and epoxy
8¼ × 24⅛ × 5 in.
Collection of the artist

Mole Greeting the Sun, 2003
Bronze
H. 6½ in.
Private collection

Two Owls and Their Night Forest, 2004
Cedar and onyx
24¾ × 21½ × 13 in.
Collection of the artist

Index of Illustrations

Sponsors

The Museum of Northwest Art's grateful thanks go to the following organizations and individuals for their generous support of *600 Moons:*

Patrons

Allen Foundation for the Arts
Anacortes Arts Festival
Morris Graves Foundation
Skagit Valley Herald
Washington State Arts Commission

Contributors

Dorothea Larsen Adaskin
Richard and Connie Albrecht
Rod and Kathi Arnzen
Brent Bartlett
Kay and Glen Bartlett
Lance and J.P. Brigham
Kelsey Britz and Nancy Neuerburg
Tim and Gail Bruce
Jeannie and Charles Gravenkemper
Mit and Maureen Harlan
Marshall and Elena Hatch
Roger and Marny Heinen
Frank Hull and Alice Webb Hull (Memorial)
Duff and Dorothy Kennedy
Kurt Lidtke Gallery
Tom and Mary Moody
Harry and Judi Mullikin
Washington Women's Foundation
William and Margaret Wesselhoeft
Anonymous contributor

Supporters

Marjorie Bickel
Douglas P. Burton
Philip G. Burton
Shelley and Angelo Castellino
Gerry and Susan Christensen
Tanya DeMarsh-Dodson
Phyllis L. Ennes
Phyllis Field Entrikin
Wallie and Mary Ann Funk
Gretchen N. Gould
Anne Gould Hauberg
Janet Huston
Vern and Jerry Jackson
Elliott and Vicki Johnson
Fred and Lynn Johnson
Henry and Phyllis Klein
Roger and Lou Ann Knutzen
Otto and Greta Larsen
Dave and Bev Larson
Lawrence and Anne Martz
Bill and Marjorie McNae
Carl and Kris Molesworth
Babo Olanie
Grace Eligian Park
George Rolfe and Lois Gamble Duncan
Mr. and Mrs. Robert M. Sarkis
Langdon and Anne Simons
Charles and Janis Stavig
Jacqueline Dinsmore Stegner
Grant and Barbara Winther

Photo Credits

© AESTUS: 128

Oliver Baker: 28 (bottom), 44 (top)

Geoffrey Clements: 26, 27 (bottom), 30, 31, 32, 36

Dick Garvey: 2, 8, 12, 40, 41, 45, 58, 60, 61, 62, 63, 64, 65, 66, 67, 68, 69 (left), 78, 80 (bottom), 83, 85, 86, 87, 88, 89, 90, 91, 92, 93, 94, 97, 98, 99, 101, 102,103, 104, 105, 107, 108, 109, 110, 112, 114, 115, 118, 119, 120, 121, 123, 127, 129 (top left, bottom), 130, 132 (top), 135, 136, 137, 138, 140 (right), 141, 142, 143, 144, 145, 146, 147, 148

John Graham: 52 (bottom)

Blake Grinstein: 51

© Art Hupy: 24, 33, 34, 52 (top), 69 (right), 117, 122, 140 (left)

Hans Jorgenson: 49 (top)

Kevin Kelley: 42, 44 (bottom), 50, 53

Ray Maichen: 81, 82, 84

Bob Matheson: 80 (top)

Johsel Namkung: 48

© Charles Pearson: 37, 38, 39, 70, 72, 74, 75, 76, 129 (top right), 139

Mary Randlett © MSCUA, University of Washington Libraries: 16, 27 (top), 28 (top), 29, 49 (bottom), 54, 56, 57, 116, 124, 126, 132 (bottom), 133

John Vallentyne: 46, 47